Svetlana Palmer was born in Moscow in 1969. She studied at Moscow State University as well as in London and Berlin. She moved to Britain in 1990 and has worked on critically acclaimed documentaries including the BAFTA-nominated CNN/BBC *Cold War* series and ITV's award-winning *The Second World War in Colour*. Svetlana also co-produces arts and music documentaries with her film-maker husband. They live in north London with their two sons.

Sarah Wallis was born in America in 1967 and moved to Britain as a child. She studied Russian and German and used these languages while working as an assistant producer on many historical documentary films including the BBC's *People's Century*, for which 'Master Race' won an Emmy award; and the RTS award-winning *Homecoming*, a film following the return to Russia of Alexander Solzhenitsyn. Now a producer, she lives in north London with her partner and their two children.

A WAR IN WORDS

*The First World War in
Diaries and Letters*

Svetlana Palmer

and

Sarah Wallis

POCKET
BOOKS

LONDON • SYDNEY • NEW YORK • TORONTO

First published in Great Britain by Simon & Schuster UK Ltd, 2003
This edition first published by Pocket Books, 2004
An imprint of Simon & Schuster UK Ltd
A Viacom Company

3 5 7 9 10 8 6 4 2

Simon & Schuster UK Ltd
Africa House
64–78 Kingsway
London WC2B 6AH

www.simonsays.co.uk

Simon & Schuster Australia
Sydney

A CIP catalogue record for this book
is available from the British Library.

ISBN 0 7434 6906 2

Typeset by M Rules
Printed and bound in Great Britain by
Cox & Wyman Ltd, Reading, Berks

Contents

To Eleanor, Ben, Tristan and Zig

List of Maps

Foreword

The notion that the First World War was futile and wasteful is one of the clichés of history. However, that idea is itself less the product of the war's history than its literature. The writings of Henri Barbusse, Vera Brittain, Robert Graves, Erich Maria Remarque and Siegfried Sassoon, to name only the best known, illustrate a paradox – that from destruction came forth creativity. Critics have credited the war with the birth of modernism. In searching for a language more able to express what they had experienced, authors shed the conventions of the nineteenth century in favour of uncluttered prose and understated irony.

It was a literary war, but that was in part because it was also a literate one. The works that have now entered the canon represent the tip of a very large iceberg. Most of the belligerent populations could read and write. This was not true of previous wars. The combination of compulsory primary education and cheap printing, both developments of the last third of the nineteenth century, created an expanding market for the published word, whose most obvious sign was the number of mass-circulation newspapers. No war before 1914 had been so written about; no war after 1918 would be so uniquely captured by a single medium. The First World War was filmed and photographed; its participants were recorded. But the technologies of sight and sound had yet to rival that of the printed word. In 1939 the radio and the newsreel would do so.

The classification of this output is easier in theory than in practice. Propaganda occupies one end of the spectrum and poetry the other. But poets could reflect the themes of propagandists, and the most effective propaganda mirrored as much as manipulated the fears and anxieties of the people. Private diaries can carry xenophobia and nationalism far more virulent than that published in pamphlets and press. Censorship was never so tight that opposition to the war was totally muzzled, nor were the voices of one side totally inaudible in the other.

The war's participants wrote not just because they had the ability to do so, but also because they were conscious that they were living through a historic moment. Today's media are fond of describing the most trivial events as historic – and so they are, because once they have occurred they belong in the past. But the epithet also carries connotations of significance and meaning. In August 1914, nobody underestimated the import of what was happening. They knew that their world would be changed by the war. For some this was a threat; the older generation feared the breakdown of a managed, secure and prosperous order. For others it was an opportunity – this would be a war to end all wars, it would be a war to cause revolutions, it would be an enormous personal adventure.

Most of the voices gathered in this book are those of young people, ostensibly more likely to be in the second category than in the first. Indeed, some of them never reached old age. Televised interviews with survivors of the war have left an image that this was a war fought by old people. But in the intergenerational frictions of 1914–18 it was a war caused by the old people, and then sustained by, and at the expense of, the young. Moreover, after the war the frustrations of youth were compounded. Those same politicians who had come to power before the war were still in power after it, and they completed their follies by botching the peace settlement as well. In that respect at least, it seemed as though the war had not been a historic moment, because nothing had changed.

The First World War was a global war from its outset. Thirteen different nationalities are represented in the following

pages. That in itself is one of the reasons for the book's importance. Represented here are people that the English-language
literary tradition, with its focus on the Western Front, and even
more on the British army's experience of that front, forgets. Too
few German and French eyewitness accounts have been translated. They are here, but so too are Russians, Serbs, Turks,
Austrians, Italians and Americans. Still there are absentees. Even
literacy had its limits in 1914–18. The First World War was the
biggest collective experience undergone by Africa up until that
date, but few Africans were sufficiently literate to write diaries or
letters. Their testimony, when we have it, is part of an oral tradition, recorded much later.

One or two names will be familiar. Rudolf Hess, who did live
to a great age, albeit mostly in Spandau prison, gives vent to the
frustrations which explain the later appeal of National Socialism.
Richard Meinertzhagen, whose diaries were published in his
own lifetime, wrote entertainingly (and, it has to be said, self-
servingly) about hunting and ornithology as well as soldiering.
But many of the first-hand accounts which follow have never
appeared in print before, even in their native languages.
Moreover, the voices we hear are not just those of soldiers and
sailors but of women and children as well. Yves Congar and
Piete Kuhr moved from infancy through adolescence in 1914–18:
it was a formative experience for them even if they did not fight.

The phrase 'total war' was not one much used in 1914–18. It
was coined as part of the rhetoric of the French government
formed by Georges Clemenceau in November 1917. But after
the war was over, those who had been through it were clear that
it had been something they called total war. Many of them also
concluded that that would be the pattern of the future. They
reckoned that the mobilisation of the nation's entire resources
would be required, and everybody – non-combatant as well as
combatant – would be involved in its conduct. Most of the
women and children we encounter here are passive rather than
active participants. They can be caught up in the fighting,

besieged as Helena Jabłońska was, or living under occupation as Yves Congar did. More often, however, they are removed from the direct experience of combat, and feel its effects through economic controls, through propaganda, or through the loss of loved ones. They are reactive, but their reactions are important, because without their consent the nation could not maintain its war effort. Indeed, as the letters from those at the front make clear, the steadfast support of those at home was crucial to the morale of those at the front. One corollary of mass mobilisation was these accounts; another was that the armies became armies of citizens rather than of soldiers.

These testimonies contain a wealth of insights for the historian. Svetlana Palmer and Sarah Wallis have woven them together with remarkable skill. First, they have given them shape, so that the place of an individual in the wider war is clear, and his or her words can therefore be read as part of that bigger event. Secondly, they have edited them so that we can engage with their hopes, fears and peccadilloes. There is poignancy and humanity here, without cliché.

HEW STRACHAN
All Souls College, Oxford

Preface

You must not tell lies in your diary

Piete Kuhr, 1st August 1914

Behind each of the first-hand accounts in this book there is a story about how it survived for nearly ninety years. To write and preserve them in the first place involved various degrees of risk. One of the diaries ends mid-sentence as its author unwittingly records his own end. Within weeks, the officer who rescued the tiny notebook from his compatriot died too. This time a combatant from the opposite side saved the diary for its propaganda value. It was soon translated and published in a newspaper interspersed with venomous editorial comments. This, along with the danger of letting slip operational information, was precisely the reason why diary writing was discouraged. Scottish POW Duggie Lyall Grant, released from German captivity during the war, was aware of this danger and had his orderly sew pages of his diary into the waistband of his kilt, concealing the rest inside the bag of his bagpipe. The trouble Lyall Grant took paid off and he succeeded in smuggling the carefully hidden diary across the border to neutral Holland.

But even when the accounts, if not their authors, survived the war, many were at risk of oblivion, stashed away in soon forgotten boxes. Few people ever go through the personal memorabilia cluttering the dusty corners of their attics. Some of the diaries have reappeared by pure coincidence. Like the diary of Russian soldier Vasily Mishnin, found in a house clearance in his hometown of Penza decades after the war. Or the three note-books, covered in tiny handwriting in Ottoman Turkish, offered to a Turkish historian browsing one day through a second-hand bookstall in an Istanbul market.

Although several of the accounts have been published posthumously in their own countries, none of the twenty-eight men, women and children whose diaries and letters feature in this book were professional writers at the time, nor were their accounts intended for publication. One exception was the youngest of them all, ten-year-old French schoolboy Yves Congar, who did write with future readers in mind. Yet even he soon forgot about this once the war ended. His journal, filling five beautifully illustrated exercise books, remained private until his death at the venerable age of ninety-one.

From the hundreds of accounts we read in the course of research for Channel 4's television series *The First World War* and this book, we selected twenty-eight for their character, vividness, humour and originality. The process was entirely subjective. Between us we have spent years living, studying and working in Germany and Russia. So we both have a natural bias towards the little-known Eastern Front and many of our discoveries came from there. The Serbian and Italian diaries were uncovered by Milan Grba and Martina Cavicchioli during extensive research for the series.

To be included, each account had to tell a unique story and sustain our interest. If we were not riveted, we rejected it outright. While trawling through stories of the war at sea in the Imperial War Museum's normally quiet reading room, an entry from a young British midshipman describing his conquests while on leave made us laugh out loud and ensured his diary's place in the book.

'Isn't it depressing to spend months and months reading and writing about the First World War?' was the question our friends and colleagues most frequently asked, surprised by our enthusiasm for the project. The answer was 'no'. Diarists and correspondents became familiar personalities, each with their own idiosyncrasies, engaging and full of surprises. Our motivation was to tell their stories in their own words. Words which were written without hindsight, often on the same day and in the same place as the events happened and as the diarists paused to reflect on their experiences. To build a narrative we have abridged the often lengthy accounts, some of them hundreds of pages long and intercut them in each chapter with one or more accounts expressing the view of someone on the opposite side. The selection process was often painful, our choices influenced by the timescale of significant episodes in the war and those we felt were personally significant to the individuals concerned or gave an insight into his or her character.

Most of the material we use are diaries – by their nature intimate and honest accounts – but four come from candid and frequent letter-writers whose missives escaped the censor and reached their parents, siblings or fiancées on a regular basis. We have made exceptions to our rule of only using contemporary accounts in three cases: Richard Meinertzhagen's diary of his experience in East Africa was published in his lifetime, but proved too irresistible to leave out; Dmitry Oskin's entertaining depiction of his exploits on the Eastern Front and his subsequent account of the Russian Revolution were based on his contemporary diary, expanded and amended for publication after the war; and finally, we have included an oral history account from Guinean soldier Kande Kamara, a remarkable testimony to an experience of the war we would have otherwise had to leave out, for no known African diaries of the conflict exist. There are many other nationalities, in particular Indian, which we have sadly been unable to include in this edition due to the absence of complete diaries or full letter exchanges. For the same reason we were unable to feature the experiences of many others involved in campaigns in Europe and beyond. Aware as we are of these omissions, we await further discoveries with great interest.

For the sake of clarity we have corrected the spelling of familiar French towns and villages, but have left the spelling of some Polish villages as they appear in the original German, Russian and Polish diaries. We have refrained, too, from altering the punctuation of diaries or letters originally written in English. Two of the young men had little formal education: Winnie McClare owes his spelling to leaving school early to help run his father's farm; and Robert Cude's punctuation seemed to be an integral part of his writing style.

We owe big thanks to a number of people who have encouraged and guided us often beyond their remit: *The First World War* Series Producer Jonathan Lewis, Professor Hew Strachan and Alan Clements, Managing Director of Wark Clements & Company, without whom this book might never have come about; Natasha Fairweather, our agent at A. P. Watt and a constant source of encouragement; Andrew Gordon and Martin Bryant, our patient and enthusiastic editors at Simon & Schuster; our colleague and mentor Isobel Hinshelwood; Angus Macqueen, whose generosity contributed greatly to the project; and Miriam Ravich and Ruthie Smith.

The following people either in their own books or in person have brought individual diaries to our attention, for which we are greatly indebted: Stéphane Audoin-Rouzeau, Julie Berranger, Malcolm Brown, Martina Cavicchioli, Jacques Clémens, Ann Dunemil, H. Basri Danisman and Turgay Erol, Orlando Figes, Bill Gammage, Milan Grba, O. Gschliesser, Joe Lunn, Verena Moritz and Hannes Leid, Michael Moynihan, Sergei Poltorak, Irina Renz and Valentin Zemtsov.

We were helped immeasurably, often at a distance, by the staff of several archives, libraries and institutions who went out of their way to be of assistance: Dr Zdravko Antonic; Naiomi Cox at the Australian War Memorial; Adam Dryś; David Keough at the US Military History Archive Carlisle; the staff of the Documents Department at the Imperial War Museum and the British Library; Dwight Messimer; Dr Mögle-Hofacker, Head of the Hauptstaatsarchiv in Stuttgart; the Przemyśl Scientific Historical Institute and the National Museum of the Przemyśl Region in Poland; Irina Renz at the Bibliotek für Zeitgeschichte in Stuttgart; Angelika Siljaew; Dr Karl Rossa at the Kriegsarchiv in Vienna and Dr Christa Hämmerle at the University of Vienna; Jane and Stuart Warren.

One of the greatest pleasures in producing this book has been to come into contact with relatives of the diary writers, all of whom have answered endless questions, provided photographs and helped to bring us closer to the authors of these accounts. Our thanks to Madame Cambon, Henri Cambon, Dominique Congar, Dr Ljiljana Klisić-Djordjevic, Daphne Robinson, Dragoslav Marković, Dale McClare, Randle Meinertzhagen, Alexandra Mishnin, and Anja Ott for their assistance.

For their patience, astute comments, criticism and encouragement on reading the early drafts of the manuscript we are grateful to Paul Bernays, Natasha Fairweather, Eleanor Jacob, Will Jacob, Sergei Palmer, John and Tamsin Slyce, Charlotte and John Wallis, Duncan Noble and Nick Richards. Stephen Sharkey has done a fantastic job unifying the translations and helping to convey the tone of the original texts.

A big thank you to Gregor Murbach for helping to source and put together the photographs and illustrations and to Reg Piggott for the maps.

A huge thank you to all of the following for the care and precision of their excellent translations: Mr H. Basri Danisman for kind permission to use his translation of Mehmed Fasih's diary; Martina Cavicchioli for the translation of Virgilio Bonamore's diary; Claire Derouesne for her translations of the French diaries; Helen Ferguson for her translations of the Hess letters and the diaries of Ernst Nopper, Dmitry Oskin, Vasily Mishnin, Dr Josef Tomann and Alexei Zyikov; Klara Kemp-Welch for her translation of Helena Jabłońska's diary; Sabine Pusch for her translation of Paul Hub's letters; Vanessa Vassic for the final Serbian translations; Mick Wright for the original translation of Piete Kuhr's diary; Tatjana Paunovic and her team for their collaborative work on the Serbian translations.

Our big personal thanks go to Ben, Eleanor, Paul, Tristan, Will and Zig who have been a constant source of support and distraction.

And finally our thanks to the twenty-eight men and women whose remarkable accounts form the basis of this book.

SVETLANA AND SARAH,
London 2003

A WAR
IN WORDS

GERMANY

POLAND

Warsaw

RUSSIA

*Prague

Krakow

R. Vistula

R. San

Lwow (Lemberg)
Olszan

Przemyśl

Tarnopol

Sanok

AUSTRO – HUNGARIAN

Carpathian Mts

Vienna

N

R. Danube

Budapest

EMPIRE

Zagreb

CROATIA

R. Sava

Belgrade

ROMANIA

Tuzla

Bucharest

BOSNIA

Zenica

Kragujevac

R. Danube

SERBIA

Sarajevo

HERZEGOVINA

Niš

MONTENEGRO

*Sofia

BULGARIA

Adriatic Sea

Ljesh

ALBANIA

Uskub
(Skoplje)

ITALY

MACEDONIA

Salonika

Valona

GREECE

Aegean

Corfu

Sea

Athens

Austria-Hungary
and the Balkans in 1914

0   50   100   150   200 miles
0   100   200   300 km

Chapter 1

THE FIRST SHOTS

28th June–30th July 1914

On 28th June 1914 Archduke Franz Ferdinand, the heir to the Austro-Hungarian throne, and his wife, Sophie, were assassinated during a state visit to Sarajevo, capital of the Austro-Hungarian province of Bosnia-Herzegovina. The fatal shots were fired by nineteen-year-old Gavrilo Princip, a Bosnian Serb who wanted Bosnian unification with Serbia and independence from the Austro-Hungarian Empire. Franz Ferdinand, as a member of the ruling Habsburg family, was a symbol of that ancient, multi-national empire and the repression of its minorities. Unknown to his assassin, the archduke, who was an advocate of political reform, had recently given an after-dinner toast: 'To peace! What would we get out of war with Serbia? We'd lose the lives of young men and we'd spend money better used elsewhere. And what would we gain, for heaven's sake? A few plum trees, some pastures full of goat droppings, and a bunch of rebellious killers.'

Now he was dead. The Austrian army's Chief of the General Staff thought differently about a war with Serbia. On 23rd July, Vienna will issue an ultimatum with demands unlikely to be met in Belgrade. Five days later Austro-Hungarian troops will invade with the backing of Germany. Two Balkan wars had gripped this *unstable region in the early twentieth century. But this time what could have been the third Balkan War will become a world war.*

*

The youngest of the assassins involved in the plot to kill Archduke Franz Ferdinand left an account of his role in the assassination. Seventeen-year-old Vaso Čubrilović, a Bosnian Serb from Basanska Gradiska, was educated in the Bosnian town of Tuzla, then part of the Austro-Hungarian Empire. The Habsburgs had only recently wrested control of Bosnia and Herzegovina from the Ottoman Empire, which had ruled large parts of the Balkans for four hundred years. While Bosnia exchanged one imperial rule for another, for over three decades neighbouring Serbia had been an independent kingdom. The very existence of Serbia inspired many still living under foreign rule to hope for independence. This, in turn, threatened the stability of the Habsburgs who ruled an empire of at least ten different nationalities, any one of which could have attempted to follow Serbia's example. Like his fellow assassin Gavrilo Princip, Vaso Čubrilović was a member of Young Bosnia, an underground organisation with one main aspiration: the creation of a southern Slav state, Yugoslavia, which would unite Serbs, Croats and Slovenes, be they Orthodox, Catholic or Muslim, in a new state free from both Ottoman and Habsburg influence.

Vaso Čubrilović is spared execution for his part in the plot, as he is under twenty. In a letter to his sisters, Vida and Staka, written while serving a sixteen-year sentence in prison, he explains how he came to participate in one of the world's most notorious assassinations.

Zenica Prison, 1918

I shall write as much as I can remember about the assassination. I first thought of it in October 1913 in Tuzla, incensed by the fights we had with our teachers, the mistreatment of Serbian students, and the general situation in Bosnia. I thought I'd rather kill the one person who'd really harmed our people than fight in another war for Serbia. All I'd achieve in a war is to kill a couple of innocent soldiers, while these gentlemen who were responsible for it would never come anywhere near the war itself.

In January 1914 I was expelled from high school in Tuzla. I wavered for a while, unsure whether to escape to Serbia or come to you in Sarajevo. Finally, I decided to come to you. It was while staying with you in Sarajevo that I was introduced to various students, mainly to those who felt the same way as I did.

Vaso Čubrilović

And then came April. I remember clearly reading in *Srpska Reč* [Serbian Word] and in *Pobratimstvo* [Fraternity] that Ferdinand was coming to Sarajevo. I immediately began thinking about an assassination. With all the anti-Austrian feelings at college, I was convinced that someone else must be planning it too. I knew that Lazar Djukić had gone to jail in 1910 for his role in a similar plot against the emperor. He was bound to know if anyone was plotting, and I decided to find out. I would join them, or at the very least persuade Djukić to hide the weapons I planned to obtain in Tuzla. While we were out walking one day he was telling me about the emperor's visit in 1909.[1] I casually remarked that now Ferdinand was coming. 'Yes,' answered Djukić.

I said, 'We ought to welcome him.' That was our code for assassination.

'Ahem, yes, if we can find the people to do it,' he said.

'The people are there, but they've nothing to do it with.'

'Weapons can always be found, if people really want them,' he responded.

Up until now our exchange seemed light-hearted, but at this point it got serious. I told him I was willing to do it and that my mind was made up. I just couldn't find the weapons.

Djukić introduced me to Danilo Ilić.[2] He would also get me two bombs, a gun and some cyanide. All that Ilić told me was that there would be three others, apart from us three, and that Serbian officers were supplying the weapons. I asked if the Serbian government knew about it. He said no, in Serbia everything was being done in secret.[3] We didn't talk about it any more.

---

1 The emperor who visited in 1909 was Franz Joseph, Archduke Franz Ferdinand's uncle.

2 For over a year journalist Danilo Ilić had been a member of the Black Hand, a secret organisation directed by Lieutenant Colonel Dragutin Dimitrijević, the head of Serbian military intelligence.

3 Rumours of a plot had reached the Serbian prime minister but he failed to investigate.

We worried that the Sarajevan police might decide to remove us all from the city [during Ferdinand's visit]. Besides, I wanted to leave you before the assassination, to avoid causing you problems. This is why I kept nagging Staka to let me leave before the exam results came out.

On June 27th Ilić, Popović and I went to Bembasa, where Ilić gave us each a bomb and a gun. We had received our cyanide pills a couple of weeks earlier. Unfortunately, we didn't know how to store them properly, so the pills got ruined in our pockets. Ilić told me my position would be by Danilo Dimović's front door, while Cvjetko [Popović] was to stand on the corner by the Prosvjeta building. Popović and I were angry to be given such bad positions, but Ilić said we could choose better ones later.

[On the morning of 28th June] I had my gun in my right pocket and the bomb tied to my belt. I tied my red tie to the belt

Archduke Franz Ferdinand and his wife, Sophie, 28th June 1914

at both ends and spread it out like a sack to hold the bomb, easy to take out but hidden from view.

At about 10 o'clock I saw a procession of cars approaching in our direction. Ferdinand's car was the first, instead of an escort car. I can see them clearly even now. I saw Ferdinand greeting the crowd, touching his cavalry hat. Next to him sat his wife. She was dressed all in white and was holding a parasol. I asked a student who stood next to me whether this was definitely Ferdinand, and he confirmed it was. I took a few steps back towards the wall to throw my bomb, but the car was already right in front of me. All of a sudden I heard a loud crack, as if from a gun. I stopped, realising someone had thrown a bomb. I saw it hit the lowered roof of the car, bounce off and fall, just a few steps away from me. I could see it smoking and hissing like a steam engine. In an instant I threw myself on the ground. The heir [Franz Ferdinand] turned to see what was happening and the car stopped just feet away from Gavrilo [Princip] and Cvjetko [Popović], but in the confusion they did nothing. Fortunately, I was unharmed but almost everyone around me was wounded. The explosion made all six of us run in different directions. I then ran to Cemalusa street, for I was hoping to get Ferdinand there.

The first assassination attempt has failed and the bomb thrower, Nedeljko Čabrinović, is arrested. But Franz Ferdinand and Sophie insist on continuing their journey to the city hall undeterred. After the official welcoming ceremony, they ask to be driven to the hospital to visit two soldiers wounded by the morning's blast. The driver takes a wrong turn and Gavrilo Princip finds himself with a chance as the car approaches. Meanwhile Vaso waits at a road close to the river hoping for his turn.

I stood waiting at Cemalusa street for ages, until I heard there had been another attack. When I got back to the riverbank I heard that Princip had shot Ferdinand and that Ferdinand had been driven away to his residency. I wish to add to this that we never intended to shoot Ferdinand's wife, we wanted to exact revenge on [General] Potiorek[1] for introducing martial law in 1912–13.

I was so certain that I would carry out the assassination and then die myself, that I hadn't thought about prison. And I didn't think anyone would betray me. To tell you the truth, we were all somewhat exhilarated by then. We were determined, yes, but we couldn't see straight. What we did we did out of our own free will, and yet I cannot help feeling that some stronger impulse drove us. Even now it seems that it wasn't us at all who did it, that it was someone else altogether. Our trial reinforced that impression.

All seven conspirators are young, only two of them over twenty.

It was our misfortune that not one of us was maturer. The oldest was Ilić, but at 24 he too was practically a child. It was especially true of me and Popović. We were determined to kill Ferdinand, but we weren't ready for such deeds. They require maturity, a cool head and caution, traits we could not have had at 17 or 18 years of age. Besides, we had no counsel, no one to encourage us, unlike the three who prepared in Serbia.[2] But even they said they had hesitated. Čabrinović told me he didn't know how he took the bomb out and threw it. The same was true of Princip. Of us all he was the coolest, the best mentally prepared. He carried out the attack mechanically – this much is obvious when you analyse the assassination.

---

1 General Oskar Potiorek was governor of the Austro-Hungarian province of Bosnia-Herzegovina and travelled in the official car with the archduke and his wife, but escaped unharmed.
2 Of the seven, three have been recruited and trained by the Black Hand in Serbia and sent to Bosnia on a mission to carry out the assassination.

*Gavrilo Princip and Nedeljko Čabrinović are arrested on the day of
the assassination. They weaken under interrogation and confess some
of the names of their co-conspirators who, in turn, betray others.
The police are able to round up all seven principal plotters as well as
members of their support network.*

If only we'd had better poison. Princip and Čabrinović would
have died instantly as soon as they swallowed the cyanide.
Instead, we all ended up in the hands of sly judges, with no
chance to agree on our stories beforehand. This was the main
reason that so much had come out about our plot.

Worst of all, Ilić, who was at the centre of it all, was the first
to cave in and confess. I still cannot understand him. A man
who was so stable and reliable, as it wasn't his first plot – but he
lost his nerve and betrayed us all. I don't blame him. I know
from my experience that at some moments in his life a man
needs great mental resolve just to maintain his balance.

When I was arrested and detained at Dubica, I didn't even
suspect it was because of the assassination. You can imagine my
surprise when the police asked me where I'd left my bomb. Had
it fallen on my head, I would have been less shocked. In a panic,
I admitted giving it to Ivo [Kranjčević]. Luckily, instead of
asking me more questions (I would have confessed everything),
they rushed off to arrest Kranjčević, while I stayed alone with the
chief spy, Pera Maksimović. He was too busy to interrogate me
properly. I admitted no more than conspiring with Ilić. The interrogation lasted all night with officers coming in one after the other.

The next day I was interrogated by the investigative judge,
Sefer. Of course, I was still a child and Sefer was able to confuse
me and lead me to confess. I took the whole thing lightly and
made a joke of it. I didn't care then, for Ferdinand had paid his
due. I had no more to say. Ilić had already betrayed Djukić and
Popović. As you can see, we all betrayed each other.

Prison, with all the beatings, the hunger and the cold, cannot
torment you as much as knowing that you could have spared

someone the suffering, and you didn't. In here you are alone. In solitary confinement there is nothing to distract you. You attack yourself. Your whole life passes through your mind and the smallest mistake, one you would never notice outside, becomes a matter for shame and regret.

In my opinion, the assassination turned out well, considering who they gave the job to. In any event, it wasn't our intention to cause a world war, and we truly believed just a couple of Serbian officers sent us the weapons. Had I got involved in a similar plot now, I would have done it all differently. But it matters little now. I was ready to die on 28th June 1914, so the life I have now is a gift I may not reject. In truth, I would rather I had died four years ago. This is no kind of life. This is a slow death, of spirit and body.

There, I've written so much my hand aches. But be careful with this, as I have told you some things the court doesn't know, to give you a better overview of my participation in the assassination.

After his arrest on 20th July 1914, and subsequent trial, Vaso Čabrilović serves the first part of his sixteen-year sentence in Zenica Prison.

*

Slavka Mihajlović is a twenty-six-year-old doctor from an affluent and progressive family who lives in a tranquil, leafy area of Belgrade, capital of independent Serbia. Newly qualified, she has lived through two local wars in the last three years and has already worked as an army doctor. She is enjoying the brief period of peace. But blame for the recent assassinations in Sarajevo has been laid on Belgrade, and Austrian demands to extradite the conspirators for trial in Vienna are unlikely to be met. The threat of war hangs once again over the Balkans as Slavka Mihajlović starts her diary.

24th July 1914

A beautiful sunny day has dawned. As I do every morning, I leave my house just before seven for the General State Hospital in Vracar. The streets are filled with people. Office workers hurry to their jobs, tardy peasants rush to take their goods to the market, while some housewives are already heading home with full baskets. Horse-drawn milk-floats clatter over the uneven Belgrade cobbles. The sun is scorching, no hint of a breeze, the air is muggy. I hurry down the street thinking, how are we going to operate on our patients in such heat?

The head surgeon goes to his office and soon returns, serious and agitated. He invites all the doctors to his office. His green-blue eyes stare at us behind gilt-framed glasses. He then says: 'Austria has sent an ultimatum to Serbia. Continue your work. I must report to the ministry at once.' He leaves us with a nod and walks out of the hospital.

We are astounded. We look at each other aghast, but must go back to work. Today's operations have to go on. After the Sarajevo assassination we expected Serbia's relations with Austria to get tense. We did not expect an ultimatum, however. The news spreads quickly around the hospital and causes alarm. Not just in the hospital. The whole town is in shock. Streets and cafes are filling up with anxious people. How will our government respond? Can a new war be avoided?

It is less than a year since our little Serbia emerged from two bloody wars, with Turkey and Bulgaria. Some of the wounded still lie in hospital – are we to see more bloodshed and more tragedy?

The two recent Balkan wars were fought between a shifting alliance of regional powers. Serbia doubled its territory at the expense of Turkey. Vienna, worried by any Serbian expansion, warned them off in 1913 and demanded the immediate withdrawal of their troops from Valona and Albania. Serbia complied. This time Austria-Hungary issues an ultimatum designed to provoke war, filled with clauses the Serbs cannot accept. It is delivered to Belgrade on the evening of 23rd July with the demand for a response within 48 hours. As the deadline approaches, Slavka records her impressions.

25th July

Throughout the day worried people gather in the streets. Everyone is discussing the news – at home, at their garden gates and in cafes. Even school children and youths wander the streets arguing.

All day long there are rumours of enemy troops massing on Serbia's northern borders, and that Zemun[1] is full of soldiers. As the day draws to an end the crowds do not even consider going home.

Just before sunset paperboys appeared with extra editions. People rushed to read hastily printed newspapers carrying the 'Proclamation to the Nation', in which the government urges people not to gather in the streets and not to panic, as there would be no war. Eventually the city calms down and falls asleep.

Serbia's reply to the ultimatum is fairly conciliatory but the government refuses to have Austrian representation in any internal enquiry into the assassination. On receipt of the reply, Austria-Hungary breaks off diplomatic relations with Serbia. Serbian mobilisation begins the same day in anticipation of an imminent attack.

27th July

Those arriving at the hospital this morning talk excitedly about the drum roll outside The Russian Tsar and other cafes, calling upon all conscripts to report to their district offices at once. After delivering its reply to the Austrian ambassador, the government is said to have declared a general mobilisation and then left for Niš. The Russian embassy staff has gone with them.

Until yesterday Belgrade was a quiet town, its gardens full of sweet-smelling roses, carnations, wallflowers, jasmine and lilacs, with walnut trees branching in the yards, and streets filled with

---

1 Austro-Hungarian fortress town on the other side of the border from Belgrade.

Dr Slavka Mihajlović with her husband and son in 1922

the intoxicating smell of lime and acacia blossoms. All of a sudden the city is a cacophony of sounds, as inhabitants begin to get ready for war.

Convoys of peasants arrive from nearby villages and proceed to report to their district command offices. Their fathers, wives and children follow, carrying food in colourful bags: boiled eggs, cheese, bread, perhaps a roast chicken, and a bottle of plum brandy.

We watch the war veterans; they pass in front of us in peasant garb and footwear, wearing military caps from last year's war. People walk the streets all day. The youngsters are singing, the veterans and pensioners sitting in front of cafes. Some shake their heads in concern. Everywhere we hear the same question: 'What is this? Are we really at war again?'

That day Austria-Hungary declared war on Serbia.

On the night of 28th July Slavka Mihajlović is on duty at the General State Hospital.

29th July

Before dawn today, at 2 a.m., artillery fire thunders from the direction of Zemun. The explosion echoes around Belgrade and the hospital shakes. We all jump out of bed and, more out of astonishment than fear and stay up till dawn. So it is true! The war has started. Big Austria has moved against small war-torn Serbia!

Since early this morning our hospital has been in a state of excitement. All ward heads and our hospital chief, all doctors, conscripts and nurses are ordered to report to their district command offices at once. They are all leaving for new posts – for war and uncertainty. All patients who are able to walk got up to go home.

Lunch is over quickly. Around noon enemy gunboats appear on the Sava and the Danube rivers and start a bombardment. Buildings near the cathedral are hit first.

There isn't a soul in the streets. It's as if the whole town had faded away. Suddenly we see thick smoke rising from somewhere downtown, followed by sparks and flames. We see something burning but don't know what it is.

The bombing goes on until dark. In the hospital everything is quiet. Only the moans and the muffled whimpering of the sick patients occasionally interrupt the quiet of the evening.

The clock strikes half past eleven. As I flip through a surgical textbook preparing for tomorrow's surgery there is a sudden explosion, a terrible noise. The building shakes, windows shatter and broken glass spills over the floor. The patients are screaming. Some are jumping out of their beds, pale and bewildered, while those unable to move cry out for help from their beds. Terrified nurses run from all sides and gather around me. We are all pale with shock, unable to understand what could have happened. Then there is another explosion, and another, and then silence again.

30th July

Hardly anyone slept last night. At dawn Dr Radovanović inspects the wards. He tells us the bridge on the Sava river was blown up last night when an enemy train tried to cross it. There was a great explosion and half of the bridge collapsed into the water. At the same time, a big ship full of enemy troops attempted a landing on our side of the river right under the bridge, so when the bridge collapsed it took the boat and its soldiers under with it. The first enemy attempt to enter Serbia has been thwarted.

Several of the soldiers wounded when the bridge collapsed arrived on our ward early in the morning. Exhausted and pale, suffering from severe blood loss, the wounded got their turn at the operating theatre early this morning. I bandaged their wounds straight away and put them to bed. These must be the first men wounded in this war!

The conflict remained local for only a matter of days. Russia began partial mobilisation on 28th July in support of Serbia and the German government backed the ultimatum which meant that war would be difficult to contain. It would be another two weeks before Austro-Hungarian troops crossed into Serbia but by then the war would reach far beyond the Balkans.

Slavka Mihajlović continued to work through the first months of the conflict in Belgrade. As a woman she was not subject to military recruitment and was soon the only doctor left to take charge of caring for civilians at the General State Hospital.

Chapter 2

SETTING OFF TO THE FRONT

August 1914–January 1915

On 30th July 1914, as the first Austrian shells fell on Belgrade, Russia, Serbia's Slav ally, began to mobilise its men. The gradual slide into war now accelerated all over Europe. An ever more frantic exchange of telegrams between cousins Kaiser Wilhelm of Germany and Tsar Nicholas of Russia did little to postpone the inevitable, for the war was now in the hands of the military. With Russian troops on the move, Germany, in turn, began to mobilise its armies.

On 1st August, as Germany declared 'defensive war' on Russia, France, allied to Russia by a pact of mutual assistance, mobilised against Germany. Two fronts, on the west and east, opened up immediately: on 2nd August German military patrols crossed into France; on the following day Russian troops marched over Germany's borders. All the nations involved were convinced they were fighting a defensive war, forced upon them by someone else. Meanwhile, the argument raged in Britain as to whether it could stay out of the war.

The question was answered with an emphatic no on August 4th. On this day neutral Belgium rejected Germany's request of free passage through its territory to attack France's less fortified border; Germany ignored their refusal and invaded. Britain, allied to Belgium, joined the war that evening at 11 p.m. Its own imperial *interests were at stake, should a powerful Germany come to dominate the high seas.*

Little over a month since the assassination of Archduke Franz Ferdinand in Sarajevo, five empires were at war and millions of soldiers were mobilised. Their armies included the first of what by the end of the war would be nearly 9 million Britons, 8.5 million French, 12 million Russians, 11 million Germans, and close to 8 million Austro-Hungarians.[1]

For the time being, Italy, Romania, Bulgaria and a few other nations remained neutral, waiting to see where their interests lay before declaring their allegiances.

*

Paul Hub from Stetten, a small village near Stuttgart, Germany, volunteers immediately in response to Kaiser Wilhelm's call for 'true patriots'. Two days before departure for training, Hub, who is twenty-four, becomes engaged to his girlfriend, twenty-one-year-old Maria Thumm. On the day of departure, he sends his first letter home.

4th August 1914

Dear parents,

My suitcase is all packed. At 2 p.m. this afternoon I'll be leaving Ulm on a troop train. My life as a soldier has begun. Please keep my washing a little longer, until I ask you for it. Unpack my clothes in the meantime, because they'll get damaged if they're squashed in the suitcase for too long. Maria's letters are in the engagement case, together with my watch chains and other keepsakes that remind me of the happy times I've had with her. Please look after them. I hope I'll be coming back. Think of me when you unpack my things. A final greeting to you all as a civilian. From this evening I'll be sending you military war greetings.

*

---

1 The British and French figures include soldiers recruited from across their empires.

Robert Cude, an unattached twenty-one-year-old from south London, also has no military experience, but enlists immediately when Lord Kitchener, the British Secretary of State for War, issues a call for volunteers.[1] Cude has no great commitment to his factory job, and fancies the adventure and change of scene promised to all members of the new 'Kitchener's Army'. Yet things don't immediately go as Robert had imagined. Having lost his first diary notebook, he recalls his attempts to join up and the first days of soldiering a few months later.

Within a few days of war being declared, I make my first attempt at joining a branch of 'His Majesty's Forces'. I try the Navy. Report at Admiralty, pass doctor, also Educational Officer, and am sent home to await orders. Within seven days am off to Devonport for my trade test. After about ten days I fail, not so much inefficiency, as my inability to stomach orders.

Next few days am unable to settle down. There is a certain amount of Personal Pride in being part, (if a very minor part), of the War Machine. Now it is plain Mr Nobody. It is impossible. However, I resume my old occupation pending my joining the Army. This latter is inevitable, if it lasts another week or two.

On September 7, meet three of the lads at the gate of the firm. The question that has been on the tip of our tongues for days now is asked. Result, four more present themselves at New Cross Town Hall and duly pass the Doctor. Not sworn in today, 24 hours grace to attend to our affairs.

September 8 at 9 a.m. we are sworn Privates of the East Kent Regiment and before 11 a.m. are on our way to Woolwich Barracks. On [September] 9, however, move off to our depot at Canterbury. Here, if we were expected, no steps were taken to receive us, and so no food awaited us and no sleeping accommodation. I sleep in, or on, Barrack Square, inside it was too 'lively'!

---

1 Britain initially relied on voluntary recruitment. Full conscription was enforced in March 1916.

However passed jolly evening and night. Very little breakfast awaited us. Was one of the unlucky ones myself. Could not stomach the fight for a bit of greasy bacon. Still, to add insult to injury, am told to wash up the plates of those who had been fortunate. During morning, am issued with 1 shirt, 1 pair pants, 1 towel and 1 small piece of soap, 'No Khaki'. This is a disappointment indeed. Do a few Movements today to keep us out of mischief. Such as forming fours by numbers, and turning right or left, also by numbers, in between whiles, take off fellow, Buffs.[1] What a cosmopolitan crew we are! All manner of wearing apparel. Parade in afternoon, and am soon packed off with hundreds of others, all the younger men, to Purfleet.[2] We are to help form another new Division, remainder go to Dover. We duly arrive Purfleet at 8 p.m., herded in tents 22 in each. No food, manage to sleep a little with someone sleeping on top of me. Breakfast arrived at last, one sausage per man, no bread, then beginning to resent treatment. Parades every few minutes. Am sick of this playing at soldiers. Dinner comes up. Menu 'Warm water with pieces of a substance which was termed meat floating on top'. Nothing to eat it out of. Cannot eat or drink broth without plate or mug. 3 p.m., camp in uproar, armed pickets on gates, only infuriated men more. Boys demand food, failing this, leave to go home to get some.

Less than impressed with his first experience of British military organisation, Cude, along with several of his friends, heads home to recover.

Leave for 3 days granted and as have not enough for a train up, Charley and Walter Household, J. Bell and myself are soon putting our left leg foremost, 18 miles to London. Get left at Rainham and soon at Blackwall Tunnel. Arrive home 1 a.m.

12 September eat a loaf before I am satisfied and soon forget

---

1 Familiar name of the East Kent Regiment.
2 Military training camp in Essex.

my troubles in sleep. Absolutely the first sleep since I enlisted. Return on Sunday night and find things working fairly smoothly. Fully 20 per cent of men did not return. Suppose they failed to see the humour of the thing, or, their Patriotism had run dry. However, we start 'soldiering' in earnest now. Reveille 6 a.m. and Parades throughout day. We are young and enthusiastic, so we cheerfully bear it although the soldier's 'privilege', ie Grousing, is beginning to be manifest.

By this date, nearly half a million British volunteers have enlisted, although most won't see action for many months. While Robert Cude and his fellow volunteers still pass their time bayonet charging at straw sacks in Essex, over 100,000 professional soldiers of the British Expeditionary Force are already engaged in heavy fighting against German troops in France and Belgium.

*

Paul Tuffrau, twenty-seven, a passionate French patriot from a family of prosperous Bordeaux vineyard proprietors, is swept up in the first wave of mobilisation. A highly educated teacher, Tuffrau has just completed his military service, entering the war as a junior officer. In one of his first diary entries, he admits to feeling 'dizzy and light-headed in the atmosphere of excitement'.

He is leading his company of soldiers deep into the territory of Alsace-Lorraine. This long-disputed territory has been in German hands for forty years, since the Franco-Prussian War of 1870–71, and now the French are determined to claim it back. Just three weeks into battle, life on twenty-four-hour alert is already taking its toll on Tuffrau's men, as he records in his diary.

23nd August 1914, Rembercourt

Yesterday, I got to the trenches at 1 p.m. I could hear the sound of artillery some way off. My men slept where they could – on the bare ground, in the sun or in the shade of the trenches. The dappled light under the plum trees, the men snoozing under the noonday sun as artillery boomed in the distance.

Paul Tuffrau in Paris, 9th August 1914

In the evening we set up the machine guns on the railway line. One of my men, Nérot – short, with little grey eyes – refuses to go to sleep with the other men in the nearby barn. He's made his bed between the rails, next to his machine gun. He has straw for a mattress and two cartridge boxes for pillows. I lend him my blanket. He's a no-nonsense sort of lad, a bit grumpy sometimes, but you can always rely on him.

25th August

In the grey twilight, dull crump of artillery fire, shrapnel exploding above the trees, smoke rising from villages on fire. Endlessly waiting in the gloom of grey roads for orders or information is very nerve-racking. We sleep where we can. I'm in a cart with my face pressed into the canvas. It is raining. The searchlights look for planes in the clouds. The artillery shuffles by, accompanied by a constant stream of stretcher-bearers.

Tuffrau's hopes of liberating Alsace-Lorraine are quickly quashed when his troop is ordered to retreat back across the French border.

29th August

All sorts of vehicles on the road – big carts pulled by oxen, full of women and children, some crying, some laughing. Liancourt, Roye. Enthusiastic welcome, wine, cider, chocolate. Very different from the people of Lorraine. The happiness of the soldiers! We pass two British soldiers on the road and the whole column cheers.

2nd September

Wake up at 4 a.m. We climb onto a wooded hill overlooking the plains. We ready our weapons in a potato field. We dig trenches in the fine soil. Suddenly, an order to withdraw. Later I heard that Major Brun had reacted to the order by shouting, 'To think we have been preparing for the war for forty years, and now this!'

Paul Tuffrau and his fellow soldiers continue their retreat in the face of the German advance. By now, German troops are within 30 miles of Paris, the government leaves for Bordeaux and a third of the city's inhabitants are fleeing the capital. Tuffrau and his men join the Allied French and British troops defending the heart of France.

The fate of Paris, and of France itself, will be decided on the River Marne, east of the capital. The French Marshal Joffre issues

*an Order of the Day: 'At the time when the battle upon which hangs
the fate of France is about to begin, all must remember that the time
for looking back is past; every effort must be concentrated on attacking and throwing the enemy back. Troops that can no longer advance
must at any cost keep the ground that has been won, and must die
where they stand rather than give way.'*

*On 5th September 1914, the Battle of the Marne, the first mon-
umental battle on the Western Front, begins. Over a million French
soldiers with British support slightly outnumber the German forces.
As the German troops near Paris, Tuffrau and his men are defending the village of Barcy, within sight of the River Marne.*

6th September

A beautiful day. We march all morning and around noon we
reach a deep gully below a little village now very familiar to us,
Barcy. German shells rain down methodically and relentlessly –
screaming, awesome explosions, dense black and reddish smoke.
I'm ordered to support the Salé company. I push forward, desperate to catch up with them, but they are advancing too quickly.
We'll make up the ground.

Bullets start whizzing by from unseen guns. I stop several
times to regroup my men. I manage to collect just one artillery
unit. We pass a colonel who points me to the left of a row of
poplars. Following a gully, I squeeze my company in between
two others in a beetroot field. They advance rapidly and, before
the angle they form disappears, I try to protect them by firing
blind. Their march forward is magnificent but too fast, too close
together. One rank kneels, one stands up. We advance with
them, but my artillery men are way behind. Finally here comes
Chamoutin, all upset: 'Poor Maire . . . a bullet in the heart. He
only just got there.' I realise the supplies won't reach us, because
we're going too fast, and certain people who talk a good war are
over-cautious, such as fat L., who will use this as an excuse not
to send them. In any case, we must push forward and if possible
support the bayonet charge, which is imminent.

Some men try to crawl to the rear, hiding in the beetroot. I go over and threaten them with my gun. They claim they are wounded or helping a casualty. Bullets whistle by non-stop, from all directions. It is quite a job to get the men to stand up. I reach the edge of the field but I cannot get the second machine-gun unit to budge an inch, even by insulting them. Of the first unit, only Nérot follows me, looking as resolute and fierce as ever. He is carrying a trivet on his shoulder. 'Why is B. not here?' – 'He says it's pointless, not enough cartridges left.' There are four hundred of them left. I am furious, but there is no time to dwell on it. The men fix bayonets, a flag is unfurled. It's too late to get to my own regiment. I pick up a dead man's weapon, slip on a cartridge belt and join the advancing troop – it is rather scattered and pushing forward in every direction, urged on by the bugles. What's that I'm stepping on? The dead and wounded, friends and foes. Bullets fly past, then the brutal blast of artillery fire right in front of us. The charge tatters, stops. Mulleret, the flag-bearer, is on his back on the other side of the road, his head lying on a sack. Behind a haystack, I come across the flag, a few men and a colonel, shaking like a leaf, his tunic undone, right arm in a sling, shirt covered in blood. He comes toward me; I can't remember what he said. All around, behind piles of grain, men are lying down, shooting or just waiting. Through the haze, you can just make out the rise of a hillside. Is that the Marne?

I am bandaging Mulleret, who is wounded below the left shoulder. His eyes are closed, his face still has some colour. 'Is that you, Tuffrau?' He takes my hand, squeezes it tightly: 'You won't leave me?' He barely complains about the pain, except for the odd wince: 'Unfasten my belt; under the shirt . . . I have some gold in my belt. Leave that. But take my handgun.' All the while gunfire, artillery. The flag had tried to advance, but must have been driven back as I notice it on my right, a little further back, behind a large haystack.

Bugles are rallying the men 'To the flag!' Some who had been

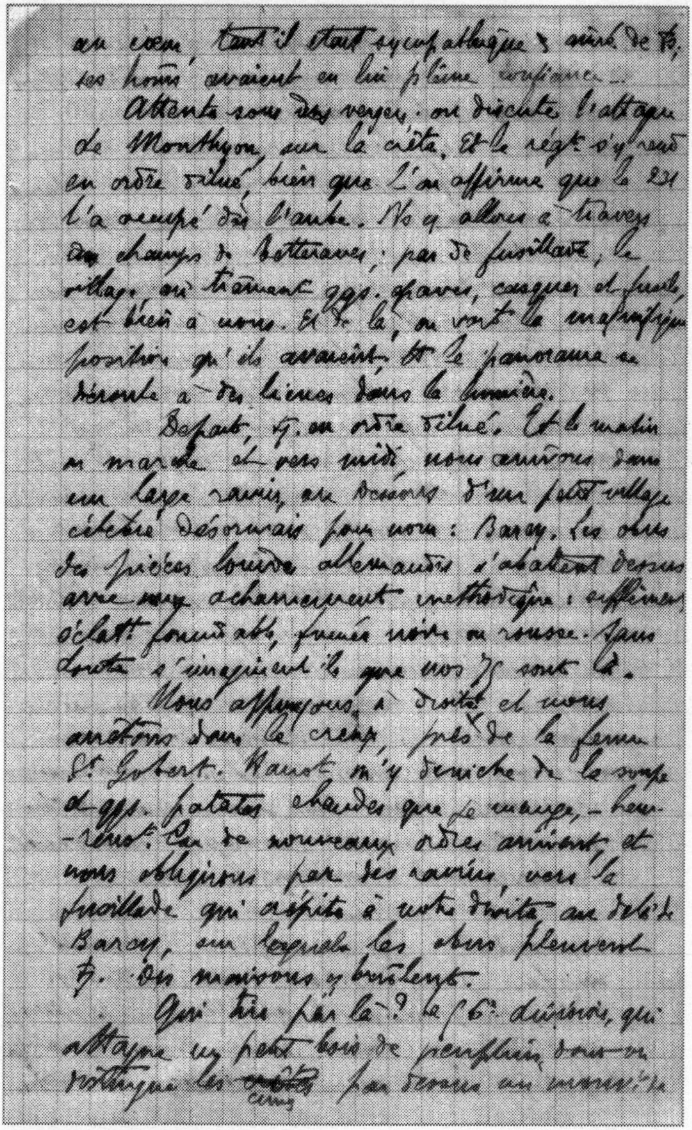

au cœur, tant il était sympathique & sûr de lui;
ses hommes avaient en lui pleine confiance.
Attente sous des vergers. On discute l'attaque
de Monthyon, sur la crête. Et le régt s'y rend
en ordre dilué, bien que l'on affirme que le 231
l'a occupé dès l'aube. Nous allons à travers
des champs de betteraves; pas de fusillade, le
village, où traînent qqs. épaves, casques et fusils,
est bien à nous. Et de là, on voit la magnifique
position qu'ils avaient. Et le panorama se
déroule à des lieues dans la lumière.
Départ, tj. en ordre dilué. Et le matin
se marche et vers midi nous arrivons dans
un large ravin, au dessous d'un petit village
célèbre désormais pour nous: Barcy. Les obus
des pièces lourdes allemandes s'abattent dessus
avec un acharnement méthodique: sifflement,
éclatt formidable, fumée noire ou rousse. Sans
doute s'imaginent-ils que nos Js sont là.
Nous appuyons à droite et nous
arrêtons dans le creux, près de la ferme
St Gobert. Haenot m'y déniche de la soupe
et qqs. patates chaudes que je mange, — heu-
-reusement. Car de nouveaux ordres arrivent, et
nous obligent par des ravins, vers la
fusillade qui crépite à notre droite, au delà de
Barcy, sur laquelle les obus pleuvent
tj. Des maisons y brûlent.
Qui tire par là? La 56e division, qui
attaque un petit bois de peupliers dans un
vallonnement les ~~[illegible]~~ cinq par dessus un marais. La

A page of Tuffrau's diary for 1914

beating retreat now head for the tricolour, rifle in hand. I gather some of them and we turn around, heading for the battle. But the gunfire is intense and we have to stop to fire back. All of a sudden we're under a hail of bullets. The entire line falls back and I can hear some of them shouting, 'Our own 75s[1] are firing at us!' I order them to be silent, they could create a full-blown panic. This time, however, more of the men are retreating, in reasonable order. We head for a small gully and pause there, while the German shells scream and explode above us continuously. 'Halt! Turn around! Forward!' I keep shouting, and these brave soldiers do turn around. I notice Dumesnil who is holding the flag. A sergeant close to me breaks into the Marseillaise and everyone joins in. But in this incredible noise Valmy's song is drowned out.

We march on. From behind a haystack on the left, almost within reach, Germans emerge, their hands in the air. Thirty men surround them to disarm them, when suddenly rat-a-tat-tat, the machine guns begin and I realise that we will not advance any further.

We're all on the ground in the beetroot, not moving, not shooting. We can't see anything. The bullets keep coming. I look at my watch, it is 4:30 – two hours of clear daylight left. To cap it all, the sun sets behind us. We have lost the support of both artillery and infantry. German rifles crackle incessantly, they are king of the battlefield.

I tell the men, 'If we all get up together, we'll get mowed down. We have to withdraw one by one, on our bellies.' I lead the way. I mostly crawl on my elbows and knees. Bullets follow my trail in the alfalfa. My coat is all screwed up, so is my shirt. As I crawl on my bare stomach, the grass and the earth feel deliciously fresh.

When the gunfire intensifies yet again, I lie at the bottom of the trench, my face to the ground, my gun in front of me – and I go to sleep. Yes, I really sleep, exhausted and deafened. A

---

1 75 mm artillery guns

minute of sleep gives me the strength to go another hundred metres, and the thought of loved ones drives me to keep going.

After four relentless days of fighting, casualties on each side reach a quarter of a million. These losses will be the highest sustained in a single battle for the rest of the war. On 8th September 1914 the German troops are ordered to fall back and dig in. Though tactically inconclusive, the Battle of the Marne is a strategic victory for the Allies and one of the decisive battles of the First World War.

The Battle of the Marne was fought as a war of movement, yet this was about to change. Within weeks, both sides would begin to dig deeper and even more elaborate defensive lines. Trench warfare that began in earnest here, along the River Marne, will set the pattern for the rest of the war.

*

Having just completed his obligatory two months of training, the young German soldier Paul Hub is now marching fast across German-occupied territory in Belgium. Hub is one of thousands of young recruits sent to make up for the heavy losses suffered by his advancing army. In a series of letters to his fiancée, Maria Thumm, Paul shares his new experiences. This is his first time abroad.

16th October, Pipaix, Belgium

My dear Maria,

I never thought I would be wishing you a happy birthday from an enemy country! The people in Pipaix are very friendly and kind to us. The only problem we have is making ourselves understood. My schoolboy French is patchy. They can just about understand me, but the locals speak so quickly, I can't keep up. Please be so good as to send me a pocket German-French dictionary. I'm living in the schoolhouse. I'm sleeping fantastically well on straw after four uncomfortable nights on the train. It's difficult for the local people to feed us. Wherever you go, everything is usually sold out. The whole time we were in Germany we were showered with presents at every station; that stopped when we got to Luxembourg. As soon as we crossed the Belgian border we were ordered not to wave at the locals, but load our rifles instead. I'm not used to walking down the street with a loaded rifle. The local people probably fired at some German soldiers in the past. That's why some places have been flattened.

The 'local people' Hub is referring to are the franc-tireurs, *or civilian snipers. A reality in the Franco-Prussian War of 1870,* franc-tireurs *are more an imagined threat in 1914, but the danger is talked up by German commanders anxious to promote aggressive vigilance in occupied territories. This results in frequent German atrocities against Belgian and French civilians.*

After a long march north Paul Hub's regiment arrives at the outskirts of Ypres where British and German troops try to outflank each other within close range of the English Channel.

23rd October, South of Terhand

My dear Maria,

I wanted to write to you on your birthday but I didn't get round to it. The English gunners wouldn't leave us in peace. So far we're all fine, although we've been under heavy bombardment. The morning of your birthday was our baptism of fire. Our adversaries are almost all Englishmen who got away from Antwerp. They're trying to break through our line to get into France. These dogs are almost on top of us and are costing us a lot of blood. They make very quick raids from their trenches, then disappear into cover very quickly. I've already seen quite a lot of the misery of war. Maria, you wouldn't believe it. In Heule, one of the suburbs of Courtrai, the shocked inhabitants were roused at 11 p.m. to provide quarters for two to three thousand soldiers. If there isn't any straw then you just fall asleep on the bare floor. We never take our clothes off. Lots of houses are being shot to pieces, set alight and burning. It was a terrible sight when night came. The civilians had all run away. Their animals are running around helpless and there's no way other

Paul Hub and Maria Thumm

soldiers will help because they're all happy when they find a
place for themselves to bed down. Maria, this sort of a war is so
unspeakably miserable. If only you saw a line of stretcher-bearers
with their burdens, you'd know what I mean. I haven't had a
chance to shoot at all yet. We're having to deal with an unseen
enemy.

25th October

My dear Maria,

I'm sitting in Vieux Chien. Will there ever be a normal Sunday again? The terrible digging continues. Every day brings new horrors. Yesterday, while trying to dismount our telephone line, we ended up in the middle of heavy infantry and grenade fire. We were incredibly lucky to get out unscathed. It's impossible to get rid of those Englishmen. They've dug one trench behind another. The weather is good, which is a good thing for the troops (though it's also good for the enemy). The weather is much milder – autumn is dragging its feet this year.

Maria, how are things with you? I long for some news of you. It was still so lovely just a few months ago. We've set up camp in a little farm near Vieux Chien. When the enemy finds us, we might be on the move again. I'm slowly getting used to the noise. My hearing has come back again after the effect of shells exploding right next to me yesterday.

To maintain the speedy advance of its army, the German Supreme Command issues orders to confiscate much of the food and supplies from the local population; troops will have to live off the land they occupy. Paul Hub has difficulties finding enough to eat.

Everyone has to find their own food. Sometimes we manage to throw together a decent soup. You can find meat on the farms. We just don't have enough bread. We find all sorts of things when we're requisitioning, just no bread. I've got a few pieces of chocolate and other tasty morsels in my rucksack that I got from you and our parents. As soon as this is over (it's lasted a week already), I guess I'll get together with my company. Then I'm going to open my rucksack and tuck in. But first I will ask for my post, because there's bound to be something there from my Maria. You just don't realise how lonely you get when you're cut off from the rest of the world like this. Now I understand why people were begging for newspapers at all the German-occupied train stations.

God bless you, Maria! I hope he keeps an eye on me too. Please write when you get this. The post here is very slow.

I remain, with lots of heartfelt wishes,

Your Paul

Hub's regiment is now thrust into their first action. They receive orders to capture the village of Gheluvelt on the Ypres Salient. On 30th October 1914 German General Von Fabeck issues bellicose battle orders, calling for the final settling of old scores: 'The break-through will be of decisive importance. We must and therefore will conquer, settle for ever the centuries-long struggle, end the war and strike the decisive blow against our most detested enemy. We will finish the British, Indians, Canadians, Moroccans and other trash, feeble adversaries, who surrender in great numbers if they are attacked with vigour.' The following day Paul Hub writes to Maria with considerably less enthusiasm.

31st October

My dear Maria,

I feel so terrible I'd really rather not write to you. That doesn't mean that I've forgotten you, though. Every day spent here makes it clearer to me how beautiful home is and what a crowd of feelings that word 'home' brings out in me. I have lived through such horror recently, no words can describe it, the tragedy all around me. Every day the fighting gets fiercer and there is still no end in sight. Our blood is flowing in torrents. When I think of our 247th Regiment my eyes swim with tears. The first and second battalions only have 250 to 300 men left, so more than half are gone. Today only a few of my comrades will be still standing. My company commander, Lieutenant Massbauer, had been at the front for one hour when he was shot through the head. Pale and close to death, he was carried past me. Today, Sunday, I stood at his modest grave and joined in a prayer.

That's how it is. All around me, the most gruesome devastation. Dead and wounded soldiers, dead and dying animals, horse cadavers, burnt-out houses, dug-up fields, cars, clothes, weaponry – all this is scattered around me, a real mess. I didn't think war would be like this. We can't sleep for all the noise. At least thirty shells explode at once, the whole time. We called for back-up yesterday and today – I hope they make it. There are only a few of us left to tackle the English. I managed to wash myself properly yesterday, for a change. My beard is getting ever longer. Otherwise, I'm feeling fine. As you can see – all this noise is not going to ruffle my Württemberg calm.

As the day ends the village of Gheluvelt, having changed hands several times, is with the British. The losses are severe on both sides, including some hundreds from Hub's 247th, later known as 'The Regiment of the Dead'.

Once the day's fighting is over, Paul Hub finally gets a close look at his adversaries, reporting back to Maria on the subject of their peculiar dress sense.

There are lots of Scots amongst all the dead and wounded. Instead of trousers they wear a sort of short, warm skirt that only reaches halfway down their thighs. Well it's not really a skirt, it's more of a sort of folded wrap-around thing. It is a strange sight. I'm amazed the boys don't freeze their bums off, walking around half-naked like that, because they don't wear any underwear either.

That said, they do have a warm, heavy coat like the other English soldiers. The colour of their uniform is much more suited to the terrain than ours. It's a sort of dirty brownish green. Their hats and wrap-around things are the same colour. The English soldier can move much more freely than we can. With their practical clothing and their light packs, they can run like hares. This really is an advantage when under fire. But we're still going to win.

I give you, my most beloved, a big loving hug. I am so lucky to have you, my love.

Yours, Paul

The fighting for the village of Gheluvelt lasts four days, forming part of the First Battle of Ypres. After another three weeks of combat, no decisive breakthrough is achieved, despite horrendous losses: 80,000 German and over 54,000 British, dead and wounded. Unwilling to give any ground, or sustain the bloodletting, both sides dig in. By December 1914 the line of trenches will stretch for 500 miles along the Western Front, from Switzerland to the English Channel.

*

By the winter of 1914 there is trench warfare also on the Eastern Front, where German and Russian troops face each other. Russia's initial advance into East Prussia, early in August 1914, was followed by a number of spectacular defeats. By December 1914 over a quarter of a million Russian soldiers are dead; hundreds of thousands are captured. To replace its heavy losses, Russia must keep delivering trainloads of fresh recruits to the battlefields.

Vasily Mishnin is a furniture salesman from the sleepy provincial town of Penza in central Russia. Mishnin, a twenty-seven-year-old conscript, is newly married; his young wife, Nyura, is already pregnant.

After two months of very basic training and occasional boozing, at 11 a.m. on a freezing cold morning, Mishnin's regiment lines up at Penza train station. Relatives are on the platform to say their last goodbyes, but unlike August 1914, there is no orchestra and no patriotic cheering. The news of the bloody carnage at the front has been pouring in, causing anxiety and panic.

Vasily Mishnin and his wife, Nyura, summer 1914

25th December[1]

The first bell – a shiver runs through my whole body. We take our places in the carriages. Pushing and shoving. Some are drunk, some sober. Everyone is clambering around the carriage. This doesn't feel like the right time to be saying goodbye, perhaps for ever.

The third whistle. Everybody breaks down. Loud crying, hysterics, whole families weeping. I kiss my Nyura for the last time and all of my family kiss me. I can hardly hold back the tears. I say goodbye to Nyura. She shouts, 'Why are you crying Vasiusha, you said you weren't going to cry!' Beside myself, I climb into the carriage with the rest and look out at the crowd. I can hear wailing, and a tumult of voices, but I've suddenly gone numb. My nerves are in shreds. I gaze at the pitiful crowd, but then my eyes find Nyura again and everything changes. I want to jump out of the carriage and kiss her again, for the last time. Too late, the long whistle of the steam train screams out, it's ready to separate us from our loved ones and take us – God knows where. I am about to climb out of the carriage, when something stirs under my feet. I feel the train moving. The crowd is whipped up into a yet more violent state of hysteria. My heart pounds as the carriage rolls on. We will perhaps never return to Penza.

We are pulled away from the doors and they are locked shut. Someone starts up our favourite tune, 'Today Must Be Our Final Day', to take our minds off all this, but I huddle up in a corner. The song upsets me so much, it is hard to compose myself. I feel ashamed. While my comrades sing, I can't stop crying, can't calm down.

---

1 Until February 1918 Russia used the Orthodox Julian calendar, which was 13 days behind the Gregorian calendar used in Europe. All dates have been converted in line with the Western calendar, here and in subsequent chapters.

On 1st January 1915 Mishnin's train arrives in Warsaw. A few days later he gets to choose his first gun.

5th January 1915

We go to the depot to get our rifles. Good Lord, what's all this? They're covered in blood, black clotted lumps of it are hanging off them. All of this horror is piled up in the yard, and we all rummage about looking for a decent one – a soldier with a bad rifle is like a teacher without a pencil. At 4 p.m. we are back in our den. We eat and clean our rifles. Knowing that soon, very soon we shall have to go into battle, we start singing 'Today Must Be Our Final Day'. We go to bed anxious. The glass rattles more loudly in our window frames tonight. That means the enemy guns are not far away.

7th January, Warsaw

'Get up, lads, and God help you – get ready to move out.' We get up, drink tea and pack our possessions. 7 a.m. We line up in the barracks . . . The order is 'To Prayer!' and we sing 'Your Birth Oh Jesus Our Lord' in a thousand voices that echo through every corner of this bleak stone building. What a solemn moment! I want to be joyful and praise the Lord, but this is only a fleeting thought. In my heart I can only feel sadness and grief; tears roll down my cheeks, and I am not the only one. Each of us hides the tears from his comrades. Afterwards, we sing 'God Save the Tsar'.

For the last time we cross ourselves and move off, slowly and gently. No use being sad any more. 'Lads, how about a song? Think we can manage that?' We strike up with 'Hey Lads, Get Ready to March' and the buildings of Warsaw echo loudly. The crowd seeing us off are not our people, they are all foreigners. They look surprised – 'How can these guys sing like this when they're going off to their deaths?' We sing for a long time, one song after another, until some big cheese stops us. It turns out we're not allowed to sing here in the town of Warsaw.

*Their march westward takes several more days. On 25th January
Mishnin spends his first night in a trench, in Russian Poland.*

26th January

At 7 a.m. the division commander walks down the trench and
orders us to oil and clean our rifles. 'As soon as you see a
German, shoot him!' (he is shaking, as if he has a fever) 'But
don't let him see you, and don't leave the trenches!'

The sun is shining but the trenches are muddy. We have a bite
to eat, we drink water from our flasks and walk about the
trenches, like we're in the park. Through our gun ports we peer
at the Germans, who are wandering about their trench to get
warm. It is getting dark, I want to go to sleep, but an order
comes – everyone has to stand to by the gun ports. So we stand
and gaze into the distance.

12 midnight, 27th January

I have to go and relieve the guard under the cover of fire that's
pouring on to the enemy trenches. My heart pounds, it is a terrifying thing to walk to your death. The seven of us climb out of
our trench and go up to the barbed wire boundary. We find a
hole in it and crawl through it like cats. Bullets and shells keep
flying out of the German trenches, lighting up our position. We
get to the guard post, let the previous lot off duty and take their
places. It is frightening even to sit or lie down here – the rifle is
shaking in my hands. My hand comes down on something black:
it turns out there are corpses here that haven't been cleared
away. My hair stands on end. I have to sit down. There is no
point in staring into the distance – it is pitch dark. All I can feel
is fear. I am so frightened of the shells that I want the ground to
open up and swallow me. Two soldiers – I can only see their silhouettes – are coming from the German side. What can you
do – we ready our guns – now I will send an angel of death for
someone – but it turns out they're ours, they've been out to recce
and throw bombs into the German trenches. These lads, they're

so brave, they've got real guts – they'll get the Georges[1] on their chests for that.

Now the next shift arrives. Thank God, we've survived this one. What next?

27th January

11 a.m. Soon our lunch is coming. Hot soup, my heart's desire. Suddenly a screeching noise pierces the air, I feel a pang in my heart, something whistles past and explodes nearby. My dear Lord, I am so frightened – and I hear this buzzing in my ears . . . I leave my post and climb into my dugout. It is packed, everyone is shaking and asking again and again, 'What's going on? What's going on?' One explosion follows another, and another. Two lads are running, shouting out for nurses. They are covered in blood. It is running down their cheeks and hands, and something else is dripping from underneath their bandages. They're soon dead, shot to pieces. There is screaming, yelling, the earth is shaking from artillery fire and our dugout is rocking from side to side like a boat.

The explosions come nearer and nearer. The injured from the 1st Company arrive and crawl into our dugout crazed and in agony, so we drop all our gear and try to crawl out, to run away – somewhere, anywhere. And at that moment a shell flies right into our dugout and my mates Kozhukhin and Blinov, who'd just crawled out, stand staring at it, as if they'd gone out of their minds.

We are running, but God knows where. Our CO had run off to the forest. I suppose he thought it was safer in there. As if. None of us can understand what's going on. Everyone is trembling. We crouch down on the ground in silence, then when a shell bursts right around our ears we move on.

Samoudrikhin and I scramble into a peasant hut. We press

---

1 The Order of St George.

ourselves against a wall, sit down and wipe our eyes. Our eyes are full of tears, we wipe them away, but they just keep coming because the shells are full of gas. We are terrified. Samoudrikhin and I lie face down and we just want to dig ourselves into the earth. Under our breath we pray to our Lord God to save us from this, just for this one day. Dear Nyurochka, pray for me in this terrible hour, and forgive me if I am guilty of anything. We will probably never see each other again – all it takes is an instant and I will be no more – and perhaps no one will be able to gather the scattered pieces of my body for burial.

Long, agonising minutes pass. Suddenly our battery begins to speak: at first the field guns, then the mortars and finally the entire division battery starts up. There is such a roaring and shaking that I think my nerves will shatter and I'll go mad. 'Well, now it's our turn to die,' I say to Samoudrikhin, and he replies: 'Don't talk like that, you've got a death wish.'

Dear God, are you really sitting up there in heaven without hearing or saying anything? My body is burning as if it were on fire, I am shaking all over and my head is icy cold. If only I could fall asleep and not hear death taking my soul away.

Dear Lord! Please end this storm, please save me, not for my own good but for my family, for my beloved who is now suffering along with her darlings! If only I could daydream and not think about death. But these wretched thoughts, each more frightful than the last, keep turning round inside my head. I'd rather be killed instantly than be left crippled. The earth is shaking more and more violently.

In the coming months, Paul Tuffrau is to fight at Verdun, Robert Cude and Paul Hub will take part in the Battle of the Somme and Vasily Mishnin will try to get out of the trenches on the Eastern Front.

Chapter 3

CHILDREN AT WAR

August 1914–September 1915

Some of the opening encounters of the war were not unlike those seen in previous European conflicts. The initial rapid advances covered hundreds of miles and were made by cavalry armed with lances and dressed in bright uniforms more suitable for parade displays. The first trenches on the Marne were shallow; yet gradually, as the early movements rolled to a standstill, the trench network deepened and expanded, forming a permanent line that stretched for hundreds of miles and would remain static for most of the war. Tin helmets would become indispensable kit for millions of soldiers making their homes in the trenches.

The world of 1914 was a mixture of the old and the new. Horse-drawn carts were gradually replaced by automobiles, electricity was spreading beyond the cities, telephones were making an appearance in better-off homes and medical breakthroughs included the discovery of powerful anaesthetics. Military technology had also undergone a substantial leap in recent years. Powerful new artillery, poison gas, aeroplanes and, later on, tanks all made their first appearances in this war. Yet at its start even the most seasoned military men could not predict which of this new weaponry would play an important role in the conflict, nor could they imagine the destructive power of the mass-produced weapons that were now available.

The most recent Balkan War of 1912–13 had left millions of civilians within Europe untouched. But in the new conflict the home and the front will become intertwined, the state of one affecting the other. After the initial German advance on the Western Front in the opening weeks of the conflict, 11 million civilians in Belgium and France were placed under occupation for the duration of the war. The unprecedented scale of the war involving millions of troops, mass production of armaments, and staggering casualties will affect people around the world. Whether fighting it, working for it, or living with it, millions of men, women and children would be involved in what later became known as the first total war.

*

Of the children growing up in Europe during this time two keep detailed diaries of their experiences. Yves Congar is a ten-year-old French boy living with his family in Sedan, a town in north-eastern France, the site of the famous Battle of Sedan fought during the Franco-Prussian War forty years earlier. His grandfather is the only one who remembers that time. In the summer of 1914, at his mother's suggestion, Yves begins to write a diary: an educational way to pass the time during the summer holidays. With war looming, Yves writes of his keenness to be a soldier and draws pictures of imaginary battles. Just three weeks into the war, real soldiers arrive on his doorstep when German troops occupy Sedan and a German officer moves in with Yves' family.

Piete Kuhr is a twelve-year-old girl from the East Prussian town of Schneidemühl, just a few miles out of the reach of Russian troops on the Eastern Front. She introduces herself in her first diary entry: 'I am called Piete. My brother's name is Willi-Gunther, he is fifteen years old. I am twelve. We live with my grandmother in Schneidemühl in the province of Posen. My mother has a School of Music and Drama in Berlin. She often visits us. Those are great times.' Piete's mother, the family's main breadwinner, had asked *her daughter to keep a diary and send the entries to her in Berlin as a way of keeping in touch. Piete starts writing on the day war breaks out.*

1st August 1914

From today Germany is at war. My mother says I should write a diary about the war; she thinks it will be of interest to me when I am older. This is true. When I am fifty or sixty, what I have written as a child will seem strange. But it will all be true because you must not tell lies in a diary.

The Serbs started it. Austria-Hungary, Germany, Serbia, Russia and France have joined in. We have no idea what war will be like. There are flags on all the houses in town, just as if we were having a festival. They are black, white and red.

3rd August

At school the teachers say it is our patriotic duty to stop using foreign words. I didn't know what that meant at first, but now I see it – you must no longer say 'Adieu' because that is French. I must now call Mama 'Mutter'. At school they talk of nothing but the war now. The girls are pleased that Germany is entering the field against its old enemy, France. We have to learn new songs about the glory of war. The enthusiasm in our town is growing by the hour. People wander through the streets in groups, shouting 'Down with Serbia! Long live Germany!' Everyone wears black, white and red pompons in their button holes or black, white and red bows. In our school people wear bows and German hair ribbons. I had one too but I've lost it.

Sentries with loaded rifles stand in front of the railway station. Sometimes they fire a shot or two. I got close enough to them to see the fixed bayonets. They are long and much thinner and sharper than I had thought. It is expected that the Russians will blow the station up. All troop transports for Russia and from east to west are routed through our town. As we live close to the station we think we're in danger.

Piete Kuhr seated with (from left to right) her mother, her brother Willi, and her grandmother

4th August

The 149th Infantry Regiment is stationed in our town, Schneidemühl. They are going to be sent to the Western Front. This evening we heard the far off sound of the drums, bass drums and kettledrums. The music kept getting louder and clearer. We couldn't bear to stay in our room and ran out into the street. 'To the station', cried Willi. Our regiment was marching down the street to the station. The soldiers wore new grey uniforms and black spiked helmets. They were looking serious. I had expected them to be laughing and rejoicing. A trumpet call rang out. A soldier as big as a tree came past me. I stretched out my hand over the fence and muttered 'Farewell!' He smiled at me and shook my hand. I gazed after him. Gradually the train began to move. It wouldn't have taken much for me to burst out crying. I went home by a roundabout way. I held my hand out in front of me, the one that the soldier had squeezed. As I went up our poorly lit steps, I stared at the palm of my hand. Then I quickly kissed it.

German regiments are heading both west for France and east to face the Russian army. In the first days of August the Russians invade East Prussia, close to where Piete lives. The initial Russian foray causes German troops to retreat. Civilian refugees fleeing from the advance begin to flood Piete's town.

14th August

You suddenly get the feeling that the enemy is quite near. People are becoming uneasy. Fresh refugees have arrived from East Prussia. This time I have seen them myself: mothers with their children, old women and old men. Some well dressed, others not. They all carry bundles and suitcases, bedding, coats and cloaks all tied together. The refugees are looked after at the Red Cross depot on the station. One woman with noisy children kept crying out, 'Where can we go, where can we go?' She said, 'A girl

like you can have no idea what it's like, can you?' and tears ran
down her chubby red cheeks.

17th August

The town is swarming with strange soldiers. I met Greta Dalüge
and went with her to the marketplace down Posener Strasse. She
was greeted by several officers. I wonder if Greta Dalüge is
happy. She is much older than me and puts make-up on her face.
She does it very carefully so the teachers don't notice. Nearly all
the big girls at the high school wear make-up.

22nd August

Japan has given an ultimatum to Germany.

A map of the world hangs in our classroom on which the enemy
countries are marked with red flags. Now we have the island
nation of Japan also flagged with red.[1] The areas that are for
Germany carry black, white and red flags. When we have won a
battle a flag is moved forward.

*New flags are about to appear on the map not far from Piete's own
home. As the German army in East Prussia regroups and retaliates,
its disgraced commanders, who were defeated in the first three weeks
of the war, are replaced. Newly appointed Generals Hindenburg
and Ludendorff lead a ruthless campaign on the Eastern Front.
Centuries-long animosity between the German 'Teutons' and the
'Slav' nations including Russia, Ukraine and Poland, comes to a
head at the Battle of Tannenberg, where German forces had been
famously defeated by those of Poland 500 years previously. Soon, the
first Russian prisoners of this battle arrive at Schneidemühl train
station. Piete rushes to get a glimpse of the enemy.*

---

1 On 23rd August 1914 Japan declared war on Germany.

25th August

At six o'clock in the evening some troop trains arrived with the first Russian prisoners. People crowded both sides of the street to see the enemy. The Russians are tall, fair and bronzed with curly beards. Their ragged uniforms are an ugly grey brown. Instead of helmets they have peaked caps or fur hats worn at an angle. Many of them had woollen rags wrapped round their feet instead of boots. The Russian soldiers searched the ground for discarded bits of tobacco. They picked up crumpled pieces of paper and rummaged in rubbish bins. Suddenly a company of soldiers marched down the street. They were armed and took the Russian prisoners away. We were excited. Our first Schneidemühl prisoners! Where were they being taken?

30th August

Whole columns of refugees came through our town. Many are crying. There are mothers with quite tiny children. The babies' bottoms are red, because the mothers haven't enough nappies to lay them out to dry. We have torn up old sheets and shirts and given them the pieces to use as nappies. Gretel and I now play a game in the yard in which her old doll is a refugee child that has no more nappies. She has painted its behind red, to show that it is sore.

1st September

The battle is won! This is really true, so it says in the special news sheet; General Paul von Hindenburg has defeated the Russians at Tannenberg. Crowds of people are milling around in the streets, laughing, wishing each other good luck and joining in singing the national anthem. We met Fräulein Ella Gumprecht. 'Such good news! The Russians all stuck in a swamp.' 'Will no one help them out? Do they have to drown?' I asked. The war is one month old today.

Russian troops are encircled in a swampy area near the Masurian Lakes in East Prussia. Thousands of men drown, as their horses, carts and munitions sink into the swamp. The cries and pleading of the slowly dying soldiers are heard for days. Some of the victorious German troops shoot them out of pity – and to get uninterrupted sleep at night. The Battle of Tannenberg lasts for four days, resulting in over 30,000 Russian dead and 100,000 captured.

Every major battle is celebrated with a day off school. Victories from past conflicts are also still honoured. The Battle of Sedan, in the Franco-Prussian War of 1870, is yet to be overshadowed by the tragedies of the new war.

2nd September

Sedan Remembrance Day! Another holiday from school. We assembled at 9 o'clock in the school courtyard in order to march to the church where a service was held to celebrate the day.

4th September

More and more people are fleeing from Schneidemühl. Whole blocks of flats are empty. The platform is swarming with wailing refugees. A young woman with a black headband is crying because she has lost her children. An old, refined-looking man grabs Grandma's sleeve and asks, 'Have you not seen my daughter? She is wearing a blue coat. I am nearly blind.' We ran around serving bread, coffee and soup. Sometimes three or four troop trains arrive in a single hour. In between these come trainloads of refugees, and passenger trains that have been converted into hospital trains. But Grandma suddenly became angry and said I must stop hanging around the soldiers, and should make my way home and get my homework done.

Frightening rumours about the treatment of civilians by the Russian army begin to spread through the town.

10th September

Horror stories. They say Russians tie German women to trees, then set up wooden crosses in front of them and nail their little children to them. When the kids have died before their mothers' eyes, the Russians mutilate the women and kill them. The Belgian guerrillas are said to be no better, but they do it all more secretly. Dear God, just bring the war to an end! I don't look on it as glorious any more, in spite of 'school holidays' and victories.

14th September

The little cemetery is the burial place for our enemies. A few Russian prisoners who have died in transit and several spies who have been shot rest there. Frau Annchen and Grandma have asked me to show them the graves. As they were not on duty at the station today we went there together. Gretel Wegner came with us too. Gretel and I broke off pine twigs and threw them on the nearest mounds. We secretly decided to look after the cemetery. It was to belong entirely to us.

16th September

Last night I heard Grandma crying. She was crying so much it greatly distressed me. The young First Lieutenant Schön is the first of our friends to be killed. I buried my head in the pillow so that Grandma would not hear me crying.

25th September

Gretel Wegner, her brother Fritz, Dora Hänsch's brother Julius, a few neighbouring children and I now play a new game of soldiers. I have bought myself a little yellow book, which contains all the drill regulations for infantry officers. Jule Hänsch and Fritz Wegner have carved rifles and bayonets out of wooden boxes. Now in every spare moment we practise the 'drill'. All the mothers complain about our clothes, which are quite grey with dust from lying down.

28th September

People talk much of the ferocity of the French colonial troops.[1] The blacks are said to have sharp curved knives, which they carry between their teeth when charging. They are very tall and as strong as lions.

11th October

At school everyone is so much in favour of the war. What a hullabaloo there was today when the teacher read out the news, that Fort Breendonck near Antwerp had been taken. You could hardly make out her words because of the screams of joy. Sometimes I think the girls keep rejoicing so much just because they hope there will be a holiday from school. They scream so that the headmaster sees what a patriotic school he has, and then perhaps they will be let off the last lesson. I do scream, but not because of the victory. Nor because I think we should be let out. I scream just for the fun of it. I think it's brilliant to shout at the top of my voice in a place where I usually have to keep my mouth shut.

25th October

There is war everywhere. In Africa too. In the Orange Free State and the Transvaal a rebellion has broken out. There is nothing in the papers about our losses. The war has indeed spread through the whole world!

As living conditions deteriorate, Piete tries to hold on to her enthusiastic patriotism by repeating adults' promises that the Fatherland will triumph and protect her and her family.

---

1 The French army includes recruits from their African colonies.

2nd November

Everyone talks of shortages. Most people are buying in such massive stocks that their cellars are full to bursting. Grandma refuses to do this. She says she doesn't want to deprive the Fatherland of anything. We're not hoarders. The Fatherland won't let us starve. It is frightening to see how uncivilised the soldiers look. Dirty, ragged and with stubbly beards. Nearly all those who come from Russia have lice. There are indeed de-lousing centres but there is often no time for the soldiers to be de-loused, so they sit in our Red Cross depot and scratch themselves in secret. When we return home after station duty we have to search our clothing thoroughly for lice. There is now a remarkable illness around, a kind of influenza. There have already been cases of it in the towns. Perhaps I shall fall ill too.

5th November

I can no longer play with dolls. Gretel asked me what I would like to play, then. I said soldiers. Many planes crash in Schneidemühl. I have seen two crashes. It is due to the fact that we train young airmen here. When they make their first solo flight they are often nervous, and then an accident happens.

7th November

Schneidemühl now has a prisoner-of-war camp. It is near the infantry barracks that Grandpa built. To the right is the starch factory, which stinks horribly. The camp is called the Russian camp because they are nearly all Russians in it. Grandma has strongly forbidden us to go to the Russian camp, because influenza is prevalent there. In the last eight days six of the town's inhabitants have died of influenza.

Piete then stops writing for nearly a month.

1st December

I was mighty ill. It was the influenza epidemic. Grandma didn't go to the station for three weeks. She looked after me continuously. I love her so much! At 42 degrees you die. Once I reached nearly 41 degrees. Then I asked Grandma whether I was going to die. Grandma, sitting by my bed in the dark room, said: 'If you have to die, my child, then we both go together.' I shall never forget that.

7th December

I am back at school now. The girls were pleased. I decided in the afternoon to call for my friend Dora to go for a walk. Dora and I went into town. 'Not to Posener Strasse!' I said. Posener Strasse is the true 'Lovers' Lane'. Dora can't bear the 'flirting', as it's called in Schneidemühl, either, so we chose the lonely way across the horse market.

9th December

I was with Grandma today at the Rohleder hospital. We took two feather pillows, chocolate and cigarettes there. The wounded lie on cotton and hay. Everyone is taking their spare feather beds and cushions there. And all the time more bedding is needed. How much longer will the war last? For a few weeks, people thought – till Christmas. But no end to the war is in sight.

*

While Piete Kuhr lives behind the front, the war marches right into Yves Congar's home town of Sedan in north-eastern France. Ten-year-old Yves is the youngest of four children. 'I can only think about war. I would like to be a soldier and fight,' Yves notes excitedly on 29th July. Four days later German troops begin their swift advance through France, pushing the French army all the way back to the outskirts of Paris. Sedan is once more a battlefield. Twenty-five civilians are killed, either executed or in fires, during the invasion of Sedan.

Yves Congar at First Communion in 1914

25th August 1914

Tuesday, cruel Tuesday.

We are just getting up when mother comes up to me and says: 'Vonet! Vonet![1] Put your soldiers away, the Germans are coming!' I go outside after putting them away and I hear shooting and I see a plane in the sky. As soon as I am back inside, my big brothers come through the door. 'They're coming! They're coming! They're right behind us!' I go and look out the dining-room window.

Ah, the rotten beasts! They pass by the window and we hear a gruff command: 'aarrarrrncharr'. They stop and line up to go to the station, when the shooting starts. They turn around and charge. Some fall down and we hear a thud – two massive ones even, as two horses fall dead in front of the window. Bullets whizz by in both directions. We can hear artillery firing as well as machine guns and rifles. We go into the living room and we hear Germans hitting Mr Benoit's door with their rifle butts, looking for French troops. Just to be safe they shoot Mr Benoit's dog, so that its barking won't interfere with their patrols. Another time we hear a patrol shuffling along our wall and shouting in French, 'Silence!'

At noon we're not very hungry, all this has spoilt our appetite. Around five, we get terribly anxious – they are blowing up the bridges, it is a spectacular sight. Grandad, who is used to it all as he saw it in 1870, wonders if it's not the town that's exploding. The Germans, fiends, thieves, murderers and arsonists that they are, set fire to everything: to our church in Givonne; to the chapel in Fond de Givonne Glaire; to Donchery, where they use incendiary rockets; and to lots more as well.

In the evening we drink bouillon to recover and father goes to

---

1 Yves' nickname.

the quay. There is a lot of smoke. We go to bed but can't sleep.
Wednesday morning at about eight, the sound of the artillery is
as loud as it was the day before. We wonder how we're still alive.
It feels so weird and everything is unfamiliar, but we'll get used
to it. Sedan is full of Germans. They confiscate weapons and we
have to hand them in. They ask for a quarter of a million francs'
worth of gold.[1]

*As the German troops consolidate their occupation of Sedan, Yves'
family is forced to bear the indignity of having a German officer billeted in their house.*

5th September

There is a German officer lodging with us, Captain Nemnick.
When he has supper, he calls eight other Germans to come and
have it with him. He has it with good Burgundy wine that he gets
from Dodelier.[2] He cooks four chickens and in the morning his
orderly eats a whole one. He's scared, so he sleeps with his
orderly and a lieutenant.

19th September

How long can this life amidst barbarians and enemies of civilisation last? It's already been a whole month with no news or
food supplies. Little did I know that the future had so much in
store for me!

*The German occupying forces order everyone to hand over their
household supplies. Demands for voluntary contributions are met*

---

1 The requisitioned money is to be handed over by the next day. The mayor
  appeals to Sedan's inhabitants, and the full amount is paid within a few
  hours to avoid repercussions. On 1st September, another 500,000 francs is
  demanded, as a collective punishment, after townspeople are allegedly caught
  shooting at German soldiers.
2 The Congars' neighbour.

with little enthusiasm and a system of hostage-taking is introduced.
Civilians are taken in small groups and locked up for a day or a
night, with the hostages only returned if their relatives pay up or
surrender their supplies. Yves' father, Georges, is on the hostage list,
together with 145 others.

25th September

Tere[1] makes us work and soon we will have no bread. Such dep-
rivation for French people!

26th September

Still no bread. Those damned Boches are forcing us to change
our diet.

30th September

Grandpa has been denounced for having wine. Oh those snitches
are worms, they deserve to be burnt alive!

3rd October

Dad is a hostage. Instead of doing 12 hours during the day or 12
during the night, he does 4 hours at night and 10 in the day. it's
so unfair. Well, if only that was all there was to put up with, it
wouldn't be too bad. It is sunny, we hear the artillery, a convoy
passes by – we go to church, still no bread. The officers leave, the
German Command changes over.

12th October

It smells as if they've just suffered a defeat at the Front, because
they've just come out with a charmingly kind idea: people who
own cars or bicycles are to take them straight away to the
German Command, or they'll suffer martial punishment.

---

1 Yves' mother.

13th October

Tere is ill. The firing is really loud. From now on, we'll only be able to cook two or three times a week because the Boches are taking the flour for themselves.

16th October

Tere is still stuck in bed and we're becoming quite good cooks. Pierre and Robert[1] are getting cooking lessons at Mrs Dervin's. Bread is very very scarce. Bastards!

20th October

The sound of the artillery is ever so loud. Grandpa is in his office when, without him having heard any footsteps, there is a knock on the door. Grandpa says come in and two Germans (a lieutenant and a private) enter the room. They ask him whether we have a phone and he answers that yes, we do. 'Good' they reply, 'we're taking it.' They unscrew the set and write on a piece of paper. Then they go, leaving Grandpa to stare at about ten screws, utterly baffled.

26th October

A notice is posted on the walls: it is forbidden to gather in the street in groups of more than two. Now I know why we were shot at. Four of us were chatting and the soldier guarding the bridge, who must have had the order already, shot at us from far away. My brothers and Dad are getting the cellar ready to put away our potatoes so that the Germans won't take them. Tere manages to get up again. Another plane has escaped the German fire.

---

1 Yves' older brothers.

29th October

Such horror! Catherine[1] had managed to keep her foal and two cows, but today they came and took the foal from her. Her only payment is a requisitioning voucher valid after the war. Pierre has a headache.

4th November

We only have one kilogram of bread left. They are going to let us die of hunger – oh well – we are French after all, and we will die if we must, but France will be victorious.

12th December

Another poster has been put up: anyone caught trying to get food or other supplies from Belgium will be fined 1,200 marks or 1,500 francs. Very well, if they want to starve us then they'll see when, in the next war, the next generation goes to Germany and starves them. They are turning the French people against them and I'm happy about it. I have never hated them so much.

16th December

The Boches must have lost yesterday's battle: a new infuriating notice has been posted. Anyone caught trying to leave Sedan will be fined and imprisoned for six months.

24th December

It is Christmas Eve and we hope that next year will be better than the one we've just had. It is very cold, Dad is being held hostage overnight. There is no midnight mass. A year ago we'd walk in our clogs in the snow, and through the church's windows we could see a woman's hat bobbing along the old road. At the

---

1 The Congars' neighbour.

other end of the church lay our saviour – so many voices singing Christmas carols would rise to the sky!! Now foreign feet trample the old road and everything is silent and gloomy. It is because of the ruins that are still smoking, because of the burnt-out church and the menacing posters. It is the rule of the strongest; it is invasion and ruin; it is the cry of the hungry who don't even have a crust of bread; it is the resentment against the race that pilfers, burns and holds us prisoners; our country, which is no longer our home, when our cabbages, our leeks and all other goods are in the hands of those thieves; the town is held to ransom, under oppression and the aggressor's injustice. Vengeance starts with a murmur, it's getting stronger and soon it will overflow like water in an already full cup, and in 10 years it will allow us to pay back the invaders with interest.

It is hard to believe that this unusually eloquent entry comes from a ten-year-old boy. It is possible that Yves, who like the rest of his family was a devoted Catholic, wrote it under the influence of a Catholic Christmas mass delivered that day at the Congars' local parish church.

26th December

Tere is a little ill but it should only last another ten days or so. It is really really cold. They must have been beaten because there is a new notice: all men between 18 and 48 years old have to report to the town hall. They are prisoners. Also the sound of artillery is very loud and it sounds like there's heavy firing towards Noyers.

*

In Schneidemühl, Piete is celebrating her first wartime Christmas. Piete's mother has come from Berlin to spend Christmas with her.

24th December 1914

Christmas! It's Christmas now! We exchanged presents at six o'clock. Before that Grandma, Willi and I went to the old town church for the Christmas service. The market was full, but everyone was silent. We went through the porch and sat on our seats. Suddenly the organ began to play 'Silent Night, Holy Night'. Everybody began to sob and cry. The whole church was full of people wearing black clothes and black mourning veils. For a long time after we came out of the church we couldn't speak. When anyone met a friend they just shook hands in silence. We walked home quickly. Grandma and Mummy couldn't join in singing carols, they were so upset. Now we are all in bed. The house is dark. Dear God, please, please, bring the war to an end.

26th December

The earth is covered in snow. Mummy loves the clean snow of the provincial town. Everyone looks at her as she goes by, so like a queen. She finds the town of Schneidemühl altered because of all these new faces from the 134th Reserve Battalion and the 1st and 2nd Reserve Flying Corps. The women and girls go to great lengths to look nice for them. A few days ago a thirteen-year-old girl, a baker's daughter, was expelled from our school because she is going to have a child by a first lieutenant. She is a big, strapping girl with blonde pigtails. None of us had noticed anything. The whole school was in turmoil.

Later in the spring Piete's diary becomes more personal and she stops sending it to her mother in Berlin. In the coming months, as Piete turns thirteen, her enthusiastic patriotism will gradually begin to wane.

11th March 1915

Another collection has been announced at school, for copper, again, but also for tin, lead, zinc, brass and old iron to make gun-barrels, field guns, cartridge cases and so forth. There is a keen competition between the classes. Our class, the fourth, has so far collected the most. I turned the whole house over from top to bottom. Grandma cried, 'The wench will bankrupt me! Why don't you give them your lead soldiers instead of cleaning me out!' So my little army had to meet their deaths.

29th April

Now I ask you, God, will you really let every dead soldier rise again, every dead Englishman, Frenchman, Russian, Turk and of course German? Why do you never answer me?

20th May

Now when the trains come from the west with soldiers being transferred to the Eastern Front, their uniforms are dirty and torn. Their spiked helmets are no longer enamelled black, but are painted field-grey. The soldiers don't say much, they are so hungry and thirsty. At the station there is ever more soup made, with meat or sausages. There are hardly enough supplies coming in. Many soldiers complain of lice. Some of our lady helpers at the Red Cross have got lice too now. They have to go for medical treatment straight away.

In May 1915 Piete's brother Willi falls seriously ill. During his illness Piete is required to live in the local girls' boarding house, while their grandmother cares for Willi at home. After five weeks he recovers and on 14th June Piete is allowed to return to the house. That summer food shortages begin to be felt in the shops.

4th July

You can no longer buy bread without so-called 'bread-cards', nor any rolls or biscuits. There used to be white bread made from wheat, now there's 'war bread' made from rye meal and potatoes. The 'Russian bread' that was on sale at the beginning of the war, and that Willi and I liked so much, has disappeared. In the bread that the prisoners now get in the camps there is potato-peel mixed with bran and animal-feed, for the sake of economy.

England, so the newspapers say, will not 'starve us out'; we'll see to that.

2nd August

The council school is closed because it's been occupied by the military. (Gretel is lucky, she doesn't have to go to school now.) The classrooms are crammed with soldiers. Every family with a spare room has to take in soldiers. They came to us too. Both our attic rooms and Grandpa's office are occupied again. In the evening we all sit on the Wegners' bench in front of the house singing songs with the soldiers or listening to their stories from the Front. Sometimes the soldiers flirt with Gretel's elder sisters, but in a nice way, and the sisters put up with it because we all know that the regiment has to go to the Front in a few days' time and the soldiers will probably be killed.

Piete is now thirteen years old and the games she and her friends invent reflect their shifting feelings about the war.

5th August

Gretel and I have a new game, as I no longer play war games with the boys. I have moved the green garden table from the summerhouse into the middle of Aunt Otter's garden. Gretel acts the part of Nurse Martha and I hobble on her arm to the hospital. That's the summerhouse, and she tends my wounds there.

8th August

Somebody else wanted to care for me in the summerhouse – namely, Aunt Otter's new billetee. He is blond and good-looking, really likeable. He came into the garden with Aunt's permission as I was swinging in the hammock on my own, reading. He wanted to know what I was reading, and I said 'Goethe!' He looked at me in a most interested way, as if he could not imagine me reading Goethe. Then he twisted one of my plaits in his hand. I let him do it because I thought he was playing. But it was quite another thing when he began to stroke my breast (I really don't have any yet) and then my hips and legs. I saw what he was up to, of course. I had a marvellous dodge. As quick as a flash, I swung round in the hammock and simply dropped out of it on to the ground. He hardly grasped what was happening as I shot past his legs on all fours out of the summerhouse. I ran out of the garden and slammed the garden door behind me. I'm just furious with this orderly! It is the first time a man has looked at me as a woman.

*

In Sedan Yves Congar is now eleven years old, and no longer a passive witness to the humiliations of living under German occupation.

12th March 1915

Yesterday I was walking to Granny's house with Robert and, because I like to taunt the Germans, I set to work in the rue du Menil. I see one and Robert goes 'pchiiiiteiiite' at him. I thought he was spitting at him so, as a medal of honour, I decorate the right hand side of his chest with a nice big gob. He stares at me for a long time but because he is only a simple private he doesn't say anything.

18th March

The Boches throw big nets from the Saint Vincent bridge. They claim that bottles with notes inside them are being thrown in the Meuse. These bottles are then taken to the Kommandantur. So the inhabitants of Sedan start throwing bottles with messages that read: 'Deutsch kaput', 'Down with the Boches' etc. . . . Father throws one saying 'Dreck für Deutsch'.[1]

---

1 'Germans are rubbish'.

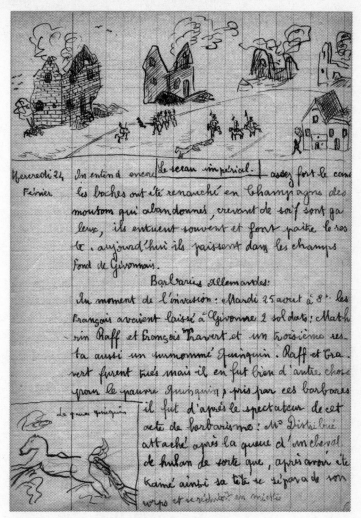

A page of Yves Congar's diary from 1915

25th March

It is rainy and windy. This morning the town was swarming
with Boches: 9,000 men plus the garrison. It was crawling with
'grey worms' as we now call them in Sedan because of their
greenish-grey clothes, and also because the more you kill the
more come back – just like grey worms.

*On 15th April 1915 the German Occupation Authority orders the
evacuation of all civilians incapable of work: the elderly, women
and children. By October a third of Sedan's population has been
moved. The Congars are unaffected as they have three suitable
labourers, Yves' two older brothers and their father.*

17th April

The Boches take away the pigs, horses, cows etc. They have
evacuated half the town. 1,200 people are in despair, leaving
their houses to be looted, with all their possessions. Oh, these
Boches! They are barbarians using their advantage to feed their
greed and cruelty.

*To secure more money from those who remain in Sedan, the German
authorities introduce a pet tax. Unwilling to pay, Yves' family reluctantly chooses to have their dog put down.*

15th May

This is a bad day, a mournful day. My dog is killed. Today, May
15th came the martyrdom of a hero who died for his homeland.
At 3.30 the vet arrives. We give the dog a chunk of meat, which
he devours, then we tie his jaws shut with string as tight as possible. While we hold his legs, the vet injects poison into his heart.
He is still warm when we bury him.

10th June

We can hear the noise of artillery. Kids who used to go out

with a toy rifle on their shoulder, wearing a red cap and a French flag or a nurse's uniform, are now forbidden to go outside. We are banned from playing soldiers, even in our own home.

In late June Yves lists the extent of German requisitioning. His resentment leads to his own small acts of resistance and retaliation.

27th June

Luckily the requisitioning of fruit hasn't happened. They didn't take any from our house and we don't think they'll follow it through. They're requisitioning – oh guess what! Shallots and garlic.

List of things taken by the Boches:

> money
> wool
> bedding
> men
> home-made food
> cabbages
> leeks
> wood
> flour
> coffee
> chicory
> sugar
> chocolate

10th July

It is terrible! Our town has to pay 1,000,000 marks! The city of Lille has to pay 3,000,000 and Mezieres 900,000. Lille says it doesn't have anything left. Mezieres simply refuses, but Sedan complies once again and asks its shopkeepers for money. It is shameful for French people to give money to help kill their brothers. Oh, oh! Beware, the cup is getting full! Not only that, but I'll give a thousand francs to anyone who can find me a litre of milk in a non-Boches-occupied house! Be careful Muller, Alexander[1] beware: there are loaded guns in Sedan!

14 September

We get up at six and go potato-pinching. We come back at eight, soaking wet. We'd make perfect sponges! It had started to rain but we kept on picking. We managed to bring back a fair amount!

17th September

I am on my way to go potato-pinching again when I see a big crowd. I wonder what is going on and I see 300 men, women, and children caught with wheelbarrows and sacks. I wheel mine behind the wash-house and go and mingle with the crowd. There are around a hundred people milling about when the *uhlan*[2] arrives on his horse. He tells us to go away. Then he pulls his sword out and makes his horse gallop into the crowd. Two people are wounded. It's shameful! I escape into the fields. It was a close call!

Both Yves Congar in occupied Sedan and Piete Kuhr in Schneidemühl continue to keep their diaries throughout the war.

---

1 The lieutenant in charge of occupied Sedan and his interpreter.
2 Mounted cavalry soldier.

Chapter 4

THE SIEGE OF PRZEMYŚL

October 1914–June 1915

In early August 1914 Russian troops advanced simultaneously into German East Prussia and Austria-Hungary's largest province of Eastern Galicia, in present-day Poland. While Russia's foray into Germany was swiftly rebuffed, its Galician campaign was more succcessful.

As the 1.3 million-strong Russian army overran the borders of the Austro-Hungarian Empire in Galicia, the Habsburgs' own prime target was Serbia. Their vengeful advance was led by Austrian General Potiorek, who only a month earlier had narrowly escaped the assassin's bullet while riding in Archduke Ferdinand's car on the fateful morning of 28th June 1914.

The Russian troops meanwhile advanced further inside Austria-Hungary's own territory. The outnumbered Habsburg forces defended tenaciously, but on 11th September 1914, having lost a third of their combatants, they were finally ordered to withdraw. The garrison town of Przemyśl,[1] a fortress town on the River San and a Galician stronghold, was ordered not to surrender. If Przemyśl fell, it would

---

1 See map on page 2 for the location of Przemyśl.

allow the Russian troops to advance across the Carpathians and into Hungary. Thirty miles of fresh trenches were dug and 650 miles of barbed wire were used to make seven new lines of defence around Przemyśl's perimeter.

Inside the fortress, a 127,000-strong military garrison, 18,000 civilians and 14,500 horses were surrounded by six Russian divisions. A gruesome siege, the longest of the First World War, began.

Przemyśl is a microcosm of the Austro-Hungarian Empire – orders of the day have to be issued in fifteen languages. Austrians, Poles, Jews and Ukrainians are locked together in the claustrophobic confines of the besieged town, pounded daily with artillery fire and overflowing with the dead, sick and wounded. Mutual distrust, racial tension and fear of the 'enemy within' are amplified when starvation and disease begin to take their toll on the fortress garrison and civilians.

Two people who endure the siege are a middle-aged Polish woman, Helena Jabłońska, and Josef Tomann, a young Austrian recruited into military service as a junior doctor. Tomann, from the town of Eger in Hungary, has been sent to Przemyśl to look after the sick and wounded at the garrison hospital. During his brief breaks from exhausting shift work, Dr Tomann starts to confide his thoughts to a diary, especially his longings for his young family. He records the different stages of the siege, leaning on his dark sense of humour for relief.

Helena Seifertóv Jabłońska is a relatively well-off fifty-one-year-old Polish woman. Originally from Sanok, she moved to Przemyśl to look after her family's property in the town. Alone since the death of her husband, Jacek, three years before, Helena now lets out rooms in her large family house to Przemyśl's garrison officers. When thousands of civilians flee before the onset of the siege, Helena chooses to stay, to protect the house she once shared with her husband and be near his grave in the town's cemetery. She begins to keep a detailed diary that in time will run to thirteen dense notebooks. Written mostly in Polish, her diary also records encounters in Ukrainian,

Russian, German and Italian, perhaps reflecting the ethnic mix of
the town as well as its changing occupiers. A month into the siege,
Helena is getting by on the rent from her lodgers, but the garrison
soldiers can barely get enough food to survive.

18th October 1914

Soldiers are out on the streets begging. A few of them were
trying to thrust ten, fifteen crowns at me to buy some bread, a
few rolls, some chocolate. One offered me five crowns to bring
him a glass of tea, saying I had to bring it and that he would
wait. He was Romanian. I went back home and fetched the food
I had made for Pegan, potato broth and some rice, and gave it to
him. He was so happy he shouted for joy and tried to thrust two
five-crown notes into my pockets. I did not accept them, of
course. He must have thought this was still too little, for he
pulled out a silver watch and wanted me to take it. Other soldiers crowded around me, taking out their money and waving it
at me. I hurried home again and fetched a hunk of bread, a few
apples, a few boiled potatoes and half a kilo of sugar, which
were all I had left. They gobbled it all up and wanted to pay.
You can make a fortune, but seeing it all is enough to break
your heart.

The municipal authorities try to regulate prices but then all
the goods vanish. All shops are closed, so you have to go round
the back. The Jewish women in basements rip you off the worst.
People say they purposely rent basements with windows onto the
street, so that they can pass goods out through a crack, never
showing more than a few items at a time, a few bread rolls or
eggs. You see whole groups of soldiers huddled around these
little windows.

26th October

In spite of all this terrible misery, I am the most miserable person
around. Every dying man has someone or something he regrets,
some grand passion, some kind of longing, someone or some-

thing in his heart that he grieves for – while I have nothing, just a dreadful, ice-cold emptiness and a great yearning for final peace.

Vast numbers of wounded are being brought in. Many of them die from severe blood loss, but the death toll would not be half as great were it not for cholera. It is spreading so fast that the cases outnumber those wounded and killed in battle. Everything has been infected: carts, stretchers, rooms, wardens, streets, manure, mud, everything. Soldiers fall in battle, where it is impossible to remove the bodies and disinfect them. They don't even bother.

A month and a half since the Russians surrounded the town, German troops help the Habsburg troops to break the encirclement. Civilians are ordered to evacuate immediately, not least to relieve the acute food shortage the siege is already causing.

4th November

This morning the gendarmerie and the police were sent out, and ordered everyone to pack up immediately, with barely time to throw some clothes into a bundle, take their children by the hand, throw their belongings on their backs and run, shoved along cruelly by rifle butts, no rest allowed. They even dragged the sick out of their beds, including a woman with a five-day-old baby. They hurried along an old crippled man wrapped only in shawls, with no warm clothing, as though he were no better than swine. Another group of soldiers were driving cattle, horses and carts, all now the property of the army. The horror! Children are separated from their families. Everyone has become heartless. A mother with two children boarded the train and her three-year-old child was left behind when it moved off. She wanted to jump off, but it was too late.

I hear a year-long siege is expected. I went to the cemetery to pour out my grief and ask for advice. No, I cannot leave my loved ones at a time like this, my heart would break. After all, if things go badly for us and the fortress is taken, I might never see this grave again. I promised Jacek that we would be together. I once swore to him 'till death and after death'.

6th November

I went to mass at the Franciscan church. The town is now half-empty – there was only me, one other woman and a few soldiers taking communion. Perhaps it would be better to leave after all, and take the more valuable things with me. But I am scared to go by car, with just a driver and no escort. If I were shot by Cossacks, at least the driver could keep going, but if the driver was shot, what would I do? They might rob me or take me prisoner.

After much deliberation, Helena decides to leave. She packs as many belongings as she can manage and abandons Przemyśl on a hired cart.

8th November

We reached Olszan. The ruins are still smouldering, the poor inhabitants have to live out in the open. They sit on bundles that hold all their worldly goods, shivering with cold. They are ghosts, not people. They are homeless – they don't have tents or shawls even to protect them. This place is worse than a desert. There is nothing to make a fire with: all the trees have been chopped down, and even the stumps have been burned. Everything has been razed to the ground to give the troops an open field of vision.

After Olszan we were stopped by soldiers driving cattle. They were supposed to be returning to Sanok but could not, because the road there was already unsafe. The driver wavered but we drove on. At the second checkpoint the guards informed us that a large regiment of Cossacks had closed off the road, and they had heard gunshots. A convoy captain caught up with us and told us it was madness to continue, that he himself was turning back.

There are only ashes ahead of us and amongst these ashes there are only suffering human ghosts, cold and hungry.

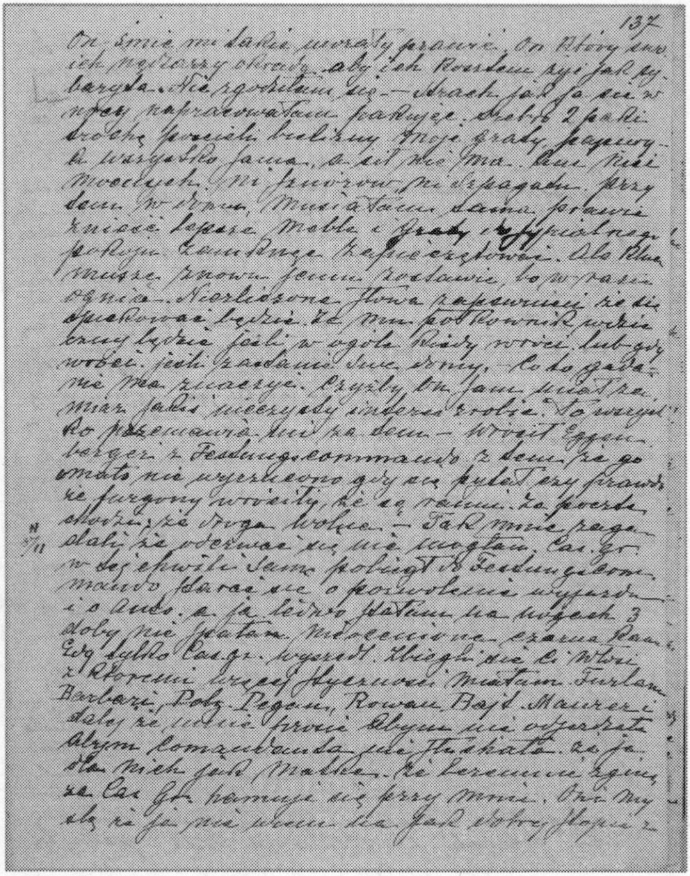

A page from Helena Jabłońska's diary for 1914

Their destination seems even more blighted than the town Helena has abandoned. She orders the driver to return to Przemyśl.

10th November

First thing in the morning I found out that we are now surrounded and completely shut in. The town is dead and silent.

By mid-December 1914 the Russian forces are pounding the fortress with constant artillery fire in an attempt to force the town into submission.

12th December

In the evening I stayed up late at my desk, listening to the shelling. Sometimes it all merges together into one furious wave of noise. You get used to it, like you get used to the tick-tocking of a clock, so that you simply cease to be aware of it. It's only when it ends that you wake up with a start, realising the clock has stopped.

Christmas approaches, breaking up the daily routine of survival, although for Helena it seems to be an unwelcome interruption.

22nd December

All my servant woman can think about is what to cook for Christmas Eve. Isn't it ironic? I gave her what little I had, let her prepare a feast for herself, while I myself will escape to the cemetery.

24th December

Three years ago Jacek was alive. I cuddled up close to him, he loved me, he was alive! These days I am dead inside, I have no heart, no feelings, no faith, no hope. I feel no physical pain, I no longer need anything, I do not pity anyone, no one's unhappiness moves me, I have no compassion. I have turned to stone really, and yet I do have moments of such intense longing! I want to stop being. I feel such pangs of jealousy when someone dies and they are taken away and covered with earth.

*

Austrian junior doctor Josef Tomann also spends his first wartime Christmas in Przemyśl. He works all hours at the garrison hospital, which is barely able to cope with the toll of daily casualties and victims of the cholera epidemic. Dr Tomann's brief period off duty over Christmas allows him some time to reflect.

24th December

It is Christmas Eve and I'm here, on my own in a hostile country. I cannot rest today, my weary mind is troubled by dreams and sweet visions, that fill the air like phantoms. When we were children we looked forward to Christmas Eve with great excitement. It was a time we always spent with our dear mother, but she will be on her own today crying over her three sons away at war.

Else was born this year. It was only last summer that Mitzl and I talked about how lovely it would be to have our first Christmas together. But we couldn't decide where to spend it. The war has made that decision for us. What is it like this year at home, I wonder? Do the lights on the tree twinkle as brightly? Sister Victoria showed me the Christmas tree, sprinkled with chalk and decorated with a few small candles. The poor chaps will be glad. I don't want to see or hear anything – I'll stay at home and try in vain to bury myself in a book. And yet twice I have felt hot tears on my cheeks. The war and its miseries have hardened me. Why am I so pathetic today? We cry every year, but this year we cry bitter tears.

Josef finishes this entry recording the deteriorating health of his colleagues who are falling ill with diseases that have become endemic in the town.

Dr Friedmann has a fever of 30·5. Typhoid perhaps. Dr Weiszt has influenza, Niemcow is still sick.

26th December

On Christmas morning our scouts found three Christmas trees

the Russians had left in no-man's land with notes that said something like: 'We wish you, the heroes of Przemyśl, a Merry Christmas and hope that we can come to a peaceful agreement as soon as possible.' There was a truce on Christmas Day, they neither attacked, nor fired.

31st December

The Russian soldiers make a neighing sound whenever they see our troops, as they know we are forced to eat horsemeat in the fortress. A few days ago one of our patrols found a note they'd left us, showing where the potato and cabbage fields were and saying they would stop shooting while we fetched some food. It was true! When our soldiers went over, the Russians shot two blanks high into the air, just to let them know they'd seen them. The next day we all went for more.

It's the last day of the year! I shan't be sorry to see the back of 1914. On the other hand, I was so happy with my dear Mitzl for seven months of the year, and on 7th June 1914 Else came into the world! I am contented, I ask for nothing more.

The worst of the war is certainly behind us. We are now moving towards peace. Peace – the idea seems almost alien to me. Will it come soon? Then I can devote myself to my family and my job. The hope that next year will see us reunited with our loved ones is what keeps us going. It gives me the heart and strength for the coming year. Onwards, I am ready!

Far from improving, the conditions in Przemyśl deteriorate by the day. Already meagre rations dwindle further, great numbers of Przemyśl's soldiers and civilians fall prey to starvation and disease. However, as Tomann notes, different rules apply to the garrison's social elite. Amidst the squalor of the town, Austrian officers lead a leisurely existence, indulged by preferential rations and favours bought from desperate civilians.

13th January 1915

Starvation is kicking in. Sunken, pale figures wander like corpses through the streets, their ragged clothes hanging from skeletal bodies, their stony faces a picture of utter despair. And then there are the fat-bellied gents from the commissariat, who stink of fat and go arm in arm with Przemyśl's finest ladies, most of whom (and this is no exaggeration) have turned into prostitutes of the lowest order.

The hospitals have been recruiting teenage girls as nurses, in some places there are up to 50 of them! They get 120 crowns a month and free meals. That comes to 17,000 crowns a month! They are, with very few exceptions, utterly useless. Their main job is to satisfy the lust of the gentlemen officers and, rather shamefully, of a number of doctors, too. None of them go without furs, even though they have dirty underwear. They just get in the way. Meanwhile, I am paid less than 60 crowns for my work as a doctor!

In the face of such injustice, several days later Dr Tomann pre-scribes a dose of humour.

15th January

What is the difference between the heroes of Troy and those of Przemyśl? The Trojans were in the belly of a horse, while we have horse in our bellies!

25th January

The Russians are demanding hostages: 10 nurses, who are virgins, nine syphilis-free officers, a non-Jewish head doctor and a general. I can find no words to describe my feelings, to say how happy I would be to leave Przemyśl. Not just because of the war, but also my disgust at the thoughtless and narrow-minded people who have no sensitivity but make light of everything with their tactlessness and their idiotic happy-go-lucky attitude.

28th January

How glorious the world could be were it not for this dreadful war. How happy I would be with my darling Mitzl, what delight we would take in our little Else. Sometimes the thought seizes me so violently that the blood rushes through my veins and my heart feels strangely warm.

In the night a few frozen soldiers were brought in from their sentry posts. Starvation is taking its toll on the civilian population. Opposition to the siege threatens to make its presence felt. The situation is critical! Surplus food stuffs are being taken from the civilian population. It snows non-stop! Will the field army in the Carpathians be able to advance at all in this snow, which must surely be two to three metres deep there?

Throughout the winter of 1914–1915 Przemyśl's inhabitants hope for relief, as the Habsburg armies fight their way to the fortress and try to prevent further Russian advance towards Hungary across the Carpathian mountains. Months of dogged fighting in the deep snow of the mountain passes result in appalling losses. Austro-Hungarian troops suffer nearly 800,000 casualties, largely from frostbite and disease, but the relieving force fails to reach the garrison at Przemyśl. With its army severely depleted, Austria-Hungary appeals to its ally Germany for assistance, but the help that comes is insufficient. Germany itself is heavily engaged elsewhere on both Western and Eastern Fronts. Austro-Hungary's own desperate advance gradually grinds to a halt. In early March 1915 Josef Tomann notes down the first preparations for Przemyśl's now inevitable surrender to the Russians.

5th March

Gunpowder and ecrasite[1] are being taken to the weapons factories

---

1 A powerful explosive invented by Austro-Hungarian engineers Siersch and Kubin in 1889.

so that the fortress can be blown up if our defences fall, which could happen any time now. Despondency is widespread. We are preparing for a trip to Tomsk, Irkutsk or Tashkent.[1] Our rucksacks are packed. I have sent postcards to Landskron and Petersdorf. Will they be my last? I hope not! I won't write anything about my state of mind. Thoughts of Mitzl and Else make me miserable and discontented.

8th March

A terrifying number of people are suffering from malnutrition; the starving arrive in their dozens, frozen soldiers are brought in from the outposts, all of them like walking corpses. They lie silently on their cold hospital beds, make no complaints and drink muddy water they call tea. The next day they are carried away to the morgue. The sight of these pitiful figures, whose wives and children are probably also starving at home, wrings your heart. This is war.

At the peak of the siege 300 people die each day of starvation and disease. Przemyśl's hospitals and morgues cannot cope, and the streets of the fortress town are lined with corpses and dead horses. The garrison officers' relationships with the town's women meanwhile result in more work for the already overstretched Dr Josef Tomann:

10th March

New officers are coming in almost daily with cases of syphilis, gonorrhoea and soft chancre. Some have all three at once! The poor girls and women feel so flattered when they get chatted up by one of these pestilent pigs in their spotless uniforms, with their shiny boots and buttons.

*

---

1 Tomann fears being deported as a prisoner of war to Siberia or Central Asia.

In early March the Austrian garrison attempts a number of increasingly desperate sorties to break the Russian encirclement. Not until another 51,000 Austrian casualties are incurred do the garrison commanders finally concede that further resistance is futile. Helena Jabłońska records the final days of the siege.

15th March

The Russians have burned nearly all the surrounding villages. In one village the inhabitants locked themselves into their huts to keep out the Russians. The Russians boarded up the doors from the outside and set fire to the huts. There is no longer any doubt that we will have to surrender. Betrayal and hunger have exhausted us.

As of yesterday, soldiers are getting better food rations to prepare them for the march. They are mere shadows, not people, they are skeletons, not men. The peasants have had everything taken from them, so as not to leave anything for the Russians. This was done ruthlessly, without any compassion. An act unworthy of the civilised Catholic nation that we are. It was cruel to give such an order, but those executing it were crueller still. How generous of them to leave the peasants their lives!

17th March

In my darker moments I am just a short step away from ending all this, so that I can finally have some peace. But I can't, I can't because I have to take care of this house, or rather watch what happens to it. The Russians are giving civilians the freedom to leave, but only on foot, of course. Whoever wants to stay will be allowed to stay. I, of course, have to 'want to stay' because I have nowhere else to go.

Among the first to flee are the Jewish inhabitants of Przemyśl. Rumours of Russian executions and the looting of Jewish property in the wider province have circulated in the town for months. Yet, like

many other exhausted and embittered inhabitants, Helena is unsym-
pathetic to their plight.

18th March

The Jews are taking their shop signs down in a hurry, so that no
one can tell who owns what. They are making formal pilgrimages
to the Rabbis' graves at Okopisko. When they get there they
prostrate themselves on the ground and wail desperately.
They've all got so rich off the backs of those poor soldiers, and
now of course they all want to run away!

The night before the surrender Przemyśl's own garrison soldiers loot
and ransack the town before abandoning it to the Russians. In the
chaotic scramble, Helena tries in vain to protect her house.

21st March

All night long I could hear the racket and din of railings, stakes
and parquet flooring being ripped up. This morning my lodgers
commiserate about the looting marauders. The soldiers are tearing up the stakes in our garden, they have smashed up the apple
cellar, they've stolen everything and hacked it all to pieces. I feel
as if I'm going crazy, the fear and worry have affected my feet
and my spine, I have such intense pains, I feel weak and I can't
walk. They come storming into my kitchen and take anything
they like. I close the door but they hammer at it, they bang and
kick it in and I have to give them my last mouthful of food. Of
the lunch we cooked today all we were spared was tea and bread.
They say in town the killings have begun.

With surrender now imminent, garrison commandant General
Kusmanek orders everything that could be of use to the enemy to be
set ablaze.

22nd March

The handover of the fortress is to take place tomorrow. All

remaining ammunition and artillery guns are to be destroyed, along with all fortifications, explosives, arms factories and machinery. After that the bridges are to be blown up; rifles, carts, harnesses, saddles are all to be destroyed – everything. Of course, no one could sleep last night. We all moved down to the cellars in case the buildings collapse, taking essential clothing and food with us to be able to survive for a few days. Fela, the Prochaskis and I joined the Kwapisz family in their kitchen, and there we sat terrified, waiting for the explosions to begin. The rumble of artillery drowned out all conversations. From time to time there was a terrifying hissing sound, as though a vast swarm of aeroplanes was passing overhead. This was the machine guns firing off the last of their ammunition in a frenzied orgy.

At around 2 a.m. they began blowing up the works. Along with the throbbing and screaming of artillery this was so horrible that we were all rigid with fear. The police were sent all over town to warn people that both ammunition dumps, three bridges and the locomotive works were to be blown up at 5 a.m. We went outside. There were crowds of panic-stricken people with trunks, bundles and children hurrying down the street, their eyes wide with fear, while we stood waiting, shivering with cold.

The first ammunition dump exploded with a terrifying boom, the ground shook and the glass fell out of all the windows. Clouds of ash cascaded from chimneys and stoves, and chunks of plaster fell from the walls and ceilings. There was soon a second boom. As the day dawned the town looked like a glowing, smoking crater with pink flames glowing from below and morning mist floating above – an amazing, menacing sight. These hours were perhaps the only hours like this in the whole history of the world. Countless people died of nervous convulsions last night, without any physical injuries or illnesses. By the time the sun climbed into the sky everything was still. Soldiers knelt on their balconies, praying. When the smoke from all the explosions melted away, people slowly went back to their apartments.

There is a corpse in our house, on the floor above the Litwińskis'. The man seems to have died of fear. I have to do something about him, but nobody wants to get involved, they are all leaving it to me. I persuaded one of the workmen to go down to the army hospital to ask what to do, but they sent him packing and redirected him to divisional headquarters. Over there he was told they would deal with it tomorrow, they've got too many corpses today as it is, littering the streets awaiting collection.

The Russian patrols marched into the city today from all directions, followed by mounted Cossacks. I don't know whether there was anyone out there to welcome them, but I can't leave the house because the marauders are still here, looting, hacking everything to pieces and burning it.

On 23rd March 1915 Przemyśl's 9 Austrian generals, 93 senior staff officers, 2,500 officers and 117,000 enlisted men surrender to the Russians.

That day Helena goes from hospital to hospital to ask for her neighbour's corpse to be taken away.

23rd March

After I got my things together in the morning I did the rounds of a few hospitals and the hospital headquarters, but no one is taking any corpses. By the time the Russians get round to fetching them, the corpses will have rotted so much that we'll all have fled the town. The weather is turning warm.

In the afternoon the police did send a cart round to pick up the corpses. It turned out the body has gone missing. Someone must have flung it into a cellar or buried it under a rubbish heap. I told the police to search for it, but they couldn't find it anywhere.

*

Josef Tomann makes few diary entries once the Austrian garrison is forced to surrender. He notes the swift change of rule in Przemyśl.

24th March

Russian officers have moved into apartments vacated [by the Austrians]. A Cossack patrol has made themselves at home in the officers' hospital. A tremendous number of rifle cartridges are being destroyed. Apart from that, all is quiet. I am gripped by a choking sense of humiliation as I walk through the streets we used to control.

25th March

Mitzl, it is seven years to the day since we first kissed! How very different things are today!!

*

The Russians, triumphant after an exhausting six-month siege, now rush in to get their share of the loot, as Helena writes in despair.

26th March

The Russians have stabbed some Jew to death after he told them he had no money. They are unbelievably bold in their looting. They are going through everyone's cellars looking for drink. They stole the wine from Bishop Pelzar, and Baraniecki's entire cellar. When Baraniecki went to the Russian headquarters to complain, he recognised one of his very own bottles standing on the new commandant's desk.

Oh, what am I to do! I have to stay here, all alone with the Russians. Why did my dear Jacek leave me, why couldn't he have taken me with him? How can you not lose your faith when such things happen to you?

The Jews bear the brunt of reprisals. The Russians accuse them of spying and pro-German sympathies. In addition, to a Russian ear their Yiddish speech sounds all too much like German. All of this quickly becomes a pretext to loot Jewish possessions. Helena records the hatred that reigns in the town, but wonders for a moment if she, too, might take advantage of the situation.

Przemyśl under Russian occupation in spring 1915

1st April

The Catholic shops are open and are already fairly well stocked with goods. The Jews have been allowed to sell only what they still have in stock. The Russians make fun of them, saying they'll let them eat their matzos in peace, but after the festivities they'll take them in hand, send them to Siberia. They're saying they will confiscate their houses and property and that anyone who wants can go to Austria and Germany, but they won't let anyone who runs away come back. If only I'd known, if only I had any money, and a host of other 'if onlys' – I'd have bought that little hut from Dym. Everyone jokes about houses in Przemyśl going for 20 crowns. The Jews pretend they don't believe all this talk. They suck up to the Russians.

8th April

The Jews are frightened. The Russians are taking them in hand now and giving them a taste of the whip. They are being forced to clean the streets and remove the manure.

*

*On the same day Dr Tomann supervises his military patients'
departure. Josef himself has been ordered by the Russians to stay in
Przemyśl and tend to the sick and wounded – regardless of which
side they come from. He makes only a few brief notes of these
events.*

8th April

House searches. All my patients are leaving except for two senior
men. Sent cards to Mitzl and Bittner.

12th April

The first cases of endemic typhoid in the hospital.

16th April

[I've got] feverish gastroenteritis, the result of some ropey goulash.
Cases of endemic typhoid are increasing at a worrying rate.

17th April

The Jewish doctors (72 out of 126) have been dismissed.

*

*The same day Helena Jabłońska witnesses a pogrom spreading across
town. As she sees the events unfold, her own attitude to the fate of
the Jews begins to change.*

17th April

The Jewish pogrom has been under way since yesterday evening.
The Cossacks waited until the Jews set off to the synagogue for
their prayers before setting upon them with whips. They were
deaf to any pleas for mercy, regardless of age. They were taken
away from the synagogues, from the streets and from their
doorsteps and driven towards some enormous barracks at
Bakończyce. What are they going to do with them? Some of the
older, weaker ones who couldn't keep up were whipped. Many,
many hundreds were driven along in this way. They say this
round-up is to continue until they've caught all of them. There

is such lamenting and despair! Some Jews are hiding in cellars, but they'll get to them there too.

18th April

This regime is getting extremely vicious. All civility is vanishing and terror is raising its head. The Jews are sought out in their hundreds and chased out. It is not just our townspeople and Jews who are being made to do forced labour. The peasantry is also set to work now, repairing the roads or burying dead horses. Children as young as eight are dragged out to work. They give them spades and keep an eye on them while they work. No one gets paid. They are allowed to go home for an hour at lunchtime, and woe betide anyone who doesn't get back to work on time. The Jews have been ordered to celebrate Sabbath on Sundays! All men, even members of the professions, are too scared to leave their houses.

*

Disease continues to spread in the town's appalling conditions. Josef Tomann's brief entries record how he himself begins to fall ill.

20th April

Everyone passing yellowish stools. Food is poor and expensive. Moved into the officer's hospital. Bright, sunny days. Sunbathing.

21st April

Four-day-long house arrest of all Austrians in Przemyśl.

24th April

Have suddenly become very ill. 40·2. Bloody stools.

27th April

Better. 3 stools. 37·5 degrees.

28th April

37·2 degrees. Appetite. Cocoa, gruel, a little sunbathing.

29th April

36·5 degrees, I'm so happy! I am so glad that I am not more seriously ill, given the conditions. I am afraid for my family. I drank my first coffee for ages.

*

While Tomann notes with relief the first signs of his recovery, Helena Jabłońska continues to write with increasing concern about the plight of Przemyśl's Jews.

1st May

Over a thousand of them leave every day, and there are still many left. They are hurriedly selling off their furniture and bric-a-brac and paying vast sums for horses. We suspect the Russians are chasing them out of Przemyśl so that they can rob them thoroughly, as the Jews are not being allowed to take much with them. As soon as they leave town, [the Russians] fleece the empty apartments and shops, carrying off anything of value. Peasants and soldiers take whatever is left. The rest is destroyed.

After little more than a month of their rule in Przemyśl, the Russians hear that a new joint Austrian-German offensive has just begun along the entire Eastern Front. Germany's chief of staff, General Falkenhayn, has agreed to help the Austrians reclaim Galicia on condition that Germany's own generals lead the advance instead of the Habsburgs' 'childish military dreamers', as German General Ludendorff dismissively calls them. As the threat of a Russian retreat from the town looms, looting intensifies.

2nd May

We have been hearing for a few days now that the Russians, aware that they're not doing too well at the Front, are hurrying up with the robbing of the Jews. Any day now they are going to pass a law stating that the entire male population under fifty is to leave Przemyśl to be taken prisoner. They need more hostages to exchange with the Austrians.

*

Two days later Josef Tomann's health suddenly takes a turn for the worse.

4th May

Have been in bed till today. Temperature 37 to 37·7. Two to three watery stools. No appetite.

This is Tomann's last diary entry. Josef died twelve days later, on 16th May 1915, leaving behind his young wife and baby daughter. Josef Tomann is one of an estimated 120,000 victims claimed by disease and starvation in the siege of Przemyśl.

*

During the brief Russian reign over Eastern Galicia, Polish farmers, for centuries mistreated by their landlords, used the invasion to ransack aristocratic residences and claim the land as their own, as Helena observes.

14th May

The character of the town has changed completely. The peasantry are becoming very haughty, especially the ones now lamenting the [imminent] departure of the Russians. We live in the middle of such horror that we don't know what we should fear more: the mutinous armies, the slaughter, the raids, the aeroplanes, the bombing, the imprisonment, Siberia? In these last few days chaos has reigned. Anything that can't be carted off or used to pay one of the prostitutes for her services is burnt, so that the Germans don't get it when they march in.

21st May

It's the peasants and caretakers that live in the tenement buildings now. The peasants duped the Russians so successfully that they suddenly occupied the buildings. They argue about who will get the better ones, knowing that the first ones in will get to stay. They lounge around on the balconies and stretch themselves out on fine Jewish bed linen. There is no end of comic sights. In church there was a woman the size of a cannon wearing a deep-cut ball gown on top of her sackcloth shirt, and a string of pearls round her neck. Her corset was undone at the waist and a calico gusset was wedged in.

On the day the Russians start their evacuation of Przemyśl, Helena hears of a Cossack plan to steal more from the town's Jews.

22nd May

We heard the Cossacks discussing what they did to the Jews. They said they guessed they probably had their banknotes sewn inside their clothes. So they chased them into bathhouses and ordered them to wash. After they had done so they gave them new outfits to put on, taking away everything they had on when they were first brought in, from their skullcaps to their shoes. Then they let them go, all clean.

26th May

The Russians are in full flight. They were in such a hurry to get away that they harnessed seven horses to a field gun and galloped off like crazy. Hundreds and hundreds of carts all crashing into one another. Everyone is running away in a panic. They grab anything they can. In short, they've gone mad.

The Russians are now forced into a massive retreat, not only in Eastern Galicia, but across the whole of the Eastern Front. In May 1915 alone their casualties reach 412,000 men. On 3rd June the first German patrols enter the ransacked fortress of Przemyśl.

3rd June

At eight I went into town. This has been my first happy day since my dear Jacek's death. Our troops marched in at seven this

Civilians and Russian soldiers leaving Przemyśl

morning, alongside the Germans. They were showered with flowers, and greeted with joy and blessings.

5th June

Jews are popping up like mushrooms after the rain. The intelligentsia are visibly delighted. With the masses though, it is quite the opposite. Despite the fear which makes the wiser among them keep it to themselves, you can feel their ill will towards the Germans, and their regret at the departure of the Russians. The hags at the market refuse to sell to them. They even cover up their goods with their aprons when they see a German approaching. I admire the patience of the Germans when confronted with such obvious dislike.

Once again, Przemyśl's fortunes change. The town's survivors have endured the siege under the pounding of artillery and amidst the ravages of starvation, death and disease. Among them, Helena Jabłońska has stubbornly held on to her house, although it's been ransacked by the incoming and outgoing soldiers. She has stayed close to her husband's grave and held on to her own life. Yet once the initial rejoicing dies down, Helena reflects upon Galicia's fate, disheartened by the dismissive comments of German officers who now rule her town.

29th June

It pains me to hear the Germans bad-mouth Galicia. Today I overheard two lieutenants asking 'Why on earth should the sons of Germany spill blood to defend this swinish country?' They were saying they'd sooner defend Tyrol or recapture Lombardy and Venice from the Italians than defend Galicia and the Poles! I had managed to keep quiet up till then, but this was really too much for me. I told them they were forgetting that it was to defend *their* Berlin from a Russian onslaught that we had been made to sacrifice Lwów and devastate Galicia. I said that, in fact, we had deserved their help much sooner than it came.

Helena wonders what the Poles stand to gain from this war, noting on 28th July 1915: 'We, the Poles, are hated by everyone in this Austrian hotchpotch and are condemned to serve as prey for all of them.' When the Russians withdraw from Warsaw, the capital of Russian Poland, and German troops march in Helena reflects: 'There is much rejoicing in town, but somehow the news makes me feel sad. Will Warsaw ever be ours? Will there ever be an independent Poland?'

The fortress town of Przemyśl remained in German hands until October 1918, when Eastern Galicia left the Austro-Hungarian Empire to become part of the newly created independent state of Poland.

The Austro-Hungarian army never recovered from the horrendous losses suffered in the autumn and winter of 1914–15. The Habsburgs were forced to rely on Germany's assistance both in their sector of the Eastern Front and in the Balkans, where their two initial attempts to occupy Serbia also failed.

Chapter 5

THE EASTERN FRONT

January–December 1915

In January 1915 the Eastern Front between Russia and the two Central Powers, Germany and Austria-Hungary, stretched from the Baltic to Romania. It was twice the length of the Western Front and the character of the warfare was very different. There were huge logistical problems, with vast distances connected by slow trains and poor roads, all compounded by the relative industrial backwardness of Russia and Austria-Hungary. In contrast to the static fighting in Belgium and France, where the front line would not alter by more than twenty miles in the following three years, there were opportunities here for manoeuvre and mobility. The first Russian advances in East Prussia had ended in defeat at the battles of Tannenberg and the Masurian Lakes, and German troops now occupied a strip of Russian Poland. However, the winter campaign against Austria-Hungary was still going Russia's way as the siege of Przemyśl entered its fourth month.

In the winter of 1914, Austria-Hungary, struggling against Russia and repulsed from Serbia, appealed to its more robust partner for assistance. The German chief of staff, Erich von Falkenhayn, had been hoping that Austria-Hungary would bear the brunt of the Russian offensive in the east, giving Germany time to concentrate on the Western Front. But although unwilling, Falkenhayn was forced to accept that he had to shift his focus to the east. Germany's military alliance obliged it to come to Austria-Hungary's aid. In a dramatic about-turn Falkenhayn moved the German military headquarters east from the Meuse in France to Pless in Silesia, no more than an hour's drive from the Austrian High Command. He also created eight new divisions by calling in fresh recruits and taking soldiers from the Western Front where fewer men were needed now that deep defensive trenches had been made. Together they formed a new army for the east.

One of the non-commissioned officers transferred from the Western Front is Ernst Nopper, a thirty-eight-year-old father of two. An interior decorator from Ludwigsburg in south-west Germany, Nopper has kept a diary since he left home in August 1914. Of the burnt-out Belgian villages he witnesses in his first campaign, he writes: 'Horrible impression; one cannot describe these abominable atrocities. Mankind is an animal of the vilest sort, pitiless.' But by the time he marches into France, he is accustomed to life as a soldier and enjoys the wine and fresh fruit requisitioned from the local population. He is wounded in November 1914 and his diary breaks off while he recuperates in Ludwigsburg. He resumes it in the new year when he rejoins his 121st Infantry Regiment on the Eastern Front near Janowienta, just inside Russian Poland.

Vasily Mishnin is on the Russian side of the front line north of Warsaw. With little sense of why he is fighting this war, he has survived his first two days of combat, panic-stricken and afraid, clutching his rifle. His thoughts return frequently to his wife, Nyura, back home in Penza. In response to two German attempts to take Warsaw in the autumn of 1914, the Russian troops have dug an entrenched defensive line to the west of the city. The trenches have neither the depth nor the sophistication of those in France and Belgium. A fortnight into his first tour of duty at the Front, Vasily Mishnin records his impressions.

28th January 1915

Time drags in the trenches. We lie pressed against each other like pigs. Dirty, soiled, unwashed, we stink like old men. There is nowhere to have a shave or a haircut. I hang my black watch on the wall and we sit staring at it.

31st January–2nd February

Monotonous exercises. Everything has become even more disgusting and miserable. You don't get used to such conditions. The one comfort is when I get a letter from Nyurochka and read it slowly, not once, but five times. Today I am dreaming about home and reluctantly writing to my sweet Nyura a little more about my troubles. What a terrible misfortune has befallen us! What are we suffering for, what do I achieve by killing someone, even a German? And why does my Nyura have to suffer even more than me?

9th February

I am writing a letter to Nyura when regimental clerk Pokrasov comes round and sees my handwriting. 'You write well,' he tells me. 'Stay in the dugout tomorrow, don't go to drill'. A kind of anxious thrill runs through my body. Such joy, not to have to do the exercises today.

19th February

5 a.m. They wake us up. I've been selected as one of twenty better-educated soldiers. We are sent to the regimental treasury. It is an eight-mile walk to the train station. If we miss the train we have to walk for thirty miles. We are drenched in sweat, but we keep going, we are so happy to be getting further and further away from the trenches.

Forty miles behind the front line, Vasily Mishnin reaches local military headquarters in the Polish fortress town of Pultusk, north of

Letter from Vasily to Nyura. This handwriting saved Vasily Mishnin from front-line duty.

Warsaw, where he lands a clerical job at the treasury. Now ade-
quately fed and relatively safe he waits anxiously for news from his
pregnant wife.

7th March

Post arrives and I get ten letters, seven are from Nyura. In a
good mood. I read the letters several times, and at night I get
down to writing back. Nyura is expecting a baby very soon,
maybe it is happening right now, perhaps this very minute.

14th March

I am 28 today. I write to Nyura about it. In the evening a gnaw-
ing sadness creeps over me. I want to leave the barracks and be
on my own for a while. I lie on my wooden bed. It is already dark
when the post arrives. With a tremor I read the first letter, and
then I open another one. This one has only a few lines, scribbled
in pencil. My eyes run down the page fast and suddenly I feel as
if I'm on fire. I feel hot and I'm short of breath. An incredible
moment: 'It's a boy, I am still in bed, scribbling down these three
lines to you, Vasya, the best I can. I will write more when I have
a minute. I'm going to call him Vasya, after you. I am sending
you a kiss for now, Vasyusha, and I love you always, yours,
Nyurusha.' Praised be the Lord. From now on, even if I get
killed, my descendants will go on. My twenty-eight years in this
world have not been in vain. In great spirits, I go and share my
joy with everyone.

11th April, Pultusk

I go with my mate Kozhukhin to get our pictures taken. Dear
God, I look like an old man in the photo. I don't recognise myself
at all. How quickly war can ruin a man. In five months I have
completely changed. I look haggard, a young man no more. I
don't want to look like this. I worry that I shouldn't send this
photo to Nyura. It is bound to upset my sweet lady. She is still
young, she still likes the look of a healthy young man, she wants

to still fancy me. But there again, she loves me and knows that I belong to her alone, and we've been so happy together. Slowly my doubts begin to dissolve. A man's heart is much more important than any photo. You see, I didn't want to change, it's the war, and I'm not the only one. But the thought of Nyura looking at this and saying 'Vasyusha, what's happened to you!' keeps troubling me.

Within days of escaping the trenches, Vasily Mishnin and several others are sent back. It turns out they had been selected by mistake. They are told that only older soldiers are allowed to do clerical work.

18th April

We take the binoculars and watch the enemy. Visibility is amazing today, everything is crystal clear. The Germans are putting their trench in order, and we can see them taking their mess tins to fetch water. We can hear their arguments and discussions, too. It is quite a peaceful scene when it's quiet and no one is firing. This is our enemy? They look like good, normal people, they all want to live and yet here we are, gathered together to take each other's lives away.

A few days later, on 22nd April, Vasily Mishnin receives a postcard from Nyura. On the front is a photograph of Nyura and baby Vasinka.

22nd April

As a keepsake for my dear Vasyusha from Nyura. Yours for ever. And to my dear Papa from your little son Vasinka. Hello, Papa! Mama asked me to write to you to help you and keep you safe from the Germans. If they shoot at you then I will come and have a go at them and they will fall down instead, and we will go home together to mama. She is waiting for you and you are her true love. She is always telling me what a good papa you are, so

Nyura and baby Vasinka on a photographic postcard sent on 22nd April 1915

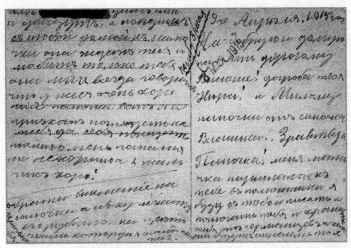

The reverse of the postcard from Nyura

I should come and take a look at you and let you have a look at me. How is my papa doing?

Your loving son Vasinka and Mama

The postcard reinforces Vasily's determination to survive and return to his family. After only one more day peering at the enemy through his binoculars, he finds an opportunity to bribe his way into another clerical job, this time at the local field hospital.

*

About 150 miles to the south of Vasily Mishnin's position, a joint Austro-Hungarian and German force breaks through the Russian lines. This vulnerable sector links the Galician towns of Gorlice and Tarnow, where the Germans have a superior number of men and guns. Combined Austro-Hungarian and German units fight together under a unified command for the first time in the war. They march forward at a rate of ten miles a day and end the siege of Przemyśl on 3rd June.

Officer Ernst Nopper is with the German troops gathered to the north on the border with Russian Poland. He has spent two months back home recovering from a wound. In February 1915, he is delighted to rejoin his old regiment which in the meantime has been transferred from France to the Eastern Front. On arrival he is given command of one of the companies. Four months into his tour of duty, with no orders to advance, he notes: 'the war goes on, no end in sight'. Ernst is stationed near the Polish town of Janowienta, where the dugouts consist of primitive shelters half underground plagued by lice in winter and ants in summer. Finally, his regiment is ordered to bombard the opposing Russian lines.

11th June 1915

Detonation of mines, then at six a heavy artillery attack on the enemy begins, which has now reached a crescendo. Twenty shots at once from guns of every calibre. The Russians answer

Ernst Nopper

as best they can, but their artillery is much weaker than ours. The enemy is hidden by clouds of dust. And all this time the weather is so beautiful that the shooting seems absurd. The Russians allowed themselves to have a bit of a joke with us – they put a stuffed soldier between our positions. But a few spirited chaps from our side went and set up a hand grenade to go off if the figure was moved. A group went out, in the middle of the artillery attack, to see what had happened. A dead Russian, torn to pieces by gunfire, had paid for his curiosity with his life. An attack is planned for tomorrow morning. We don't sleep at all, but read aloud to one another to keep ourselves alert.

12th June

Our artillery has begun such a bombardment of the Russian positions on Hill 137 that it feels as if we are in hell. After a short time the Russians respond with fire so heavy that fragments are as big as a child's head. Every moment is filled with an extraordinary amount of dust and noise. Suddenly our infantry breaks out of their positions and storms the hill with incredible speed, taking one position at a time. I see it all in shades of grey, not because it is dusk but because of the sand and dust. Above many of the trenches bayonets appear with white handkerchiefs waving to and fro. The infantry jump straight in and bring the Russians out. Now there's a long train of Russians coming back with their hands held high and their weapons discarded. They are taken in to our old trenches. The infantry cleans up thoroughly. One of the Russian divisional leaders tells me that our artillery had two platoons under heavy fire. When the third came under fire he surrendered.

15th June

How I would love to get undressed in peace and go to bed without worrying. You have to keep on your guard and be ready to march at any time, so you can't even take off your boots or gaiters.

In a quieter moment Ernst finds time to write home to his wife and two young children back in Ludwigsburg.

20th June

Dear wife and children,

I received letters 18 and 19 yesterday and today, thank you so much; I was especially pleased to hear news of the children. I will draw Ernst a victory at the next opportunity. And I will send something to Erika too. I should also tell Ernst that Daddy has to sleep in trenches. In the trenches we shoot at Russians or capture them and take them prisoner. Has Erika had her injections yet? If she has then she can come and join us in the trench, she can make our coffee, so we can keep shooting all the time. Then she can replenish the straw in our camp and turn on the lamps when it is night time.

I send you warm greetings and kisses,
Your Daddy

A few days later, Ernst records a Russian attack.

25th June

The cry 'the Russians are coming' rang out, and indeed hordes of them were dashing towards us. A quick burst of gunfire put paid to the first assault. They ran at us a third and fourth time. One man got as far as our defences and prodded with his bayonet, but then fell down, hit by several bullets. Others had got past our defences and might have captured a small trench. The spotlight, which had failed to work earlier, now came in very handy. That was a terrible night. You had to admire the Russians, I hadn't expected them to show such incredible guts.

27th June

Suddenly the artillery fire died away. The front line became visible. But then we began firing again. Our artillery put the Russian trenches under heavy fire. I demanded that the reserves go in. We had a firing line, man against man. The Russians didn't advance and those who tried to retreat were blown away. We killed hundreds of them. It is irresponsible, how ruthlessly the Russians drive their men forward. My men were exemplary. An unshakeable wall. The night passed without incident. We left the Russians alone so that they could collect their wounded. Many were screaming all day in the wheatfield.

*

On 13th July an attack by the three German armies massed along the border with Russian Poland begins the second major offensive on the Eastern Front. The Russian army is ordered to retreat. Vasily

Mishnin is caught up in the fighting as the field hospital where he now works flees east with the army. Up to a million civilians join the exodus, some under force, others fearing reprisals by the advancing German troops. The Russians leave nothing behind to feed or shelter the enemy. Villages and crops are burnt, animals slaughtered and civilians uprooted. Vasily records his departure.

14th July, Obetsanov

It is raining when we get the order to leave. We move off, leaving one dead soldier behind in a shed. Planes are dropping bombs everywhere, mainly on the road. Our troops are retreating. All the villagers are leaving Bogaty village. Krasne is on fire. I hear the wailing and crying of women and children. Bogaty is burning, everything is on fire. Panic. What is going to happen? How can we escape from this misery?

16th July, Makov

It is raining heavily. Shells are already exploding nearby. Refugees are walking and driving from all directions. We are ordered to pull out of Makov immediately. It turned out that two of the injured were actually dead, so they were taken to the cemetery and I think they managed to bury them. The battle is raging, everything is shaking. In Makov there is a crush of people, an endless procession of carts, no way to get out of here fast. Screaming, noise and crying, everything is confused. We are supposed to be retreating, but in two hours we only make it down one street. In the end, we hardly make it to the bridge, where the longest queue is. Everyone is desperate to avoid being taken prisoner by the Germans. We cross the bridge and just about reach the road when the shells start exploding all over town. Several fall next to the bridge. We march six and a half miles in an hour and turn off to the side of the road to await further orders.

17th July, Pshiradovo[1]

All the villagers have been ordered to evacuate. They are in despair, and protest bitterly. At eight in the evening we are on the march again. We come out onto the road. It is dark. But what's that noise? Oh my God, what's happening on the road ahead? It is blocked by carts, full of kids and household stuff. The cows are bellowing, the dogs are barking and yelping. The poor people are going God knows where, anywhere to get away from the fighting. But the old nags don't have the strength to pull the loads; the air is filled with the sound of horses being whipped and the Polish 'tso', and still the carts won't move. We don't have the heart just to drive through them. It's such a heartbreaking scene, we drag one cart after another out of the mud, get them onto the main road and then onto the bridge over the river Narew. I pity them all, particularly the little children, sitting in the carts or in their mothers' arms. They don't understand what is happening around them. My thoughts turn to my own family, I feel depressed and before I know it tears run down my cheeks.

*

The Germans advance five miles in two days and take a quarter of the retreating Russians prisoner. Ernst Nopper writes in the evening of his first day on the move.

17th July

Advance to Bartniki. I have a rather strange but happy feeling as I march over the enemy trenches which I have lain opposite for months. Perfect positions in Bartniki and we sit around all day, putting up our tents in the evening.

---

1 The place names in this chapter are reproduced as they appear in the original Russian and German diaries. Some are hard to trace on contemporary maps but this may be due to the existence of different spellings and sometimes different names in the languages of the two occupying forces and the local Polish population.

18th July

Leave Bartniki at 9.30 for Karwacze. Nothing has been destroyed here yet but it is all terribly dirty. All three companies stay in a simple grain barn 100 metres long and 17 metres wide. We advance quickly without exchanging fire.

19th July

I have been told that because of our advance the Russians gave orders to the entire population to remove or destroy all animals in our path, and because this village did not do so the Russians themselves burnt them all. Our base is in the woods, surrounded by birch and larch trees. Nice little woodlice. The landscape is immensely charming. We stay in an abandoned wooden hut.

*

The retreat continues relentlessly for Vasily Mishnin, but he finds a brief respite in the village of Dombrovo.

18th July

Arrive 5 a.m. This is a cherry heaven. We tear down and eat as much as we want, till we feel sick. When the locals realised we were here, they were very pleased to see us and gave us a warm welcome. Then in the evening the Cossacks move in, behaving despicably and viciously driving the people out of their homes amid tears and curses and anger. At 8 p.m. we leave Dombrovo and it starts to rain heavily. We march on through a thick forest, where you can't see a thing. We trip up again and again but pick ourselves up each time and keep walking, as the forest gets darker and darker.

19th July, Boyevo village

Arrived 8 p.m. Completely wet. Found a barn, got warm in some straw, then in the evening we are back on the move. I can hardly move. I stumble around half asleep. Sometimes I fall asleep as I'm walking.

21st July

As we retreat we walk for 20 to 25 miles every night, and sometimes more. By 10 a.m. we reach Ostrow, near Warsaw. It is a small town but it's clean. I think we'll be here a while, so I am writing a letter home.

23rd July

A zeppelin attacked Ostrow in the night and dropped a few bombs, many killed. One woman and her two kids got blown to pieces that blew away in the wind.

25th July

It is raining but we have to get out of Ostrow. At 9 p.m. arrive in Nagashevo.

25th July, Pshuymy

Rumours that Warsaw is being evacuated. The whole company is in shock. German aeroplanes are flying overhead, pounding our batteries.

11th August

Arrived in Topchevo village. Our hospital has received many casualties. Civilians are burying their possessions in the ground and leaving. Some children are crying about a cat, their parents are refusing to take it with them. Here it is at last, the border. So much sorrow for these people. They are carrying books and maps. New casualties arrive and have to lie on the floor, their cries mingling with the marching songs of the infantry, off to the front line.

They do not stop at the Polish border but retreat deeper into Belarus. General Yanushkevich, the Russian chief of staff, complains that his armies are 'melting like the snow' before the German onslaught.

*

One by one the Polish fortress towns fall to the invading army. Ernst Nopper advances swiftly and sends his next letter home from the prized fortress of Rozan, north of Warsaw.

2nd August, Rozan

Dearest wife, dear children,

I watch the town's inhabitants returning in small groups and breaking into cries of dismay when they see their church in ruins. Only the walls of the houses are still standing, the owners search the rubble for what remains of their belongings. Inside the fort I was particularly surprised by how clean the barracks are, everything is scrubbed and bleached. It is all in perfect order. Not unlike our barracks in Ludwigsburg in terms of cleanliness. We are wrong to accuse the Russians of being sloppy and untidy all the time. In one of the areas abandoned by the Russians I found several paintings wrapped up in newspaper. I was very surprised to find that they were of a rather high quality. We should really ask ourselves why we think so little of the Russians. But it is true that culture hasn't really got through to the ordinary people here, unlike in Germany.

Lots of warm greetings,

Your Ernst

9th August

We march on to Jestowo-Katschka. There are dead bodies everywhere you look. The villages have been completely destroyed. The fields are covered in so many graves it looks like moles have been at work. There are shells everywhere.

Two weeks after Vasily Mishnin fled from Ostrow, Ernst Nopper reaches the outskirts of the town. With the arrival of the German soldiers the town's multi-ethnic population, displaced by the Russian retreat, makes its way back home carrying whatever they are able to take with them. Many of the region's Jews look to the Germans for better treatment. But while thousands of German-Jewish soldiers

Ernst Nopper's letter of 2nd August 1915 to his wife and children fight in the German army, anti-Semitism is widespread. Ernst records his arrival.

11th August

The Jews are in and around Ostrow. Whole carts crowded with Jewish families are coming back. Even if there's only one old nag pulling, no one thinks of getting off and lightening the load. On the contrary, the poor horse is forced to trot. I couldn't bear to watch as a Polish family, heavily weighed down by only their most essential belongings struggled forward on foot, while the entire lazy Jewish population travelled on carts. I spoke to them through my interpreter and ordered them to stop. I hauled one Jew off and gave his arse a good beating before making the three Poles with all their baggage climb up onto the cart. I let everyone know that I would have all the Jews shot if they didn't let the Poles continue on their journey. The nearer we got to Ostrow, the more Jews there were.

15th August

Marched to Luniewo Duce, an attractive, unspoilt town. Everything along the way had been destroyed. A charred corpse lay against a pile of burnt bricks. Horrific scenes. Smoke rose on the horizon from the villages burnt by the Russians. Does anyone need to ask who the *real* barbarians are?

17th August

The Russians must have retreated very fast as we have to keep running day after day. We advance to Bransk, a small town that used to belong to the Russians. It is dirty beyond belief and full of Jews. All the shops are in their hands, but you can't buy anything here because it's all so dirty. One of them put a filthy finger on the picture I was drawing and I was forced to punch him in the head, a pleasant release for my general rage.

27th August

A handful of Jews are the only inhabitants left in Orla. They go around the deserted houses taking anything of any value. They are a thievish lot. The Russians have succeeded in driving out both the people and their animals, thus worsening the food situation.

11th September

Bialystok is full of soldiers. The Jews have their own Hebrew newspaper. They stand on the street corners and watch the latest developments with attentive eyes. They have adapted their businesses with incredible speed. The hat-maker who made Russian caps before is now making German ones, the photographer who took Russian military photographs is now taking photographs of German soldiers.

14th September

Set off for Radulina, a 15-mile march. The route is uniformly boring, with no trees or houses. An area of forest about 4 miles deep has been burnt down by the Russians. Only the charred tree-stumps remain. A sorry sight.

16th September

Anything which can be smoked fetches a very high price. The thicker the soldier's epaulettes, the more expensive the cigar. Major Brummer paid forty pfennig each for some very bad cigars, while some lad paid only ten. You have to buy everything from the Jews, even matches. Hotels, chemists, cafes, they're all run by dirty, mean Jews.

18th September

We are ordered to leave tomorrow. I am glad. This is not somewhere you'd want to spend much time.

The next day German units halt their advance hundreds of miles east when they take Vilnius, the largest city in Russian-occupied Lithuania. Around 850,000 Russians have been taken prisoner since the beginning of the offensive in May. Lithuania, the whole of Russian Poland as well as parts of Belarus and the Ukraine are now under German control.

After their spectacular success in Russia, Ernst Nopper's division is ordered south where a new joint Central Powers' offensive is being prepared against Serbia. The journey takes Ernst back through Germany for the first time in seven months.

22nd September

We are approaching the border of our homeland. The roads are bad, and only improve on the other side of the border. At the border post we strike up 'Deutschland, Deutschland Über Alles', and everyone joins in with gusto. But the cheering is lacklustre. How different it would be if we were crossing the border on our final march home. In Germany the beautiful houses have been destroyed, nothing has been spared. The red brick walls are the only sign that large houses once stood there. We all regret that we behaved so decently while we were in Russia.

All transports of German troops from the east, perceived as disease- and lice-ridden, undergo compulsory vaccination and disinfection.

25th September

Typhoid vaccinations today (the sixth time for some people).

26th September

Today the men and horses will be deloused and decontaminated. The lice do not survive this procedure. They are roasted brown and can be brushed off. The men receive a full set of new underclothes and must hand in their old ones. During the train-ride we are pleas- antly struck by the cleanliness, which differentiates Germany so much from Poland. The tall chimneys – and I saw none in Poland – are a ubiquitous sign of German hard work and diligence.

27th September

The journey is quick. We crossed the border at Oderberg at 1 p.m. and entered Austria. On our left a train appeared, crossing the mountainside – a very pleasant sight after the endless flat plains of Russia, Poland, East and West Prussia. A welcome change of scenery.

30th September

To the south, mountains appear through a blue haze. That is the other side of the Danube and the Sava, where the Serbians are positioned. Belgrade, Mitrowitza.

The Austro-Hungarian troops wait for German reinforcements before launching an attack on Serbia. Their previous attempt in 1914 to defeat Serbia on their own had ended in failure. The joint attack opens on 5th October with a formidable artillery bombardment, and within days Belgrade is evacuated. Ernst Nopper oversees the building of a pontoon bridge across the River Sava. He continues his diary in the border village of Dec.

9th October

The German flag is flying in Belgrade. We drilled the men on the wide pastures near the village.

12th October

Set off at 6 a.m. We approach the Sava in thick fog. Lively artillery and infantry fire, the first in a long while. You can see Belgrade. It is quite beautiful up there on the hill with its many domes, spires and battlements. The old fortress has been shot to bits. Apart from that it seems fairly untouched.

In the morning we saw a convoy of prisoners, old men, women and children at the back; a motley group of people of all ages and nationalities, some in uniform. There were some really impressive figures among them, genuine mountain folk.

14th October

The people we are billeted with are clearly terrified of us Germans. They are very keen to keep us happy and are always offering us coffee.

18th October

We moved into Bazevac. An old man and a dwarfish but very lively little man were still in the house, and watched in dismay as their supply of wine, cheese, chicken, pork and mutton disappeared. They made a tame protest at first but quickly calmed down. It is quite disconcerting how much a battalion can polish off.

For the second time in four months, Ernst Nopper participates in a major advance which forces civilian refugees and soldiers alike to flee.

*

With Belgrade occupied, the German and Austro-Hungarian troops advance further south. At this point neutral Bulgaria joins the Central Powers and its army begins to attack Serbia from the east. The Serbian army is now trapped between the two advancing forces. With them is Serbian officer Milorad Marković, the future grandfather of Mirjana Marković, wife of Slobodan Milošević. Faced with defeat, on 25th November he and hundreds of thousands of Serbian soldiers and civilians set out on a punishing three-week-long march across treacherous mountains to the Albanian coast. Milorad writes his account of the retreat when he reaches comparative safety in December 1915.

December 1915

I remember things scattered all around; horses and men stumbling and falling into the abyss; Albanian attacks; hosts of women and children. A doctor would not dress an officer's

wound; soldiers would not bother to pull out a wounded comrade or officer. Belongings abandoned; starvation; wading across
rivers clutching onto horses' tails; old men, women and children
climbing up the rocks; dying people on the road; a smashed
human skull by the road; a corpse all skin and bones, robbed,
stripped naked, mangled; soldiers, police officers, civilians,
women, captives. Vlasta's cousin, naked under his overcoat with
a collar and cuffs, shattered, gone mad. Soldiers like ghosts,
skinny, pale, worn out, sunken eyes, their hair and beards long,
their clothes in rags, almost naked, barefoot. Ghosts of people
begging for bread, walking with sticks, their feet covered in
wounds, staggering. Chaos; women in soldiers' clothes; the desperate mothers of those who are too exhausted to go on. A
starving soldier who ate too much bread and dropped dead. A
soldier selling anything and everything for bread: his gun,
clothes, shoes and boots, coats, horses' feedbags, saddlebags,
horses . . .

*Although they are marching through Albania which, like Serbia, is
on the Allied side, local tribesmen who suffered at Serb hands in the
earlier Balkan wars attack their fleeing neighbours.*

That whole day, from the early morning, we march along Esad's
road. Straight and flat, it stretches forever. Hunger, exhaustion,
weariness and boredom drain our strength. We are not walking
but dragging ourselves. We look like pale, exhausted, skinny
ghosts, images of long dead spirits condemned to wander aim-
lessly.

Silent, dark, apathetic we stagger. We have been doing this for
days. After our defeat we moved towards Albania, where we
thought we would be safe from our enemies. But with the first
steps we feel all her horror: the rage of the Albanians, the bru-
tality of nature, the terrors of hunger. Pursued by men and God,
half dead, we race to leave the country tracked by packs of
hungry wolves and gangs of Albanians. Hunger and death are

with us all along. So many remain in that mud! But we have to run further, to Ljesh. There's the harbour! There we'll have bread and rest. No bread there either, and the Germans are pursuing us. We must flee again. Further, too far for us, worn out, exhausted and half-dead – to Drach.

We are not alive; we walk and move, sometimes eat or speak, but half-conscious. We left Ljesh six days ago. We get caught in the mud; some are bogged down in the mire, mad, with mouths full of sludge, letting off terrible, mournful cries. We wade across rivers. There, too, some perish, drown or freeze to death. Then we go over rocks, ravines; many fall there, too. Others go on ignoring the stragglers. And here we are on Esad's road. There are villages around. It is hard to go on. We are fewer and fewer in number. How many will reach Drach? We can see the sea from a hill. Someone says he can see Drach too. Some even look in that direction and confirm it. But the rest are unmoved, silent. Is this Drach?

Pursued to the coast by the German and Austro-Hungarian forces, the Serbian troops and civilians have to keep going to reach the Allied boats ready to evacuate survivors from the Albanian port of Valona.

What awaits us here? Hunger. We have already heard that we will be sent to Valona. Will we be able to go? We don't think of that! We all expect to fall on the ground, never to get up. We enter Sijak. We go on, towards a hill where we meet several officers. The camp is here, and here we stay. They have everything. Bread and other food. Ah, bread, just bread! We unload the guns and feed the cattle. Then we fall on the ground, with no strength left, no sign of life. We are yanked out of our numbness by the cries of the supply unit – they are bringing the bread.

We jump to our feet. Bread! Starved of bread for so long, we come alive again. Our faces flush, eyes brighten. We fight over the bread like wild beasts. Having grabbed a piece each, we devour it ravenously, tearing it with our teeth. We don't chew, but swallow big hard pieces. And so we satisfy that wild animal hunger a little, unsated for so long. Only then do we sigh with relief and smile blissfully, like dogs after a good bite. When the cattle food arrives, and we have cared for our animals, we lie down and get up late the next day.

Tens of thousands of Serbian civilian refugees and half the army, over 200,000 men, die on the road, from hunger, disease and ambushes. British, French and Italian boats evacuate Milorad Marković and the remaining soldiers to the island of Corfu in what has been called the 'largest sea evacuation in history until Dunkirk'. On Corfu, Milorad pauses to reflect.

During a sudden attack, in the panic and confusion, a calm man can do a lot, and appear to be a hero. I remember myself at Ljuma: everyone running away in the confusion, panic, chaos; I take charge of the majors and the higher ranks; I shout at everyone; I do not run, but take even greater risks and look like a hero. They beseech me to take care of myself. I grow very big. I could have become a dictator. It is at such moments that leaders, dictators and the like are created.

Milorad remained on Corfu until 1916 when many of the surviving Serbs crossed back to the mainland and joined Allied troops defending the Salonica Front. Serbia continued to be under occupation. He would return home with the advancing Allied troops in the autumn of 1918.

In December 1915 Ernst Nopper was transferred from Serbia to Ypres on the Western Front. Six months later, on 2nd June 1916, he was killed by shrapnel during a German attack. Ernst left a wife and two children in Ludwigsburg.

At Christmas 1915, Vasily Mishnin went home on leave where he was reunited with Nyura and met his by now nine-month-old son, Vasinka, for the first time. On his return from leave he would continue as a clerk with the field hospital now in Belarus.

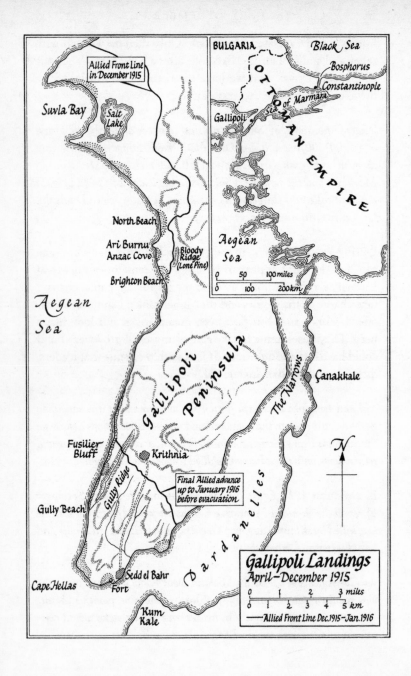

Gallipoli Landings
April–December 1915

Chapter 6

GALLIPOLI

April–December 1915

On 29th October 1914 the Turkish Navy shelled Russia's Black Sea ports without warning. The next day the outraged Russian Empire declared war on her neighbour and centuries-old foe. By 2nd November 1914 Russia's allies, Britain and France, were also at war with Turkey's Ottoman Empire. Backed by Germany, Turkey declared Jihad – Holy War – on Britain, France and Russia, threatening to foment Islamic revolt across the Middle East. Britain feared for the safety of her interests in the region, her trade routes, prestige and power. If Afghanistan and Egypt fell under Ottoman control, the British Empire, including India, would be imperilled.

To entice Turkish armies to join the Central Powers, Germany offered £5 million in gold. The ailing Ottoman Empire, the 'sick man of Europe', had its own interests at heart. Having lost a third of its territories in a succession of disastrous wars, Turkey hoped to re-establish itself as a powerful presence in the East.

For Germany, Turkey's prominent position in the region was worth every mark spent. Turkey immediately opened a new front on the Caucasus against Russia, already heavily engaged on the Eastern Front against Germany and Austria-Hungary. The first Ottoman offensive across the Caucasus mountains threatened the *southern provinces of the Russian Empire. Caught off guard, Russian troops quickly descended into a chaotic retreat.*

On 3rd January 1915 the Russian government appealed for British help to deflect the Turks by launching a campaign elsewhere. By the time the Allies reached a decision, however, the urgency had subsided: Russian troops retaliated, defeating Turkish forces at Sarikamish. Their victory was aided by severe frosts that killed thousands of ill-equipped Turkish soldiers that winter; the few survivors retreated. The Allies, nonetheless, decided to attack the heavily defended Dardanelle Straits. If successful, the campaign could open supply routes to Russia via the Black Sea, support Serbia by fostering a Balkan alliance with Greece and enable Allied warships to threaten Constantinople, eventually forcing a Turkish surrender.

On 18th March 1915 a combined Franco-British naval force opened fire on Turkish defences in the Dardanelle Straits. When, despite heavy casualties and significant loss of ships, the Allied bombardment failed to achieve the necessary breakthrough, they instead planned amphibious landings. Their chosen place was a peninsula on the northern shore of the Dardanelles. The Turks called it Gelibolu – Gallipoli.

Two young soldiers keep diaries of the Gallipoli campaign – an Australian corporal, George Mitchell, of the Allied Mediterranean Expeditionary Force, and a Turkish second lieutenant, Mehmed Fasih, defending Gallipoli with the 5th Imperial Ottoman Army. Both men turn twenty-one during the brutal battle for the peninsula.

In the early hours of Sunday 25th April 1915, the 70,000-strong Allied Expeditionary Force of British, French and Anzac[1] troops makes a silent approach by sea under cover of darkness. While the British are to land at Cape Helles at the tip of the peninsula and the French make a diversionary landing at Çanakkale, the

---

1 Australian and New Zealand Army Corps, formed in 1914.

17,000-strong Anzac group heads for the Gallipoli beaches further north. Corporal George Mitchell is on one of the Anzac boats attempting a surprise landing. Late that evening he writes down what he witnessed.

25th April 1915

Lord, what a day.

At about 2 a.m. every man was awakened and in grim silence mustered on the deck. A glorious moon lit up the scene as our ship lay with engines at rest on the calm sea. Many eyes gleaming with lust of adventure were turned to that scowling line of hills, rising out sphinx-like, holding the mystery of life and death. The only sounds to break the silence were the shuffling of feet and the muffled curses of men who scrambled down. It was eerie.

My breath became deep. I tried to analyse my feelings but couldn't. I think that every emotion was mixed, exultation predominating. We have come from the New World for the conquest of the Old. Fierce we expected it to be, but fierce as it was, we never dreamed. The price of failure we knew to be annihilation, victory might mean life. I remember turning to poor old Peter and asking him how he felt. 'Good'. That was the last time I spoke to him.

For hour after hour our grim procession held on its way. The chill wind seemed to pierce our bones. Then came the events. A blue light blazed somewhere among those formless hills. 'Seen,' hissed someone. Then it came. 'Knock-knock!' Tension snapped. 'Good,' I remember saying. 'The -------s will give us a go after all.' 'Klock-klock-klock. Wee-wee-wee', came the little messengers of death. Then it opened into a terrific chorus, and then we knew they had been waiting for us in strength.

The key was being turned in the lock of the lid of hell. Some men crouched in the crowded boat, some sat up nonchalantly, some laughed and joked, while others cursed with ferocious delight. That last hundred yards was a lifetime. The crowded

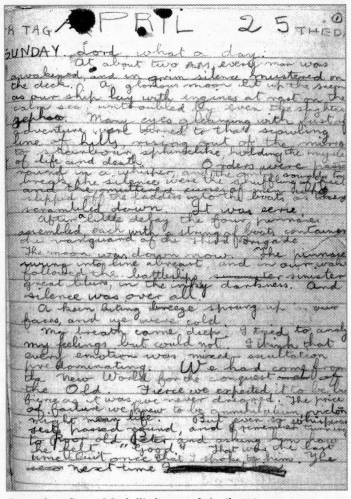

A page from George Mitchell's diary, 25th April 1915

boat made slow progress at best; [now it was] almost impossible. 'Over the side, boys!' I yelled and followed the words.

I plunged ashore and yelled for my section to assemble. In those precious minutes while we lay behind that bank, waiting for the whole party to get on land, the bullets spat venomously into the sand all round. A wave of cold fear swept over me when I realised the meaning of those terrible cries which arose at short intervals all round.

A galling fire rained on us from the left where there were high cliffs. One man dropped down alongside me laughing. I broke the news to him gently: 'You've got yourself into the hottest corner you'll ever strike.' I had shown him where the enemy were, he fired a few shots. And again I heard the sickening thud of a bullet. I looked at him in horror. The bullet had fearfully mashed his face and gone down his throat, rendering him dumb. But his eyes were dreadful to behold. How he squirmed in agony. There was nothing I could do for him, but pray that he might die swiftly. It took him about twenty minutes to accomplish this and by that time he had tangled his legs in pain and stiffened. I saw the waxy colour creep over his cheek and breathed freer.

The surprise Allied landing is by now in disarray. Instead of advancing inland, the Anzacs who managed to make it to the beach are mown down by an unseen enemy, pouring gunfire upon them from their concealed positions in the scrub-covered hills. George Mitchell and the remains of his section lay in wait under unceasing heavy fire for most of the morning, when a new order arrives.

Now and again above the fiendish din of battle came a terrific WOOM-PAH at which ground, sea and sky seemed to get up and sit down again. It was Big Lizzie[1] arguing with her fifteen-inch toys. 'Fix bayonets and prepare to charge,' came an order.

---

1 The super-dreadnought HMS *Queen Elizabeth*, which had 15-inch guns.

The remnants of our line hauled out bayonets, snapped them on rifles and gathered ourselves up ready to spring off on the instant. What a storm of lead greeted us when they saw the white flicker of steel among the bushes. About four men were hit in the instant. I think that about one man in six in that line was capable of advancing, the others were all dead or wounded.

After waiting until the fire decreased in volume, I drew myself together and prepared to make my bid for cover from the corpse-held line. I forget how many corpses I took in my stride, but I do know that the air was full of bullets and that I had no fear of them. Reached the crest four yards beyond it, then without checking speed crashed down on my back and rolled over to find myself alongside Jock. 'Hit?' he asked. 'Don't know,' I said. 'I'll find out.' But I did not find a single bullet hole. So we lay there until night when we could crawl up and dig in.

George Mitchell's section is not the only one that fails to break through. Instead of the surprise landing and rapid advance they had planned, the Anzacs meet ferocious resistance. To make matters worse, they have landed in the wrong place. Rather than a flat desolate beach, they have struggled ashore on to a narrow strip of sand surrounded by steep hills where the Turkish soldiers have built defensive positions.

Over the next few days the Anzacs make desperate but futile attempts to advance under incessant Turkish bombardment. They find shelter in a small but naturally sheltered inlet measuring just 1,100 yards across, which becomes known as Anzac Cove. The British Commander of Anzac troops, William Birdwood, suggests immediate evacuation due to strategic failure, but the Commander of Allied Forces, General Ian Hamilton, rejects his appeal. For the rest of this campaign the Anzac troops will remain here, never managing to make contact with the rest of the Allied forces at the southern tip of the peninsula.

In the first week of fighting Anzac casualties reach around 8,100, with 2,300 killed. A few days after the disastrous landing, George Mitchell reckons the cost.

4th May

Our battalion at last has been asked into reserve. I have to take charge of number 9 platoon as everyone senior to me has been killed. But the roll calls shows that the casualty rate is only about 50 per cent instead of about 80 per cent as I believed at first. The weather lately has been bright and cloudless and cheerfully warm, all in keeping with the harvest of death. The trenches have been fairly quiet today, the enemy being held perfectly in check.

6th May

There is a tremendous joke in that the Turks have given us 24 hours to clean out – baggage and all. Otherwise we will all be killed. Poor us. Great vindictiveness prevails against the Snipers, and our best shots put in some effective work. There is no excitement in waiting for the enemy who never appears.

7th May

The Turk gets very little mercy from us. How can he expect it? They are very liberal in their use of explosive bullets and had they the chance would commit their usual atrocities. Snipers are pretty well cleaned out from inside of our lines. Whenever one is caught he is put to the bayonet immediately.

The Turks suffer severely in their half-hearted bayonet attacks, usually delivered at night. They approach calling on Allah. We hold our fire till they are within twenty paces. Then they get a couple of stunning volleys and we hop out and bayonet anyone who cannot run away quick enough. I have not been lucky enough to catch one yet.

12th May

When I was awakened to stand to arms, I began wondering about the glory of war. Daylight came, so did more rain. At 9 o'clock we shifted into reserve trenches for 24 hours. Lounged around all morning and slept all afternoon.

17th May

Began to organise the work when a snarling shrapnel pierced
our trench. For a couple of seconds the air was full of hissing
bullets. When the dust and smoke cleared, there lay its victim –
Alec Richmond drilled though the brain – breathing his last.
His pals with faces grey with grief carried him away.

After work was concluded at 12 o'clock, Cheney and I made a
good stew. Onions, potatoes and bully beef. Everyone was quite
in high spirits all day. One forgets tragedy as soon it is out of
sight, often before.

*Two days later the Turks launch an audacious attack, aiming to
drive the Anzacs into the sea.*

19th May

Every bush seemed to hide a Turk. Suddenly from the gulley 150
yards from in the front came clear and distinct 'Allah!' And at the
same second I caught a flicker of a bayonet in the scrub not far
ahead.

It was a massacre. In half an hour it was over. Daylight
showed the ground in front littered with dead laying in all pos-
tures. On the right a Turk kneels in the wheat fields four yards
from the trench. He is very dead. A grenade intended to lob into
our happy home went off prematurely and improved on the
work of two well-aimed bullets. Dozens of rifles with bayonets
fixed and heaps of ammunition were brought in. I did some very
good shooting with one of them. The butt was covered with
blood but it shot straight.

A wounded Turk told us they regard Australians as fiends
incarnate. The Germans told them that we were an undisci-
plined rabble, armed mostly with sticks, axes etc. But he
reckoned we were a lot of mad devils when it came to the
bayonet.

*After days of ruthless killing and sweltering heat, the stench from
No-Man's-Land becomes unbearable for the inhabitants of both sets
of trenches, often a mere twenty yards apart. A general call goes out
for men from both sides to collect and bury their dead during a brief
ceasefire. George Mitchell is among the volunteers.*

24th May

We stepped over the parapet and were on the debatable
ground. I have grown blasé with strange sights but the novelty
of this impressed me more than anything else in this war.
They said so themselves. In this part, the trenches were from
seven to thirty yards apart – a bewildering maze. Groups of
Turks, Australians and New Zealanders wandered around the
zone of death. Mixed parties squatted together exchanging
cigarettes etc. The Turks and their officers were frankly
friendly, but the Germans stood sullen and aloof. There were
some gorgeous uniforms among them and the swank of the
Huns was intolerable.

Suddenly a word came along: 'Everyone into the trenches'.
We lost not a second in getting out of the field of vision of those
innumerable Maxims and Mausers.

All day I only saw one man who answered to the general con-
ception of an old-time Turk. He was a satanic individual in light
blue uniform. They seemed well fed and well equipped.

*In the ensuing months, frontline duty in George Mitchell's sector
consists of sniping and patrolling, with the daily routine interrupted by sporadic raids. By early June the Anzac troops abandon
all attempts to advance inland. Their actions are now aimed only
at improving their positions. In the British sector, on Cape Helles
to the south, the fighting is also now infrequent. Monotonous
frontline duty is followed by equally boring days in the rear.
George Mitchell tries to break up the routine by going for daring
daily swims.*

13th July

Unlucky thirteenth. Early in the morning I went in for a dip. The sniper was putting in great work. He had four shots of me. When he got too hot I would swim under water. Got back. Lugged all my goods to the Eleventh trenches. Put on sentry duty at entrance to headquarters. Hour on and two off. Was feeling ill. Big shells bursting overhead all day. At night I would sleep on my post, but wake up every time anyone approached. Could I not sleep in bed? Rotten. Wish the Turks attack then there would be some sport.

In the scorching summer heat the Allied troops suffer from exhaustion and dehydration; supplies of fresh water and food are scarce. As the futility of the Allied effort becomes clear the men grow increasingly apathetic and demoralised. Swarms of insects, unknown beetles, strange centipedes and, worst of all, flies attracted by the rotting flesh, human faeces and sweat, add to the troops' discomforts. The trenches, though frequently disinfected, become a breeding ground for dysentery and typhoid, soon far greater killers than the Turkish guns and bayonets. Hundreds of men fall ill daily, including George Mitchell. Over the next few days his usually neat handwriting becomes a barely legible scribble.

23rd July

The Mohammedan festival of Ramadan and we are in hopes that the Turks will not let this victorious season go by without having a go at us.

Very sick.

Paraded to the quack and got a pill.

Ate nothing all day.

25th July

Ill

Got a pill and no duty

Ate nothing.

SUNDAY JULY 25
Ill
Got a pill and no duty
Ate nothing

A page from George Mitchell's diary, 25th July 1915

On 4th August 1915 Corporal Mitchell is taken to a hospital in
Alexandria; he is one of around a thousand evacuated daily from
Gallipoli. Hundreds of less fortunate soldiers who stay behind have
barely the strength to drag themselves to the latrines, where many
remain to die a slow and agonising death.

The Anzacs make one more significant raid to assist a new British
landing at Suvla Bay north of Anzac Cove between 6th and 9th
August 1915. They manage to overrun the Turkish trenches at Lone
Pine, killing and taking prisoner thousands of Turkish soldiers. The
additional landing does not change the overall course of the Gallipoli
campaign, however.

With the onset of cold weather, the flies disappear and dysentery
subsides, but almost 15,000 are evacuated from Anzac Cove and
nearby Suvla Bay due to frostbite. The Turkish soldiers fare even
worse. Both sides frequently stamp about in full view of the other in
their efforts to keep warm.

*

The Turkish campaign on Gallipoli is led by German General Liman
Von Sanders, but on the day of the Allied landing Turkish
Lieutenant Colonel Mustafa Kemal takes the initiative, organising
a successful Turkish defence without waiting for orders from above.
In a fiery address, Mustafa Kemal urges every Turkish soldier to
fight to the end: 'Every soldier who fights here with me must realise
that he is honour-bound not to retreat one step. Let me remind you all
that if you want to rest, there may be no rest for our whole nation
throughout eternity. I am sure all our comrades agree with this, and
that they will show no signs of fatigue until the enemy is finally
hurled into the sea.' Invoking religion, as well as the threat of bullets and bayonets, on those attempting to turn back, Mustafa Kemal
ensures that the Turkish troops prove all Allied assessments wrong.
Gallipoli is no easy pushover, the Turkish soldiers and officers hold
on to every inch of ground and are recognised as a force to be reckoned with.

Turkish officer candidate Mehmed Fasih from Mersin interrupted

*his studies at the military academy at the end of July 1914, when
general mobilisation was declared across the Ottoman Empire.
Fasih's 47th Regiment arrived at the Bloody Ridge positions (known
to the Allies as Lone Pine), south-east of Anzac Cove on 15th May
1915, three weeks after the Allied landings. By the time the Mehmed
Fasih reaches the front, he is promoted to Second Lieutenant.
Injured after just a few days of fighting, he is evacuated to Istanbul.
On return to Gallipoli in late October 1915, Mehmed begins keeping a diary, which he calls 'a record of the fleeting moments in the
life of an owner of a fatalistic heart'.*

18th October 1915

After 01.00 hrs. My little dugout is small with a roof of logs and
to keep out the grenades its entrance is covered by wire netting.
I sleep on a wooden bed with a straw mattress under my blankets
and a kilim. Other furnishings include my crystal paraffin lamp,
my coffee set and a tin brazier. Thank God, I am quite comfortable. My orderly is in the adjoining dug-out. He is a good and
obedient fellow, with a pure heart.

02.00 hrs. Exploding enemy shells shake the ground but miss
their target. They land either in front or behind our positions.
Today they're sending over more of their little presents than
usual. I sense fear in the enemy's every move. Perhaps the
rumour was true. Their infantry is being thinned out and
replaced by fire power.

21st October

12.00 hrs. After lunch, have a look at fortifications on our second
defensive line. When I was here with my former battalion, we
transformed this place into a little paradise. Now it's a wasteland.
Everything is in disarray, chaos reigns. The place is now so
depressing, it makes me want to cry. Return to my dugout and
fill my water pipe with tobacco, the first time in ten days that I'm
able to smoke my own water pipe. Bombardment continues. A
few howitzer shells land close by. Enemy grenades continue to

It has been suggested that the officer to the right inside the Turkish dugout at Bloody Ridge is Lieutenant Mehmed Fasih.

explode near to where they killed one of our men yesterday. Now nobody hangs around in that area any more.

19.20 hrs. Very tired and ill, go to bed.

22nd October

06.00 hrs. Wake up. I had a comfortable night. Feel slightly better. My men fetch some firewood. It is overcast and windy. I stay in bed.

07.00 hrs. The firewood arrives. I get up, have coffee and smoke my pipe. I allow my mind to dwell on what my happiness could be like. Alas! All paths to happiness are closed to me. I recite the old prayer lamenting the lack of Divine Inspiration and find peace of mind in the realisation that Divine Inspiration can only come from God. I emerge from my dugout. Comrades invite me over for tea but I don't go. Don't feel up to it. Feel ill.

4th November

20.30 hrs. The firing intensifies to our left. I run to the trenches. Our soldiers are blazing away, our left is really getting it. The enemy is raining shells down on us. Thank God, they aren't landing inside our trenches. The enemy uses a lot of flares to illuminate both our rear and our front lines. We benefit from this light as much as he does. His shells are really pouring in.

21.00 hrs. From the rear comes 'Allah! Allah!' – the rallying cry of our soldiers. It is followed by noise, then there is silence. Then all of a sudden intensive firing erupts and shells come pouring down on our rear.

24.00 hrs. I fill up my water pipe and put a kettle on the brazier. The weather is clear and mild. A dumdum[1] explodes

---

1 This reference is somewhat controversial. Mehmed Fasih definitely refers to dumdums, bullets designed to shatter on impact with the human body leaving devastating wounds, and outlawed by the Geneva Convention. It is sometimes suggested that such stories arose as a result of propaganda or

occasionally. Though I keep picking off lice, there are plenty more – I just can't get rid of them and am itching all over. My body is covered with red and purple blotches.

01.00 hrs. I am sleepy. I have not slept for two nights. However, I must stay awake all night. This is important. On May 28th the enemy launched his offensive after midnight. I hunt lice for a while, then stretch out. Unable to stop myself, I fall asleep.

*

Two and a half months since his evacuation, George Mitchell is still recovering from the typhoid he contracted in the trenches of Gallipoli. In the military hospital in Southampton in England, thousands of miles away from the dangerous peninsula, and with nothing to do except eat and sleep, George is beginning to find his forced inaction intolerable.

2nd November

Why do people always treat wounded or sick soldiers as kids? Perhaps a dear old lady will come along and gush, 'Oh you poor dear boys, how you must have suffered. Have some cigarettes!' We have to grin at their patronising way, and the assurance of them. Sometimes we are lying on the grass. 'Aren't you afraid of catching cold?' My sense of humour prevents me continuing with the naughty words that come to me and I say sweetly: 'No, I am too slow to catch a cold.' Beautiful day.

5th November

Went to a concert in the evening. Came back and when I was going into the bathroom heard a commotion in the next ward. Poked my head through the door. Pillows were flying through the air in clouds. When they saw me, Queensland sang out: 'Here's Mitchy, let him have it!'

---

because soldiers were not accustomed to the damage that a conventional .303 round could do.

So all the pillows came at me. I let half a dozen come through the door, gathered them up and moved forward to the attack. In very few seconds I had to retire before superior weight of artillery.

Then they counterattacked in force and I had to retreat in confusion into the bathroom, locking the door. They swarmed round and laid a siege. Then they started sending in howitzers of water over the partition wall. I hopped up on a locker with a jar of cold water and caused the attackers to retire to the ward with heavy casualties. Then I escaped into my own ward.

*

Back on Gallipoli, Mehmed Fasih cherishes every brief moment of peace.

5th November

05.30 hrs. Sometimes for whole minutes there is no firing. During these fleeting moments, when silence is in perfect harmony with a lovely morning bathed in sunlight, I think about the future and the past. Oh, such bittersweet memories of days that now seem like mere fantasies of my imagination! They remain lovely and it breaks my heart to think about them, and I try not to, but I can't help it.

08.00 hrs. Battalion commander asks me to accompany him on a tour of the trenches. He points to a lovely spot, commenting: 'Let's sit down over there with our water pipe'. The place offers a splendid view of our surroundings, but is hidden by a rock formation. An ideal location for morning and evening smoking. We start our tour. As we walk along I notice a group of first-aid men gathered around a stretcher: 'It is Sergeant Nuri.'

Oh my Lord! How many more tragedies will you make me witness? Nuri has injuries to his chest, head, one arm and both legs. His head and chest are ripped wide open. His hair is all messed up, his uniform is soaked with blood. He is pale, his mouth hangs open. You can see his bright white teeth between his lips. His eyes are half open, staring at the sky. His pure, handsome features are still evident. His hands are locked together on his chest. He seems to be cursing those who have destroyed him. I can't stand it any more.

This boy was responsible for training the battalion's replacements. He had absolutely no business at the frontlines. During lunch breaks, however, he just wouldn't stay put.

Only last night he was at my door. 'My Bey,'[1] he said in his pleasant voice: 'I've brought you some ammunition.' Just think of that! The loss of a soldier like him upsets me greatly. I have already witnessed so many deaths and tragedies, but none has affected me so deeply. Very few upset me anymore, as a matter of fact. The first-aid men pick up the stretcher and move off.

We resume our tour, but I can hardly go on. Yet I am determined to perform what will be my last duty in honour of the sergeant I have cared for so much. I take leave from the battalion commander and run towards the cemetery.

I obtain special permission to bury Nuri in the officers' plot, the olive grove at the Karaburun gully. I pick a spot under a fine olive tree. Many of our martyrs lie in this place, Nuri is now one of them. We place his body into the grave so that his head rests under a tree. I gather olive and laurel branches and lay them around his body. As I gaze into his face, my grief overwhelms me so much that when I throw the first handful of earth into the grave, I break down.

I let my tears flow freely, and address Nuri, 'Oh, my son! It is so very painful for me to put you to rest.' Everyone present is now crying too. One of his comrades tells us how Nuri said to him when they arrived at the Front together: 'I implore God to let me become a martyr!' Oh Nuri! Your prayer was answered.

We bury Nuri. It was God's will that I would say the opening verse of the Koran over him. Who will be next? I again find it very difficult to control myself. Hot tears stream down my cheeks. One day this will come to an end, as all things do. I turn away from the grave and walk away.

---

1 Turkish way of addressing a superior officer.

A page from Mehmed Fasih's diary written in Arabic script

7th November

22.30 hrs. It is cold. The wind is blowing harder. A great chasm exists between the poor fellows who do all the fighting and those who merely talk about heroism and victory while getting ready for their wedding night with their penises in their hand, as the saying goes. What a tragedy it will be if all men who are still fighting here have to die like their predecessors. Just so that a handful of cowards can enjoy a taste of fame.

23.30 hrs. The NCOs leave. Tired and sleepy, I lean against the wall and sing.

9th November

16.00 hrs. Our commander gives us sweet news. Three hundred railway wagons of ammunition have arrived, as well as 21 and 24 mm guns and 15 cm howitzers. We shall now be able to bombard the enemy for 70 hours instead of 22 and follow that with a new offensive!

The prospect of success in the near future pleases me so much that I tell the battalion commander that I am prepared to become our regiment's 'fedai'[1] when the new offensive starts. He is delighted.

21.00 hrs. I return to my place. Abdulhalim Efendi offers me some tahini halva and bread. I'm hungry, so eat both.

22.00 hrs. Go to bed and fall asleep while listening to the noise of exploding grenades and dumdum bullets.

*

A world apart from the trenches where Mehmed Fasih has just volunteered for a suicide mission, George Mitchell seeks out every bit of ammunition he can find on Southampton's beaches during his numerous unsanctioned escapes from the confines of the military hospital.

13th November

Nothing doing. Another fine day, with a very strong cold wind.

Had a bomb attack with electric light bulbs washed up by the sea.

14th November

Hatched a dark plot for liberation on Wednesday. A corner to corner bombardment was in progress with slippers. One

---

1 Means a 'man of sacrifice'. An ancient Islamic concept akin to Japanese kamikaze.

smashed an electric light, one went through a window. Then beds were capsized.

15th November

Had complaining from the sisters that the row last night kept them awake. But that is nothing surprising as the noise of a bombardment carries a considerable distance. Marking time and hatching schemes.

*

Two days later conditions on Gallipoli are driving Mehmed Fasih to despair.

17th November

18.00 hrs. Heavy rain, driven by violent wind, drenches everything. My dugout is leaking. Would love to see those people who say 'soldiering is easy, the military are overpaid!' spend one night sleeping in the mud. Would they say such things ever again? I don't think so. I'm 21 years old. My hair and beard are already grey. My moustache is white. My face is wrinkled and my body is rotting. I can't bear these hardships and privations any more. Being an Ottoman officer just means putting up with shells and bombs.

22nd November

05.00 hrs. Daydream about a happy family and nice kids. Will I live to see the day when I have some? I know I should be infinitely grateful for what I do have, but why have I not, to this day, been able to find real happiness, the kind that sets the heart free and brings comfort to the soul? Dear God! Will you ever grant such things to be my lot in life?

And what about my men? We have had seven groups of reinforcements so far. Originally there were 200 soldiers in each of our companies, but now we are down to 50 or less apiece. The rest have become martyrs, or are either missing or wounded. As for the officers, none of us has escaped unscathed. This continuous fighting has exhausted us.

08.00 hrs. Bitter cold gnaws at the flesh of our hands and faces. It makes my heart flutter to think we are in such a state already. What is in store for us? Whatever happens, we will get used to it. If we had to die twice, we would get used to that too.

24th November

15.30 hrs. When I finally reach our trenches I find a large pool of blood. It has coagulated and turned black. Bits of brain, bone and flesh are mixed in with it. Shell fragments are scattered around. The trail of blood leads to the front of my dugout. This is the route followed by stretcher-bearers carrying our dead away. Very upset, I enter feeling very apprehensive. I have become cowardly. I tell myself that fear is futile, that wherever you are, death will find you if it is your time. I must always take what precautions I can, but beyond that whatever will be will be.

27th November

10.30 hrs. We find Agati [a fellow officer] distraught. Even though he prodded his men with bayonets, some of them refused to leave the trench and started crying like women. Those who did go suffered heavy casualties from the enemy fire and shells. The entire unit is demoralised.

4th December

04.30 hrs. My orderly tried to wake me for report, but couldn't. Am writing it now. All is quiet, so I go back to bed . . . I was dozing off when there was a terrific explosion close by. Earth falls into my dugout. I pull the blanket over my head and fantasise about the future. Will I ever have a sweetheart? Dear God, maker of Heaven and Earth and all creatures! Please let me live to see the day when I can taste such bliss. Otherwise I will live my whole life full of longings and grief. I try to sleep but I am mostly half-awake.

9th December

15.00 hrs. Had hardly taken 10 steps when I hear the hum of an approaching howitzer shell. Realise that if I'm to survive, I need to throw myself into a side-trench. The shell seems to be coming straight at me . . . The explosion is awesome. A violent shock follows. I'm thrown against the ramp. Feel pain on the left side of my groin. Clamp my hand on that spot and run towards my dugout. The path is shattered and covered in earth. Shell fragments are everywhere and a strong smell of acid fills my nostrils. You can come face-to-face with death here any minute . . . Oh my God! For the sake of your holy name, please protect us!

13th December

10.00 hrs. Go to see how my men are doing. Each time I pass by the olive grove I am profoundly affected by the memory of all our martyrs buried there. My heart keeps telling me that at the end of the war they will come back to life. Oh my God! Show mercy to those of us who are still living! And guide us!

18.00 hrs. My men are singing their traditional songs. They tell of deep sadness and a sense of mourning. They were singing these same sad songs when we left Mersin. But most of the men who were singing then now lie covered with earth.

19th December

03.35 hrs. Battalion commander arrives. 'Hurry! Prepare a reconnaissance patrol. The enemy has withdrawn from Anafarta and the entire right flank.' Offer him tea. The patrol is readied. Explain it will move into no-man's-land from the spot where the mine was detonated.

Mehmed Fasih stops writing his diary here. For nearly eight months the Turkish defenders of Gallipoli have managed to keep every inch of their land. Their demoralised, exhausted and battle-

weary troops have withstood their enemy and kept Gallipoli Turkish.

*

On 20th December 1915 the last Australian soldiers depart from the peninsula, leaving little soil unturned by graves, trenches and shells. The next day, at Southampton hospital, Corporal George Mitchell receives the news of Allied retreat.

21st December

Got the news of the evacuation of Anzac. Felt completely knocked out. The more I think of it, the more horrible the whole show seems. All that sacrifice, all that labour, all that suffering – for nothing at all. The flower of Australian manhood lies on and below the earth. Wandering parties of Turks in search of loot will trample over them. I feel bitter about it.

A faultless evacuation without a single casualty was the biggest success of this campaign for the Allies. Having confidently predicted an easy victory in this desolate corner of the Turkish coast, they failed to achieve any of their strategic objectives. After losing a third of a million soldiers, with 142,000 killed in battle, the Allied forces completed their withdrawal when the last British troops left the peninsula on 9th January 1916.

The Australian forces on Gallipoli suffered 27,594 casualties during the campaign, including 8,141 dead; 2,721 New Zealanders, one in four of those who landed on Gallipoli, also perished here.

Turkish casualties were between 165,000 and 220,000; 87,000 died defending Gallipoli, but their troops emerged triumphant. The victory will come to symbolise the beginning of a national revival.

*

George Mitchell and Mehmed Fasih both survived Gallipoli and saw out the war. Having finally recovered from typhoid, Mitchell went on to fight in France, where he was promoted to Captain and awarded the Military Cross in addition to a Distinguished Conduct

Medal. Mehmed Fasih fought with the Turkish forces on Sinai. In October 1917 he was captured by the British in the desert near Gaza during their advance on Jerusalem and spent the rest of war in a POW camp near the Suez Canal.

The Isonzo Front
May–July 1915

AUSTRIA-HUNGARY

CARINTHIA

Villach

Tolmezzo

Monte Nero

Caporetto

Julian Alps

Tolmein

R. Tagliamento

Udine

ITALY

Doberdo Plateau

Gorizia

S. Vito al Tagliamento

R. Isonzo

N

Monfalcone

Trieste

Gulf of Venice

ADRIATIC SEA

0   10   20 miles
0   10   20   30 km
Zone of conflict 1915–17

Chapter 7

A VERTICAL WAR

May–August 1915

Against all expectations, Italy failed to side with its traditional ally Austria at the start of the war. Instead, in October 1914 Italian Prime Minister Salandra announced that Italy would pursue a policy of Sacro Egoismo, or sacred self-interest, and side with the highest bidder. Secret negotiations ensued between Rome, London and Vienna.

With Austria-Hungary close to collapse on the Eastern Front, on 26th April 1915 Italy signed the secret Treaty of London, committing her to an invasion of Austria in return for the Allied promises of significant parts of Habsburg territory as a reward. Vienna too, came up with an offer, but it was too little and too late. On 23rd May 1915 Italy declared war on Austria-Hungary. The Allies hoped this new front would further expose Austria's vulnerability, force it to divert its troops away from their already heavy engagements in the east, and eventually lead to the collapse of Germany's ailing ally.

The new front stretched for 375 miles along the Austro-Italian border, but most of the fighting took place on the sixty miles of jagged uplands, rugged mountain ridges and precipitous valleys along the Isonzo River. The Habsburg garrisons had an initial advantage, perched high in the mountains overlooking the Italian troops. However, led by ambitious Italian General Luigi Cadorna, and determined to reach the Adriatic port of Trieste, regiments of Italian troops were poured in, soon greatly outnumbering the Austro-Hungarians. As predicted, the Austro-Hungarians were forced to divert some of their troops from the Eastern Front. A brutal 'vertical war' in the mountains began.

An Austrian officer of whom no details, not even his name, are known and a young Italian volunteer called Virgilio Bonamore fight, one above the other, in the merciless battles of the Isonzo in the summer of 1915. Both their diaries were found amid this terrain of mud, rock, shrapnel and human bone, one while the war still raged, the other many years later.

Although it is the height of summer, Bersagliere (infantryman) Virgilio Bonamore endures chilling high-altitude temperatures in trenches flooded with torrential rain. While his comrades die around him, Bonamore has a number of 'miraculous' escapes from death, feeling somehow shielded by the love of his girlfriend, Itala, who sends him almost daily letters and parcels.

The Austrian officer writes of the conflict between his sense of patriotic duty and a deep longing for his lover, Maria, an Italian and thus now his enemy. Torn between love and duty, he confides his thoughts to a diary. Writing in the officers' mess while awaiting his turn to go up to the front line, he seeks consolation and strength in his faith.

Dear Lord, come to our aid, for we fight in the name of Justice, the Empire and the Faith. Dear Lord, steer the flight of the double eagle so that these beauteous lands, which had one time belonged to Austria, once again fall under the shadow of its mighty wings; so that the Pope, your representative on earth, may once again walk freely the streets of the Holy City and rule mankind with justice.

That ensign,[1] Herr Sporer, is a wonderful pianist. While the

---

1 Rank equivalent to Lieutenant.

others were out drinking, I stayed in the music room. I was over-come by sadness; tears welled up in my eyes when he played Grieg. I can't get Maria out of my mind . . . she was so fond of his *Peer Gynt* suite. A wicked thought entered my head. God for-give me! . . . For a moment I thought about giving myself up, so that I could search for her all over Italy, just to spend one more night with her.

19th June 1915

Since yesterday my mind has been troubled by the thought of the many Austrian heroes who have given their lives defending the honour of Austria and the Habsburgs, while I entertained my thoughts of treason, all for the love of an unworthy woman. I am disgusted at myself. Habsburg, I live for you and I shall die for you, too!

25th June

A radiant, divine moonlit night. Sporer is playing Beethoven's Moonlight Sonata. I last heard this piece when Maria played it in Rimini. What could have happened to her? Has she sunk even lower?

In the evening I am going to meet my friend Dr Dinoczy. He has also arrived here from the Serbian border and wants nothing more than to exchange his hospital for the trenches, so that he too can exact his revenge on Italy.

My darling sister, how kind she is to me! And yet, because of my love for Maria, I didn't take her to Italy with me last June. And this after I'd been promising my sister a trip to Italy for two years! If I get home from this war in one piece, I will honour my promise, my dear little Else!

Just over a week later, the officer is transferred nearer to the front line, where the Italians are beginning to break through the weak Austrian defences.

Austro-Hungarian artillery observation point at an altitude of 3,500 metres

4th July

We are in reserve, one kilometre behind the Isonzo Front. Old bronze cannons, restored to good working order, have been positioned beside the trenches, even though they are incapable of keeping off the enemy. The enemy planes are showering us with bombs. Three of our men are dead, five are badly injured. Tremendous artillery fire. Today the enemy established themselves amidst the corpses of our fallen heroes. God help us!

*

The next day Italian Virgilio Bonamore begins a hazardous uphill march to the trenches, high in the Julian Alps.

5th July

It's terribly hot. We clamber with difficulty up a narrow path weaving between two precipices and sandwiched between scorching rocks. I can't recall a more tiring march; many men pass out. The enemy fires random shells at us. One passes just above my head, the blast almost throwing me to the ground. We stay on at Spleca until the evening and eat a tin of food. At 7 p.m. we start to ascend again. We go on until 3 a.m. in the morning. If God preserves me, I shall never forget this long night-time march at an altitude of 1,800 metres. There is something epic about our cautious approach in the dark, in total silence. Now and then, in the more difficult passes, someone falls off the edge. They fall without making a sound, as we have been ordered. All we hear is this pitiful sound of a body with a rifle hitting the ground. Some start marching again, others lag behind. Artillery shells fly past with a sinister howl; continuous rifle volleys echo from all directions. During each brief stop, exhausted men fall asleep on the ground. Finally, we reach the front line trenches, 150 metres away from the enemy. I'm in the first-line trench, right on the edge of a precipice. As I put down my rucksack, it rolls off the rock before I can catch it and falls into the ravine. I'm worried it's lost for ever, together with all my provisions and many things that are precious to me, but I can't go looking for it.

6th July

I sleep till eight, oblivious to artillery and rifle fire. As soon as I wake up I worry about my rucksack, as I'm starving. I get permission to go and look for it, crawl down into a very deep ravine and two hours later find my rucksack, stuck between two rocks. I try to find an easier route on the way back and so make it even longer. My little expedition takes me four hours and I feel shattered, but I have my *'canterano'* [chest of drawers], as we affectionately call our rucksacks, and all its contents.

While Bonamore searches for his rucksack, the Austrian officer, on the Doberdo plateau, comes under heavy attack from Italian artillery.

6th July

At two in the morning the Italians resume their attack. A grenade falls inside our trench. I am buried under the rubble. Someone pulls me out. Around me four are lying dead and nine are injured. The wounded groan and cry for their mothers. You have to shut your ears to it. Italy will pay for this, for the Lord sits in judgement up on high and he is wrathful. The Italians attack us again from four to six. We lose another 89 men and have to retreat a little.

7th July

A bullet hits Corporal Haari right between the eyes and he drops down without making a sound. He was the company's best shot. Lord, have mercy on his soul. I cross his arms over his chest and let them carry him away.

Towards eight o'clock we must retreat again. The silhouettes of our soldiers stand out sharply against the scattered gold of the evening sky. It reminds me of the row of saints on the walls of San Apollinare Nuovo in Ravenna and of Maria, who inspired artistic feelings in me. God bless her, wherever she may be.

8th July

My men are dropping like flies. Death is on the rampage. He who gives his life for the Fatherland and the honour of the Habsburgs shall be honoured and remembered for eternity.

*

Later that same day Virgilio Bonamore also comes in close contact with death.

8th July

At 11 p.m. the *zappatori*[1] start digging the trenches for our advance, but the sound of their pickaxes immediately attracts enemy attention. The enemy pours lively rifle-fire from his positions on the rocks to our right. Shells rain down, but narrowly miss me. When I turn around, all my companions have disappeared. I run down the slope, but in the darkness I've gone the wrong way and can't find the trench entrance. I'm terrified – I am caught in a crossfire. I throw myself to the ground and crawl.

---

1 A unit within the engineering corps for digging trenches.

I don't know how I make it. I'm sure I owe my salvation to the prayers of my darling Itala.

9th July

The Austrians are now pounding our trenches from the other side of the mountain. As luck would have it, they seem to be short of munitions, or else we wouldn't be able to hold on to our positions. Today they aren't firing many shells and they wounded some Bersaglieri[1] from the 2nd Company. One explodes right in my trench and wounds Goi, who's right next to me. He gets a piece of shrapnel in the eye and is taken away. We are given stinking soup and meat again, completely inedible. I stick to the bread, but I won't be able to keep going like this!

*

Conditions in the trenches on both sides are now atrocious. The Austrian officer's diary entries begin to become much shorter.

9th July

Cases of cholera. This is all we need. Is God no longer on our side?

*

In fact, disease spreads in both sets of trenches, largely due to water being poisoned by thousands of decomposing corpses scattered in the unreachable ravines. Soldiers are also weakened by the appalling weather conditions, as Virgilio Bonamore writes.

10th July

Towards 8 p.m. there's a terrible hailstorm. We flee into our trenches, but the water soon begins to run into them. The hailstones are as big as walnuts. We're all soaking wet, and an hour later it starts raining. We are in a tragic state, drenched to the bone and completely numb. As if all that wasn't enough, a false alarm wakes us up at 1 a.m., which makes us waste a thousand rounds.

---

1 Italian elite infantry soldiers.

I'm overcome by terrible pains in my gut. In the morning we're all shaking from cold. We've nothing to dry ourselves with. Finally, with God's will, the sun appears and our clothes dry out. At midday, I receive eight registered parcels from Itala, a letter and two postcards. Itala has sent me woollen socks, writing paper, cigarettes, chocolate, soap and other useful things. I don't know how to thank her.

14th July

Thank God, I'm feeling better. Towards evening an Austrian shell lands next to me with a thud, burying itself in the ground, but doesn't explode. I really am lucky. I get two letters from Itala.

*

While Bonamore has had another lucky escape, the Austrian officer wonders if he is foreseeing his own death.

15th July

I slept badly. I have a terrible feeling that something will happen to me. I saw myself lying pale like a dead man on a stretcher. My mother and sister stood by me. They kissed me and shed floods of tears.

*

After ten days of relentless fighting, Bonamore's regiment is finally relieved. They hand their trenches over to fresh arrivals and descend towards the villages on the Italian side of the mountains.

18th July

A terrible night. Towards midnight a fierce thunderstorm breaks out. In the meantime, the first platoons of the 23rd arrive to take our places in the trenches. We stand waiting, up to our knees in water, for the order to leave. Rain pours down nonstop. It's cold, pitch dark and I'm drenched to the bone. At 2 a.m. we set off. We can't see a thing, so we hold on to each other's cloaks. After a few hundred metres, we stop in torrential rain on a narrow muddy path, about 20 centimetres wide. We stand,

unable to move, right on the edge of a sheer drop. It is inde-
scribable torture. I shake convulsively with cold, I can feel the
water dripping down my skin, but if we move one more step,
we'll fall straight to our death. We stay standing like this, in the
rain, in total stillness for at least three hours. Finally, instead of
continuing on our journey, we turn around. We are told that the
swollen rivers have blocked our route. We are stranded on top of
a mountain.

*

*While Bonamore is left perilously stranded amid torrential rain, the
Austrian is enduring a different kind of downpour.*

17th July 1915

Terrible bombardment, worse than any man can bear. It is a
wonder I am still alive. Grenades fall like hailstones, each one
looking for its victim. The sound of artillery is the voice of
Death. The number of wounded is incredible. We no longer
have enough stretcher-bearers. Fear is driving people mad. I,
too, think I'm heading that way. Yes, I am shaking with fear and
despondency. It is all very well to talk of putting up a fight, but
in reality it is not humanly possible. We are retreating into the
valley.

18th July

In the night the artillery fire became insanely heavy. This is the
end, I thought, and prepared to die like a proper Christian. But
I am still so young! To die without a confession, without the
words of comfort and faith of our holy religion! Oh Italy, may
God punish your king and your treacherous people.

19th July

It is enough to drive you insane. Dead, wounded, massive losses.
This is the end. Unprecedented slaughter, a horrific bloodbath.
There is blood everywhere and the dead and bits of bodies lie
scattered about so that . . .

The diary breaks off here in mid-sentence as the Austrian officer unknowingly records the moment of his own death. A Hungarian officer finds the body when the firing dies down at the end of that day, adding to the diary underneath the Austrian's last words: 'I found this diary in the hand of a dead officer on the Doberdo plateau: God bless him.'

*

Monte San Michele, which the Austrian officer has been defending with his compatriots, absorbs around 2,500 shells that morning. Razor-sharp splinters of brittle limestone kill as many Austrians as the shrapnel. The Italian bombardment is followed by close combat, and results in the Italian takeover of the mountain peak. The next day Virgilio Bonamore has a brief respite from fighting.

20th July

Today I was a laundryman, a cobbler and a tailor. Now my things are all in order. In the evening we were finally given some hot food, pasta in soup, fairly good. It's incredible how important food is here, it's the main topic of conversation. I receive two dear letters from Itala and two packets of cigars, which I immediately share amongst my pals.

21st July

This morning at three a bullet bored right through our tent and wounded Vismara Angelo, piercing his right thigh while he was sleeping right next to me. That's two of my friends now, wounded next to me. Goi was asleep on my left when he got hit in the eye by a piece of shrapnel, Vismara was on my right. We get news of a great victory from Gorizia. They've captured 2,000 Austrian prisoners and many machine guns. The final victory will be ours.

22nd July

Towards six o'clock the Austrians above us open fire with rifles and machine guns. The bullets rain down but we are well protected by the rocks. A few Austrians that we managed to hit tumble all the way down the mountain and drop next to our feet. After a couple of hours the enemy withdraws in haste, while we hold on to our positions.

26th July

It's seven o'clock when we begin our march towards the peak of Monte Nero, which our men now call Monte Rosso because so much blood has been spilled here. We're 2,200 metres above sea level. Our barely visible path winds its way along a ridge. The enemy greets us with shells and grenades. We are stuck on this steep path unable to move while they keep firing. A huge pile of rock falls, sweeping away about 20 Bersaglieri. When the smoke lifts, we find two of our men crushed to death by rocks right in the middle of the path, amongst a dozen or so wounded. A rock hits me on the head leaving me in shock and bruising my left cheekbone. The battle rages on. Lieutenant Pampuri summons me to take an order downhill to Smast, eight hours away. I leave immediately. I take the wrong way and arrive at Tremenza at 11.30 p.m. It's pitch dark. Nevertheless, I continue to Caporetto and stay there for the night. I sleep at our guard post in Caporetto. It is about three o'clock in the morning when I wake suddenly, startled by a gunshot. A man on my left has shot himself in the throat. The poor wretch dies immediately. I'm so tired and drained that this tragedy doesn't shock me in the slightest, so I go back to sleep.

Here the diary pauses for a few days while Bonamore rejoins his company going back up the dauntingly high Julian Alps for a new advance on the Austrian positions. After four days of battle he begins writing again.

2nd August

In the past few days I have experienced the saddest horrors of this most terrible war. It hasn't stopped raining for a single day.

The cold was so intense that the whole battalion, except for about 50 men, went down with frostbite.

On the 29th I spent 24 hours in the trench, squatting among the corpses of men from both sides. The stench was unbearable. On top of that we had to endure a ferocious enemy assault, which we have repelled. Many of our men fell, hit in the head as they poked out of the trenches to fire. I haven't eaten or drunk anything for two days. The stench from the corpses, the cold, the incessant rain, the lack of sleep – which is rendered impossible by the continual alarms – have reduced me to a pitiful state.

On the night of the 31st we wait to be relieved. Finally, on the morning of the 1st we make our way down. We have to walk slowly in single file along the dangerous ridge under enemy fire. I'll never forget this for as long as I live. It's about 10 p.m. when it gets to my turn to go. The path takes almost an hour. I'm on top of the ridge and I go on step by step ducking the shrapnel fire. Nothing. I continue. After two paces I'm still unscathed. At the third, Zani from Vicenza, ten metres in front of me, is hit in the head. He screams and falls down the precipice. The poor wretch's head smashed on the mountainside. I see his body tumbling down. He was a good lad. I keep going, constantly asking myself when my turn will come. Someone behind me is hurt, screams, but keeps going. At one point the bullets are coming thicker and faster. The ridge is interrupted by a crevasse. I throw myself in. Fandella, the corporal of the 15th is already down there. We're lying on the corpse of a poor Alpine soldier. The firing is constant. A rock above our heads is hit and covers us in rubble. Fandella's lip is cut. I'm still unscathed. We get to Spleca at about 5 p.m.

I'm shattered. Five of us put up the tent and we crash to the ground. After five nights on the move, we can finally shut our eyes. My clothes, my blanket, my cloak are thoroughly soaked, but I sleep anyway.

On the Isonzo Front

During the devastating battles fought from the end of July to the beginning of August 1915, over 42,000 Italians are killed and wounded. After a few days' rest, the remaining soldiers of Bonamore's company are once again ordered to march into the mountains for a further assault on the Austrian positions.

14th August

As soon as the sun came up the Austrian artillery discovered us and began to fire at our positions from all directions. Poor Trecchi fell by my side, hit by shrapnel. He was smashed to pieces when he hit the bottom of the ravine. Two others died like this. There are countless wounded, but I don't know how many. We spend a horribly anxious period waiting to be hit. Towards ten o'clock we begin to fan out for the attack. We're going to have to throw ourselves at the Austrian trench, which is 200 metres above us, cut the barbed wire and leap at them with bayonets. My company, the 4th, will be right at the front.

It is 12.15. In front of us are all the barbed-wire cutters. On our left is an impassable abyss. At exactly 12.35 (I'm in the habit of looking at my watch at crucial moments) we begin the attack.

Captain Rossi rouses the Bersaglieri and sets off with determination. We follow closely behind with our bayonets at the ready. He runs really fast and in a few minutes we've run 200 metres up a steep hill under a hail of Austrian fire and have reached the barbed wire. The wire cutters behind us are still only halfway and already have many casualties. We all try to pull out the posts and cut the barbed wire with our little axes, but it's too thick.

Every minute one of us falls either wounded or dead. Our sappers have been decimated and are still far behind us. They seem to hesitate. It is then that our Major Mazzucco throws himself forward to encourage the men. He doesn't get very far when he falls, hit by a bullet. Meda and Bellora run to help him and are struck down as well. After that, the terrible tragedy unfolds very quickly.

Two Austrian field guns, whose existence we hadn't suspected, mow down everything in sight. We watch the horrific carnage from above. No one is advancing any more and we're up there, about a dozen of us, right underneath the barbed wire. We throw ourselves to the ground. Below us, a few minutes of bombardment have destroyed everything. The dead are piled on top of each other. After a few minutes, we no longer see anyone who isn't dead or wounded. Our retreat is blocked by the shelling. We lie where we are on the ground for some time, determined to stay alive in case the Austrians decide to leave their trenches.

Although there are only a few of us, 14 in all, we don't dare move and lie with our stomachs pressed to the ground, firing fast and continuously to make them think there are many more of us.

We have almost run out of ammunition and our captain decides to beat a hasty retreat. Corporal Villa goes first, crawling across the ground, but after just a few metres he screams and stops moving. Another one follows and suffers the same fate. After a few moments, Vergani gets off and almost reaches the bottom, when a bullet hits him and knocks him to the ground. Finally, Negri tries and he is hit too. Poor lads! The fire is deadly accurate and spares no one.

We consult each other and decide to stay where we are until nightfall, then go down under cover of darkness. We wait for many slow hours. It is raining and we are literally soaked in freezing water. Finally, crawling slowly, we begin our descent in the dark. The Austrian fire isn't so precise now and almost all of us get through. On the way down we tread over innumerable corpses. What a massacre! So many young lives wasted. It is raining nonstop. We lie down at the bottom of a ravine where we spend the night in the wet and cold.

15th August

Only today can I grasp the enormity of the disaster. The 21st battalion no longer exists, apart from the 50 or so survivors. The 7th and 9th Companies of the 36th Battalion have been halved. The 23rd Battalion has been decimated. It's a terrible, humiliating defeat. Today what remains of our battalion has reunited in a little gully 50 metres below the trench. From my own company only my captain is alive. I go down to our first trench and begin the patient task of collating the list of the dead, the wounded, the missing. At night I somehow manage to sleep, despite the mud and the freezing cold.

Once more Virgilio Bonamore escapes unscathed. After two weeks away from the front line in which he writes little, he prepares to go into battle again.

31st August 1915

I hand in documents to the Administrative Department and receive our marching orders.

This is Bonamore's last diary entry. Nothing is known of his subsequent fate. His account came to light many years after the war, when an anonymous visitor left a diary inscribed with Virgilio Bonamore's name at a local museum in the village of Caporetto, now known as Kobarid in present-day Slovenia. Much was done by the Kobarid Museum staff to trace the diary's author, yet to this day Bersagliere Virgilio Bonamore remains elusive.[1]

By the end of the summer of 1915, a single mile of rocky ground was gained by Italian troops. Over 100,000 died on both sides that summer; over 200,000 were captured, many more were declared missing in action.

Ten more battles were fought on the Isonzo Front between September 1915 and October 1917, with over a million Italian and an estimated 650,000 Austro-Hungarian casualties. A few Austrian mountain peaks and some square miles of land changed hands several times in the course of the war. Italian troops did not reach their objective, the port of Trieste, until after the Armistice.

---

1 The staff of the Kobarid Museum in Kobarid, Slovenia, are keen to hear from anyone who might know about Virgilio Bonamore's fate.

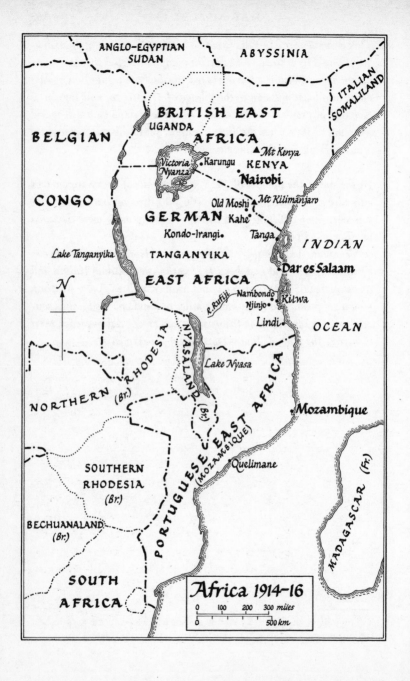

ANGLO-EGYPTIAN
SUDAN

ABYSSINIA

ITALIAN
SOMALILAND

BELGIAN

BRITISH EAST
UGANDA AFRICA

▲Mt Kenya

Victoria
Nyanza
•Karungu

KENYA

CONGO

Nairobi

GERMAN
Old Moshi ▲Mt Kilimanjaro
Kahe•
Kondo-Irangi•

Lake Tanganyika

TANGANYIKA

Tanga

INDIAN

N

EAST AFRICA

Dar es Salaam

r.Rufiji Nambondo
Njinjo • •Kilwa

Lindi

OCEAN

NORTHERN (Br.)

RHODESIA

NYASALAND

Lake Nyasa

(Br.)

PORTUGUESE EAST AFRICA
(MOZAMBIQUE)

Mozambique

SOUTHERN
RHODESIA
(Br.)

Quelimane

MADAGASCAR (Fr.)

BECHUANALAND
(Br.)

SOUTH
AFRICA

Africa 1914-16

0   100   200   300 miles
0   500 km

Chapter 8

IN THE BUSH

November 1914–October 1916

In August 1914 most of the African continent was divided between Europe's imperial powers. Britain, France and Belgium all had African colonies, as did Germany, a latecomer to the colonial scramble, having acquired its first territories on the continent in 1884.[1] When the European nations went to war, the conflict spread to their colonies around the world. Africa's peoples, material resources, strategic ports and lines of communications were all caught up in what became the first global war.

The Allied belligerents were better established in Africa and had naval control in the region, while Germany's recently acquired territories were little explored and poorly defended, with weak administrative control. Germany's four African colonies, Togoland, Cameroon, South West Africa and German East Africa, were prime targets in what became a renewed scramble for territorial gains. Togoland was the first German colony in Africa to be overrun by British and French colonial forces; German South West Africa was

---

1 Italy and Portugal were the other belligerent nations with colonies in Africa but did not join the war until May 1915 and March 1916 respectively. Spain also had colonies in Africa but remained neutral for the duration of the war.

*captured by South African forces in mid-1915 and Cameroon sur-
rendered in February 1916.*

*The campaign in German East Africa, a colony which occupied
areas of present-day Tanzania, Rwanda and Burundi, was the
longest and most destructive of all the African conflicts. Hoping for
a swift takeover, the British drew on their extensive colonial forces to
challenge a small local garrison, led by German Lt. Colonel Paul
von Lettow-Vorbeck and initially made up of 218 German officers
and 2,542 native Askari soldiers. Designed for border patrols and
internal security, Lettow-Vorbeck's army was poorly equipped for
war and at the start of hostilities effectively cut off from all external supplies by the British naval blockade of the Indian Ocean.*

*

*As the dawn breaks on 2nd November 1914 an 8,000-strong British
Expeditionary Force, accompanied by three transports of Zanzibari
porters, lands 3 kilometres south of Tanga, a port in German East
Africa. Overnight, war comes to the town, until now a quiet back-
water inhabited by several thousand locals and a small community of
German civilian settlers: administrators, plantation owners, doctors
and teachers. From now on Tanga, with its busy harbour and on one
of the two railway lines in the colony, becomes a strategically important target for the British.*

*Two very different men are drawn into the East African cam-
paign. Dr Ludwig Deppe is a German settler who moved to Tanga
from Dresden with his wife, Charlotte, a few years previously. Dr
Deppe works at Tanga Hospital; his wife, a nurse, assists him with
surgery. The arrival of British troops interrupts Dr Deppe's measured pace of life.*

*Richard Meinertzhagen, a thirty-six-year-old British officer
from an upper-middle-class family of German and Danish origins,
was brought up in the London borough of Kensington and was first
introduced to colonial service by his uncle. Initially more interested in
zoology than the call of the bugle, Richard was bribed into travelling
to India in 1899 by his family's promise of an elephant (which was
obligingly procured). He went on to pursue a successful military*

career in India, Kenya and South Africa. On 2nd November 1914,
Meinertzhagen is among the British colonial forces landing near
Tanga, where his path will cross that of Dr Ludwig Deppe.

On 4th November 1914, Meinertzhagen writes in his diary.

4th November 1914, Tanga

Last night Aitken[1] decided to attack Tanga today, but after
everyone had had a good breakfast. We only heard a few shots in
front of us and were within 600 yards of the town when the
enemy opened a heavy fire and bullets came thick, men falling in
all directions.

Keeping a sharp look-out for any chance of a shot, I saw a
small group of Germans peering round a house not 150 yards
from me. One tall man with a fine face gave me a splendid chance,
and I fired at him, but missed. I saw my bullet splash on the wall
just by him. So I gave him another and again missed. Never
before have I had such an easy target or made such bad shooting.
It annoyed me intensely for two reasons: it was my first fair
chance at a German, and, secondly, I had shot abominably.

The British force consists of one Lancashire and eight Indian reserve
regiments. The first battle of the war in the unfamiliar bush is a real
test for all the troops, as Meinertzhagen records.

On my way back, I found seven Rajput sepoys[2] cowering under
a bank in deadly terror of their lives. I ordered them out and into
a position whence they could shoot. Two obeyed, but the others
demurred and finally refused to move, so I threatened them with
my rifle, when they all got up and moved, but one man still
refused and on threatening me with his rifle I shot the brute as he
lay half-crazy with fear.

---

1 General Aitken was commander of British troops at Tanga in 1914.
2 Indian soldiers in British service.

I'm sorry for the Lancs. They behaved well under very trying circumstances. They were not supported, [but] they did their best. During the fight one of their men said to me: 'We don't mind the German fire, but with most of our officers and NCOs down and a bloody crowd of niggers firing into our backs and bees stinging our backsides, things are a bit 'ard.'

The British troops are insufficiently trained and poorly prepared for bush warfare, and retreat when challenged by the smaller but more experienced German garrison.

That morning Ludwig Deppe and his wife are woken from sleep by the thunder of an intense bombardment. Dr Deppe heads for Tanga Hospital to prepare for the imminent arrival of the first casualties.

An hour after the battle began the casualties started arriving, all of them English. I was very busy all day. In the afternoon we had just begun operating on an Englishman when the British cruiser *Fox*, moored right next to the hospital, began to bombard the town. Her endless barrage made such a din that we couldn't hear each other speak. The salvoes sent forth gusts of wind, shaking the entire building and making the curtains flap as if we were in the middle of a storm. My wife, the anaesthetist and the nurse – we all thought we were going to die, thinking that either the hospital would be hit, or it would collapse from constant shaking. We just wanted to finish treating the Englishman, who was close to bleeding to death. The hospital grounds were crowded with English and Indian soldiers.

One British shell lands a direct hit on Dr Deppe's hospital while he is operating on the wounded – all of them British and Indian soldiers.

*

The next day the shelling stops as suddenly as it started. Richard Meinertzhagen is sent on a conciliatory mission to apologise for the inadvertent shelling of the hospital – and to negotiate the release of its British patients. That evening Meinertzhagen describes his encounter with his German opponents, including an amicable chat with Deppe.

5th November, Tanga

After a breakfast of warm water and rum, drunk out of a bucket, and mighty good it was, I went to the hospital. I borrowed a white sheet, which I rigged up as a flag of truce, taking with me some bandages and chloroform for our wounded in the enemy's hands and a letter of apology from Aitken to the German commander for having put a six-inch shell into the hospital.

The Germans were kindness itself and gave me a most excellent breakfast, which I sorely needed. We discussed the fight freely as though it had been a football match. It seemed so odd that I should be having a meal today with people whom I was trying to kill yesterday. It seemed so wrong and made me wonder whether this really was war or whether we had all made a ghastly mistake. The German officers whom I met today were all hard looking, keen and fit and clearly knew their job and realised its seriousness. They treated this war as some new form of sport.

I concluded an agreement to remove our wounded tomorrow under condition that none of them served again for the duration of the war. Whilst I was waiting in the hospital a German doctor called Deppe regaled me with old brandy and we conversed freely about the war. And just outside the window were a few Germans lying among the trees sniping at the *Fox*.

*

Dr Deppe is just as surprised as Richard Meinertzhagen by the gentlemanly way in which this war is being fought so far, and himself recounts a friendly conversation with the British peace envoy.

On 5th November an English mediator, Captain Meinertzhagen, came over, accompanied by two German officers, to apologise for the inadvertent shelling of the hospital. Over a hastily prepared breakfast, the Englishman gave us bits of news, such as that the Russians were in Danzig. I retorted, 'We are near Warsaw!'

whereupon he laughed, 'According to Reuters.' We soon adopted
this as our catchphrase.

*By late afternoon of that day Dr Deppe realises he might have
unwittingly acquired an important piece of information in the course
of his friendly breakfast with Meinertzhagen.*

Shortly after he left the battle resumed. At about 5 p.m. a little
white flag appeared on the English side. No one knew what it
meant. Suddenly I remembered that during our conversation the
mediator had asked me whether the condition of the wounded
Englishmen in our hospital was such that they would be able to
leave if the English pulled out of Tanga. I told him they would.
I now rushed out of the hospital with this unbelievable news, for
we'd all thought that Tanga would be English by the following
day. But we had won! Dr Perlmann, the former ship's doctor on
the *Markgraf* had returned from town downhearted. No one
believed the English were leaving. Quite the opposite. The last of
our own troops were hurrying to leave the town.

*It is indeed hard to believe that the several times larger and better-
armed British force begins to withdraw from Tanga as unexpectedly
as they had arrived. German troops begin to withdraw at the same
time, as Deppe records.*

Each side abandoned its position without knowing that the
other was doing the same. They deceived each other simultaneously. All evening transport ships left the port, and it was soon
as quiet as before. Our joy was immense. I heard that during the
battle the English were suddenly attacked by a swarm of bees.
There is only one defence against them in the tropics: to run
away as fast as possible. And this is the really funny bit: the
English said in all seriousness that we, the wicked Germans, had
trained the wild bees, to use them instead of mine throwers and
pilots.

The defeat in the Battle of Tanga, later to become infamous as 'The Battle of the Bees', is a significant blow for the British forces. Instead of crushing the small German garrison in East Africa there and then, they are drawn into protracted bush warfare in uncharted terrain. The German troops use the British ammunition, rifles and machine guns captured at Tanga to engage and tie down numbers of British soldiers.

*

While only some extracts of Dr Deppe's journal survive, Richard Meinertzhagen's diary records his scouting missions across the unfamiliar terrain as he seeks to locate his opponents. It is just over a year since the Battle of Tanga. After four days of searching for Lettow-Vorbeck's positions, Meinertzhagen and his small patrol are finally in luck and on Christmas Day 1915 manage to sneak right up to a German camp. On his return to base, he details his patrol's lone hit-and-run raid.

28th December 1915, Karungu, Victoria Nyanza

At 5 p.m. we located four tents, fires burning and, by the mercy of God, no precautions, no sentries and men lounging about. The country was good for stalking and we were well in position for a rush at dusk. In fact, the men having left their rifles in their tents and there being no sentry, we rushed them silently from not more than a few paces. We used bayonets only and I think we each got our man. Drought got three, a great effort. I rushed into the officers' tent, where I found a stout German on a camp bed. On a table was a most excellent Xmas dinner. I covered him with my rifle and shouted to him to hold his hands up. He at once groped under his pillow and I had to shoot, killing him at once. My shot was the only one fired.

We now found we had seven unwounded prisoners, two wounded and fifteen killed, a great haul. I at once tied up the prisoners whilst Drought did what he could for the wounded. We covered the dead with bushes and I placed sentries round the camp and sent out a patrol of three men. Drought said he was

Richard Meinertzhagen in Nairobi in 1915

hungry, so was I, and why waste that good dinner? So we set to and had one of the best though most gruesome dinners I have ever had, including an excellent Xmas pudding. The fat German dead in bed did not disturb us in the least, nor restrain our appetites. After that excellent meal, I searched the German's kit: I have shot a Duke, the first Duke I have killed. His luncheon basket was a most elaborate arrangement, with plated dishes and cutlery, all marked with a coronet. These Drought and I purloined, thinking it a pity to leave them to be looted by the natives. We cleared out after dark, but were unable to bury the bodies, having no tools with which to dig. With our prisoners we marched till midnight and then slept with sentries out and were off again on the 26th and reached here without incident yesterday afternoon.

Frustrated with their inability to conduct an effective campaign in the bush, the British make a deal with their old rival South Africa. Only a few years previously, South African troops fought against the British in the Boer War of 1899–1902. Now South Africa has its own interest in helping the British. By conquering German East Africa, the South African government hopes to exchange land with Portugal, and gain an essential strip of land extending South Africa's borders to the Zambezi River.

Richard Meinertzhagen, by now frustrated with a series of ineffective British commanders, records his first impressions of the new arrivals.

1st January 1916, Nairobi

The first of the South African contingent arrived today in the form of a Mounted Brigade commander General Van Deventer.[1] He is a fine figure of a man. He fought against us during the South African War. Van Deventer talks with a husky voice, the result of a British bullet in his throat in 1900.

I spoke to many officers and men. They all seem quite confident that they will finish the campaign in a few months. I tried to explain to them that they had not the slightest idea of the climatic and health difficulties, neither had any of them any experience of fighting in thick bush. They smiled and told me I did not understand the Boer. If that is typical of their spirit, I admire it. The Boers are a fine virile race and well deserve full expression of their national spirit.

---

1 South African cavalry officer; rose to the rank of Major General during the East African campaign and in 1917 was appointed Head of the British Expeditionary Force.

From now on, the British campaign in East Africa will be led by
South African minister of defence General Jan Christiaan Smuts,
whose experience of African guerrilla warfare during the Boer War
should serve him well against Lettow-Vorbeck's troops.

23rd February

Smuts arrived in Nairobi today. I had a long talk with him today.
We had a lot in common, for he knew Mother, also one of my
aunts. And, of course, he knows that disreputable relative of
mine, Emily Hobhouse, a perverted, dangerous female.[1]

Smuts is as keen as mustard, but underrates the fighting qual-
ities of the German native soldier. The Dutchman boasts that he
can drive them with a whip. Before the campaign ceases there
will be more than one instance of the kaffirs[2] giving the
Dutchman a licking. We also spoke about malaria and the dense
bush, which Von Lettow likes for his manoeuvres. Smuts dislikes
bush, he will like it less in a year's time.

With General Smuts eager for action, Meinertzhagen is at last
hoping for some real fighting. In March 1916, he sets off on another
dangerous scouting mission through the bush.

18th March, Old Moshi

Last night I made a personal reconnaissance of the enemy position at Kahe. I went by myself carrying a rifle, bayonet and
thirty rounds of ammunition. I followed the railway line for
some distance and then struck off into the bush. There was a
decent moon and by exercising every precaution I was able to
approach within a few yards. I had the greatest difficulty in sup-

---

1 A Quaker sister-in-law of Meinertzhagen's aunt who agitated against British
   concentration camps set up in South Africa during the Boer War. During her
   second visit to Cape Town she was deported by Horatio Kitchener, who
   referred to her as 'that bloody woman'.
2 South African racist term for African natives.

pressing the feeling that every enemy soldier was expecting me and every sentry was watching me. I crossed the line between the station and the bridge and had a narrow squeak. I crawled over the line and when almost over a flashlight came down the line which seemed to illuminate me, but kept perfectly still and nothing happened. When the light was extinguished, I crept on into the thick bush, where I felt quite at home. It was noteworthy what a lot of noise a camp makes even in the dead of night. Snoring, talking, changing sentries, patrols coming and going, all kept me fully informed of the main camp. Several patrols passed me almost within touching distance and my heart beat with thumps in efforts to hide my self-consciousness. Sometimes I felt inclined to scream just to tell the enemy I was there, sometimes I was giggling at my ludicrous position, sometimes I was petrified with terror when a sentry or patrol would look hard apparently straight at me. I estimated the enemy force at Pangani Bridge at 1,400 men and there was no sign of movement. I cut back to the line and had to swim the Rau river, a cold dip with thoughts of crocodiles. I was hurrying back.

Saw Smuts late this evening to explain to him more fully the results of my reconnaissance. At the end he said: 'Meinertzhagen, you're mad, stark, staring. It's not your business to undertake this sort of risk, so please don't do it again.' I tried to explain that I am better qualified to do this sort of work than any of my subordinates and that I enjoy it. 'You're mad,' he repeated, so I left him.

25th March

Had a long talk with Smuts today on general situation. He is a bit worried about the enemy's intentions and he has not the slightest idea where he is . . . He is irresistibly drawn to Von Lettow and if he persists he will lose the initiative and the campaign will end in simply following Von Lettow about wherever he chooses to wander.

A month later Richard Meinertzhagen welcomes another opportunity to engage the enemy.

9th May, Kondoa Irangi

We were sitting having supper when suddenly the loud rattle of musketry electrified us. The whole camp blazed and we could see the spiteful little flashes of rifles and hear the cheering of troops on the ridge to the south-east. Night work has always fascinated me, for I have especially good sight by night and never feel so much at home as when working in the dark. So I rushed out and made my way towards the firing.

I was just bursting for a bayonet charge. An enemy machine gun crept up to within thirty yards of us and opened from behind some rocks. We could not dislodge it, so we led out a platoon and smothered it, bayoneting all its personnel. I ended up by using my rifle as a club – with disastrous results – for my stock broke, but it was great. The South Africans behaved splendidly: quite steady, quiet and collected. Their fire discipline was perfect. The enemy were yelling orders and trying to rally for a final rush and I could distinctly hear words of command in German. At midnight the enemy made their final rush, a few of them entering a trench near me. There was a bayonet scrimmage and I crept along a bit of trench, but this time having nothing but my fists and my boots, when I suddenly realised there was another man close to me. Thinking he was a native German soldier I said in Swahili, 'Who are you?' just in case it might have been one of our own men. His reply was a smart blow, meant for my head, which landed on my shoulder and then we closed and had a rough and tumble in the trench. He was carrying a native knobkerrie which I finally wrenched out of his hand, got my knee well into his stomach and then set to on his head with the knobkerrie until he was silent. I was furious with him for hitting me on the shoulder, but having knocked him out I left him. I then returned to the battalion, where firing had died down and the enemy had apparently drawn off. By 3 a.m. all was quiet.

As soon as we could see I returned to examine my victim and was surprised to find he was a German officer, a man called

Kornatsky, a company commander. His head was well battered in and I retained his knobkerrie, a handsome bit of native work, half black and half brown and beautifully balanced.

It is a first real knock Von Lettow had. My God, I should have liked to have caught old Von Lettow instead of poor Kornatsky.

Lumme, I'm tired.

11th June, Old Moshi

It is remarkable that on no single occasion have we won a fight and been able to reap the whole fruits of victory. The enemy always manages to slip away. The reason is not far to seek. Overcautiousness and failure to develop a real flank attack.

Under General Smuts, British troops occupy the Usambara highland in June 1916 and finally take Tanga on 7th July 1916, twenty months after their first unsuccessful attempt. Yet they still fail to capture or defeat Lettow-Vorbeck. Two weeks later Meinertzhagen is pessimistic about his side's chances of achieving a decisive victory.

25th July, Lukigura

The campaign does not wear such a rosy look. It is now an established fact that the South African is not going to fight an offensive action. He hates casualties and does not understand bush warfare. His supreme contempt for the German native soldier, formerly dubbed 'kaffir', has given place to a feeling of supreme respect.

*

Deep in the forests and valleys of the Rufiji River Dr Ludwig Deppe is having a rather peculiar war. In charge of a field hospital he is constantly on the move, with rarely a moment to do any work other than follow Lettow-Vorbeck's intricate manoeuvres.

30th September 1916

We have no concept of time here. My own private calendar is no doubt out of sync with that of world history! My boy Hassani served me well today. He brought me four pigeons for lunch: two of them boiled – one with and one without sago, and two fried, which were really tasty, and some soup to boot. I had the boiled pigeons for lunch and the fried ones for supper.

1st October

I decided to give up my 'four-poster bed', it always made me feel like Snow White in her glass coffin. My good friend Kenya made a hash of making my bed in the tent, so I spent the night in a tangle of blanket and sheets, as it was too difficult to sort it all out in a confined space.

We set off early today and for the first time got a sense of the scale of this fertile valley with green meadows all around, a real sight for sore eyes. Then it was up and downhill again, until we found a spot to set up a new camp. While others stayed down in the valley, I went up the hill and requisitioned the southern part of the village, as it was a little more secluded. There were three huts. The people were turned out by the village chief and within two to four hours we made a new large village of huts and tents for 240–250 men. Our numbers increase daily, which is no wonder, because every sick white man brings at least six men with him, in fact one had brought fifteen.

Our current system seems to be functioning well. Even when we let some people stay behind in a village, we still get to keep everything, even if there isn't much that we like (because the ever growing demand for food cannot be satisfied). In this sense, the war is an endurance test for this system of governing and, judging by my experience here, I would say that it is a success. But it is dreadful how the amount of baggage increases. It took me an entire day to reduce it to three loads, and yet there is still so much I think I will need ten porters!

Looting is one of the necessary evils of the war in Africa. We have managed to teach our Askaris to behave more humanely, but not to desist from looting *per se*. All the troops, including the whites, have been directly dependent on plunder for munitions,

A company of German Askari riflemen on the march, German East Africa

clothing and food. All the blacks are mad on looting, whether it is the Askaris or the porters, man, woman or child. It is also difficult to stop the blacks from raping women, because they see them as property, like cows or huts. The women who come along with us usually don't want to go back to their husbands, having tasted the freedom of soldiering life.

Yes, life here is just like it's reported to be. Our billeted men move into a village and seize the huts, placing rather more importance on getting what they want than on obtaining the owner's consent. There were many arguments yesterday: one of my sick Askaris had taken three hens and promptly slit their throats. Their owner appeared and started complaining and trying to reclaim his hens. As a punishment, the hens were handed over to other Askaris. But this Askari couldn't be punished with 25 lashes because he's got worms.

Lettow-Vorbeck's army lives entirely off the land, feeding on what their native labourers manage to hunt in the bush or what their soldiers requisition in the villages.

The strain of this campaign affects most harshly the native porters and labourers recruited by both sides. With few roads passable to vehicles and the disease-carrying tsetse fly making pack animals unusable, thousands of human carriers are employed instead to transport the army's entire supplies and belongings. Malnourished and exhausted, they are the first to succumb to disease. While German soldiers receive vaccinations, the native corps, regarded as an expendable resource, receive none. Dead and sick labourers are left behind, replaced with fresh men recruited in the villages the army passes through. Communication problems with his local recruits is of particular concern to Dr Deppe.

2nd October

I'm feeling glum today. Hassani is cooking with too much 'samli'[1] and it doesn't seem fresh to me. It can be improved if it's boiled up again with unripe bananas. I told Hassani this, but instead of bananas he used unripe pineapple. After a while he returned, very well pleased, with pieces of pineapple fried in samli. Do I blame the good boy's inability to take things in, or my poor grasp of Swahili? Probably the latter! He also tried to make milk rolls yesterday, only without the milk, as we haven't had any in a long while. Anyway, for lunch today there was fillet of springbok, tapioca cooked in ashes – excellent!

Deppe spends most of his time attending to logistics and supplies, all the while making sure his hospital stays well clear of the British. Richard Meinertzhagen is meanwhile growing despondent about the way the British campaign is being carried out.

---

1 A type of cooking fat.

8th October

The campaign drags on. The Germans' main force is roughly on line of the Rufiji river; but although driven back, they are still undefeated. I asked a captured German officer the other day why they did not surrender now that we have occupied most of their colony. He replied: 'Why don't you give us a chance of surrendering? We cannot surrender without a fight and so far every time we have offered you a battle you manoeuvre us out of position and will not fight. Give us a good fight and if you win we may surrender.' All very true . . .

How the Germans must laugh at our strategy. An entirely false impression is created by the fantastic cables that Smuts sends home. Fierce engagements are fought against overwhelming odds, our camps are subjected to intense bombardments, the South Africans have shown themselves to be stubborn and determined fighters. But what are the facts? The fierce engagements have cost us perhaps five killed. The heavy bombardments are carried out by one or two guns short of ammunition and the South Africans prove themselves unreliable fighters and unwilling to suffer casualties. Van Deventer, Brits, Enslin and Crew are incompetent gasbags, their official reports amounting to mere flatulence. Discipline does not exist, bush warfare is not understood, looting is rife, hospitals are full to overflowing with strong healthy men suffering from cold feet or an excess of patriotism.

*

Though Richard Meinertzhagen is increasingly frustrated with his commanders, under General Smuts British troops manage to take over significant parts of German East Africa and begin to close in on the German forces. Dr Deppe and his hospital are forced to decamp hurriedly.

9th October

All of a sudden at 5 p.m. a caravan of four Askaris and eight porters arrived, reporting that Njinjo has been taken by the

English. Thorough questioning revealed that they hadn't actually seen the English themselves, but had heard some shooting. So we went to bed. I had hoped that my sleep will not be disturbed by rats tonight because L's dog will sleep beside me and chase them. My neighbour B spent last night hunting rats, which seemed pointless to me. Then at about 3 a.m. we got the news: the field hospital and equipment are to be moved to Nambondo as soon as we get the message. In less than an hour we are ready to leave. I take the lead; I am merry and whistle various tunes. Orion is above us, the moon shining, then it grows dark and starts to rain. Then the birds begin singing, probably inspired by me! We have breakfast in Mkama. I have sugar cane with red stripes, which tastes like elderflower, and bread.

We reach Nambondo in the afternoon. For five days there were no chickens or eggs to be found anywhere. While we were discussing this, we suddenly heard shooting nearby. There is fighting in the vicinity of the hospital. My huts are not yet ready when we are told to move out with our whole field hospital! Despite the rush to pack up, not one piece of the slaughtered ox was left behind.

We are five hours from Chumo. The march across the ridge took four hours. It was particularly hard as it was up and down all the way and I could scarcely push the wheelbarrow. The camp is right on the road. I am sleeping in a tent as it is easier to set up and it looks as if it might rain. Our supper is frugal: chicken with rice and parsley, goat's liver with cucumber salad, beetroot, turnip, papaya. The enemy is right behind us.

Dr Deppe's hospital party is now on permanent alert, rarely able to stay in one place for longer than a couple of days. It is one of Deppe's responsibilities to ensure his native recruits are ready at all times.

13th October
This morning 35 people ran away from the lookout point in

Mtingi, so I had to put almost all the other porters 'on the chain' (they all have iron rings round their necks, which are attached to a chain with six to eight others). This is the only way to control the troublesome new recruits and guarantee that we can leave quickly if need be. The enemy will probably arrive tomorrow morning.

14th October

The sight of my retinue is enough to make you weep; at the front of the procession is my wheelbarrow with two men, harnessed to it like a team of horses. The wretched tracks are sandy, stony and rutted. To my left are two boys whose job it is to pick vegetables and mangoes and buy eggs, hens and pigeons. One carries a rifle and cartridge bag, a pith helmet and a lamp. The other carries the portable medicine chest and the hospital flag on a seven-metre-long bamboo stick. And then comes my caravan, which consists of 27 people. I have decided we must depart tomorrow morning at 4 a.m., because apparently we will have to march for nine hours through the barren steppe.

I finally did some doctoring again this afternoon. It is unbelievable how little of it you do when you're on the road. Travelling is a strain: you have to make sure the equipment is unpacked, the huts built, food prepared for the men and for yourself, you have to prepare the menu, look after the supplies. In short, it's hard work.

We passed through Namatawa, which had four houses but no water. I sent a boy to the first house and someone from the second house went hiding in the grass. In these remote parts people are very timid and they run away, leaving the houses empty. When will a white man come this way again?

*

Though in January 1917 General Smuts reported success in East Africa, claiming 85 per cent of East African territories were under British military control, he had failed to capture General Von Lettow-Vorbeck and his army. In late November 1917, the

*remaining German troops crossed into Portuguese East Africa,
where Von Lettow-Vorbeck continued to engage the Allies until the
end of the war. He surrendered reluctantly on 25th November 1918,
two weeks after the Armistice in Europe. His elusive army, which
had for the duration of the war managed to tie down nearly half a
million Allied troops, still numbered 155 officers, 1,168 askari soldiers, 1,500 carriers and 1,726 followers, including 427 women.*

*While the German forces lost 743 officers and 1,798 African
soldiers, the British toll was over 10,000. Death rates among
African porters and labourers employed by both sides were much
higher, and though no precise figures were recorded, an estimated
100,000 to 120,000 employed by the Germans and as many as
250,000 African recruits on the British side perished from malnutrition, disease and accidents during the war. A further 300,000
native East Africans died as a result of famine caused by war
recruitment and requisitioning.*

*Richard Meinertzhagen sailed home in December 1916. By then
thoroughly frustrated with the East African campaign, he had learnt
with some relief that his medical report advised immediate recuper-
ation in a milder climate. After a brief stint at the War Office in
London, he served as General Allenby's Intelligence Officer during
the 1917 British campaign in Palestine, where he befriended T. E.
Lawrence, the leader of the Arab Revolt. General Allenby's confi-
dential report on Meinertzhagen states that 'this officer has been
largely responsible for my successes in Palestine'.*[1]

*German settler Dr Ludwig Deppe provided medical support to the
army of General Von Lettow-Vorbeck for the duration of the campaign he later nominated for the title 'The Cheapest War in the
World'. A year after the war, Dr Deppe noted with regret: 'Behind*

---

1 In 1917 British troops swept through Palestine despite fierce Turkish resistance and occupied Jerusalem in late December 1917.

us we have left destroyed fields, ransacked magazines, and, for the immediate future, starvation. We were no longer the agents of culture; our track was marked by death, plundering and evacuated villages.'

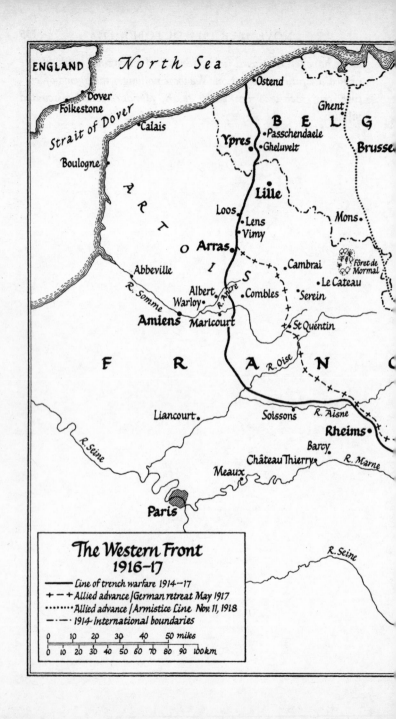

**The Western Front
1916-17**

——————	Line of trench warfare 1914-17
+—·—+	Allied advance / German retreat May 1917
··········	Allied advance / Armistice Line Nov. 11, 1918
—·—·—	1914 International boundaries

0 10 20 30 40 50 miles
0 10 20 30 40 50 60 70 80 90 100 km

Chapter 9

THE SOMME AND VERDUN

May 1916–April 1917

An elaborate system of trenches stretched for 500 hundred miles along the Western Front from the English Channel to Switzerland. By May 1916 nineteen months had passed since the first dugouts had been made to protect men from heavy artillery and machine-gun fire. Orders for spades had multiplied and the trenches, separated by a narrow strip of 'No Man's Land', now ran many lines deep on both sides. They had been there for long enough to be named and numbered. Some German troops were even quartered in heated dugouts built of concrete and steel. But mostly the trenches were cold and wet or hot and humid and infested with rats and lice. Trench life had its own routine with bombardments by day and trench mending, patrols, delivery of supplies and new troops by night. This was siege warfare with modern weaponry adapted and invented to inflict maximum damage. Little territory had changed hands. But by 1916 both the Allied and the German High Commands came up with plans to break the deadlock.

The new Anglo-French plan was to coordinate a strategy which would pull the German armies in different directions. Offensives were to start as near simultaneously as possible on several fronts.

While the Russian and Italian armies engaged the Central Powers in renewed fighting on the Eastern and Isonzo Fronts, French troops with the support of the British were to launch an attack on the Germans at the Somme in July.

But as soon as the date for the Anglo-French offensive been agreed, the German Commander in Chief, Erich von Falkenhayn, stole the initiative from the Allies with his plan to break the deadlock. On 21st February 1916 a massive German bombardment launched an offensive on a small sector of the front line near the fortress town of Verdun, a place of great psychological significance to the French and a symbol of the Franco-Prussian War. After an initial advance, and six days of fighting, the Germans were halted. The casualties were very high on both sides. The French were ordered to hold out and defend Verdun at all costs. By May the fighting was still intense. The planned July offensive on the Somme would have to be led by the British.

*

Paul Hub is nearing the end of his officer's training course and a period in reserve back in Germany. Since fighting at the First Battle of Ypres in Belgium in October 1914 he has survived a further eight months of fighting in the same area before being badly wounded by shrapnel in an attack on 8th May 1915. While recuperating in hospital from his wound and already devastated by the loss of his younger brother, Otto, near Warsaw in March, he receives news of his older brother Robert's death in Galicia. With only a year between them Robert and Paul were particularly close. He writes from hospital to his fiancée, Maria Thumm, in June 1915: 'One more sacrifice and you will have to bury your love.' Soon afterwards he returns home to Stetten on leave to complete his recovery before going on his officer's training course in nearby Ulm. He is welcomed home by his parents, his widowed sisters-in-law, his remaining brother, Alfred, and the Thumm family. Once he has completed his course, Paul Hub is put on duty in a reserve battalion in nearby Ulm. He has spent eleven months back in Germany. Maria is now twenty-three and they have been engaged for almost two years. She is keen to get married. Paul writes to her from his military barracks.

18th May 1916, Ulm

Dear Maria,

How I would love to have you here with me now to talk over your weighty letter. A war wedding! I think about it so often. Every hour that goes by here is an hour of happiness and joy lost for ever. But I mustn't think about marriage because I am not earning enough yet.

Then there's my worry about becoming a cripple. Maria, you say I shouldn't think about it. But I have to. If you were tied to me, what would your life be like? I know you would give up everything for me, as I would for you, but the sacrifice would be too great.

You must believe me when I say that I would much rather bring you home as my wife now, than put it off till tomorrow. But I think under the present circumstances that it is too soon. Don't take it badly that I am replying to your dear letter with such thoughts.

Paul Hub gets a few days' leave from his duties in the reserve battalion which he spends with Maria and his family in Stetten. He then returns to the barracks in Ulm and writes to Maria prior to his departure for the front.

11th June

Dear Maria,

What are you thinking now? I feel as if your thoughts cross with mine. Last Sunday we parted. The last time I looked into your eyes. But it was not for the very last time. Maria, we will see each other again. It might be a long time before I can hold you in my arms again. But take comfort. Look to the future – we will see each other again. Dear girl, think of that beloved time and it will lessen the pain of parting. I would so love to be with you still, to

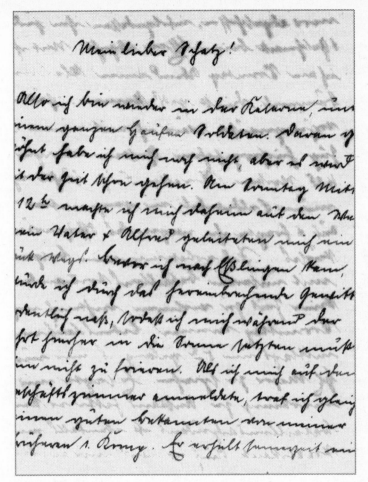

One of Paul Hub's letters to his fiancée, Maria Thumm

comfort you and wipe away your tears. I know how hard it is to part. Yesterday evening, reading your words, I felt it all over again. The pictures that you sent brought back all those wonderful hours. After such happiness, parting is not easy. But I know that my brave girl will manage to stay strong, as always. I am off to Reserve Infantry Regiment 247. 250 of us are leaving now, the rest will follow. Suddenly, the demand for men at the front is great. I am so happy I spent my holiday with you. I can go off, taking with me the happy memories of those beautiful days with my little fiancée. If that is not enough, then I can dream of the future which has helped me through so many dark hours. You should do the same. You know that I understand you. I am taking my ring with me. I cannot be parted from it. I found leaving home very hard. It broke my mother's heart. Mine too.

2nd June, Audenarde

Dear Parents,

I am well. The journey took us through Bietigheim, Bruchsal, Mannheim, Mainz, Bingen, Koblenz, Bonn, Cologne, Aachen, Loewen, to Brussels. I took the most beautiful images of our homeland with me. Our German countryside is so lovely. We crossed the Rhine at Mainz. The singing! It rang out like thunder. Half of Mainz must have heard it. God, the Rhine looked beautiful. After Aachen there was silence. All the men's cheering and shouting stopped. I crossed for the second time into enemy territory. The Belgians are as dull as ever. We can hear shooting in the distance.

*

British Private Robert Cude has just spent his first eight days' leave back in London after ten months in France. Young and single, he indicates that he had a very fine time but gives no details of how or with whom he spent his leave. Now a private in the East Kent Regiment, known as the 'Buffs', he is part of Kitchener's newly trained army. Based in the Somme area, Robert is already very familiar with the soldier's routine but has yet to participate in a major battle. He sets off to the front line for the second time in his war to resume his duties as a battalion runner delivering messages by bicycle between battalion headquarters and the front line.

27th May 1916

I present myself at Waterloo 4 p.m. for my return journey. It is rotten this return in the middle of the day. It is rotten going back at all. Life is so uncertain out in France. Still, must hope for a repetition of my good luck. This is the dreaded part of leave, for they are terrible, these rail journeys in France. Would sooner be in line at anytime. Next five or six days pass quickly. I soon settle down again as we have plenty of work. It is not safe to go to bed before midnight as messages are coming out fairly often. Very showery today, made cycling anything but a pleasure. Next few days pass quickly. Am beginning to long for trenches again, for I get fed up with civilisation.

A severe toothache puts Robert Cude in hospital, delaying further his arrival at the front line.

11th June

Have difficulty in finding unit, as place is full of troops, both English and French. Cannot but help notice the change in this place. Almost every civilian has left. Something will happen soon.

12th June

Plenty of work today. All roads in and out of town are full of traffic both day and night. The quantity and calibre of guns and shells is appalling and troops pouring in in 1,000's. Never did I think that we could make such an imposing spectacle. I lose my watch under suspicious circumstances, so for a few days war takes second place. Time goes on smoothly and we know that our days are numbered.

23th June

Tonight we push up to the trenches. Not lucky enough to get a dugout, so rig up waterproof shelter instead.

24th June

Today 3.30 a.m. the guns start the preliminary bombardment. As day succeeds day we notice more and more artillery getting into action. Jerry is getting it now. Plenty of rain first two or three days. We are getting a goodly number of casualties, for a good many of our shells are falling short, also pieces of shell flying back. Day and night German trenches and villages behind are wreathed in smoke. Occasionally we put gas across.

The seven-day continuous bombardment on the Somme, the longest in the war, is meant to damage the German defences in preparation for the infantry to leave the trenches or 'go over the top'. The opposing defences, however, remain largely intact as the Anglo-French troops launch their massive attack along a 16-mile front. In the sector where Robert Cude is on messenger duty the bombardment begins at 7.22 a.m. on 1st July, a beautiful sunny summer's day.

1st July

The day of the attack arrives and the guns are really deafening, never a German can live over that side. As the time wears on and gets nearer to the appointed hour I am wondering how many such bombardments will be necessary before war is finished. This must be the beginning of the end.

7.22 a.m. Every gun for eight minutes gave of their best and the din was terrific.

Punctual to time 7.28 a.m. two minutes before the line advanced Captain Neville, 8th E. Surreys, kicks off the football that is to take the boys across to Jerry. He is killed as his leg is uplifted after kicking the ball. I am too busy to take in the surroundings other than our immediate front. E. Surreys and Queens go over singing and shouting and the ball is punted from one to another. They are followed by 7th Buffs who are mopping up, their time will come if Jerry is refractory. Soon after the lads get going; we can see that, contrary to expectations, we are not to have things all our own way. Here I may add that I am up forward on a message and determined to stop and see a bit of the fun. Jerry's machine gun opens a terrific fire on our chaps and the first wave is speedily decimated. Others jump forward and fill the gaps. I am aghast at the accuracy of the fire. He has plenty of machine guns, and is making a frightful carnage. I long to be with battalion so that I can do my best to bereave a German family. I hate these swines.

It is a wonderful sight and one that I shall not forget. War such as this, on such a beautiful day seems to me to be quite correct and proper! On a day such as this one, one feels a keen joy in living even though living is, to say the least of it, very precarious. Men are racing to certain death, and jesting and smiling and cursing, yet wonderfully quiet in a sense, for one feels that one must kill, and as often as one can. My hand strays to my pocket. Have two 'Mills'[1] in each, and there are some Jerries against me. They are prisoners and had it not been for the fact that they are being closely watched, I would have put at least one of my bombs amongst them.

10 a.m. Boys are still fighting in the trenches and dugouts and I must say that considering the gruelling Jerry has had and the opposition he is met with, he is fighting a battle for life itself. No quarter is asked or given in a good many places and today I was astounded to think that men could fight so bitterly. The reason is not far to seek, for tens of thousands of our men are lying low, never to rise again. They are England's flower. The men that England can ill afford to spare. As far as my eye takes me, I can see rows of dead. I am afraid that had it not been for the fact that

---

1 Bomb introduced in spring 1915, egg shaped, time-fused with cast-iron case which broke up as shrapnel. More than 33 million were eventually issued to the British and AEF units.

I was too busy dodging the shells I should have broken down. Poor Newcombe and Sgt McClusky, Sgt Whipps, Lt Baddeley and almost all my old platoon was there, and most would not rise again. Have lost my old pals today. Still, some will be left, if I am. Our boys gave no quarter for a long time, but even the wholesale slaughter of a beaten but not disgraced enemy is, or grows, obnoxious. After 10 a.m. prisoners began pouring in. They had even caught a general with members of a big staff. Prisoners were thoroughly fed up.

11 a.m. Off again to get through to battalion. Have plenty of chance to observe the havoc wrought by the guns, ours mostly. Constant streams of wounded are passing backward and some with terrible gaping wounds. But the stretcher-bearers cannot hope to cope with a tenth of the wounded, and so if a man can crawl at all, he is asked to do so. Plenty of souvenirs about, watches, purses, rings and brass hats, helmets are kicking around everywhere, but still, having just returned from leave, am not going to be littered with carrying too much. Several of the prisoners I spoke to speak of our artillery as fiendish, and I saw tears in the eyes of many a German when thinking of it. One point worth mentioning. The burnt faces and hair of some of the Boches bear excellent testimony to the effectiveness of our liquid fire,[1] which was used considerably.

Next three days pass in burial parties and consolidating our positions. Whole squadrons of cavalry are doing the burying fatigues.

Robert Cude records 3,000 casualties in his 55th Brigade. Made up of volunteers grouped together by community or workplace, the losses in the battalions of the New Army leave shattered networks of

---

1 First developed by the Germans and then adopted by everyone, a tank of inflammable fuel oil used as an anti-personnel weapon.

neighbours and school friends. On the first day of the Battle of the Somme 19,240 British men are killed or die of wounds. The total of 57,470 casualties amount to the heaviest loss suffered in a single day by the British army in its history. Some 30 per cent of the British shells fired that day are duds, which, along with the lack of heavy guns, contributes to the failure to break through the German lines or reach their planned objectives.

*

Two months later the battle continues. It has become a battle of attrition with each side wearing the other down. By late August the Allied troops have advanced and are pushing back the German front line, trench by trench. Paul Hub, now promoted to second sergeant, receives orders to depart. The 247th regiment is to reinforce depleted front-line troops. Thinking of his brothers Otto and Robert buried on the Eastern Front, Paul writes farewell letters to his parents and Maria, just in case he too doesn't make it.

29th August

Dear Parents,

We are busy packing. We leave in the next few days. None of us knows exactly where we are going. The days ahead will probably be difficult and bloody. Don't worry if you don't get any news of me for a few days. Even if we take a beating, we hope the worst will not come, God willing I will survive. Thank you once again for all the good things you have done for me. Farewell! I remain to the last breath, your grateful son Paul.

29th August

Dear Maria,

I had to write to you again from here. We are moving out. All the signs are that we are going to the Somme. We won't be down there for long. Normally a regiment spends two to three weeks there before being relieved. Not many people can cope with more than that. Where the losses are greatest, nerves are most likely to fail. God willing, I will survive this hell. I am not particularly confident, but I am sure the worst won't happen. Dear girl, I so want to be happy with you. I am sending you my ring as a token of my true love. Your Paul.

30th August

Dear Maria,

Now that we are leaving, I want to take as little as possible with me, you never know what is going to happen. I do not want any of your lovely letters, which give me so much pleasure and which show how devoted you are to me, to fall into strangers' hands. I will send them all to you in the next few days. Darling, thank you for all your dear sweet words and for all the good times we have spent together. I am going once more into a bloody battle. I am not worried for myself but feel sad for you and my parents. If I die, you will be all alone again and my parents will lose a third son. I hope to God it doesn't come to that. Oh dear girl, if only I could take you into my arms and tell you how much I love you, how devoted I am. I would comfort you and give you strength. Be strong. The last trial and our regiment will have a quieter time. We have been forbidden to let anyone know where we are going but I can't leave you in the dark. If I do fall, it won't be completely unexpected.

Paul Hub now joins the Battle of the Somme. Sending brief letters to his parents whenever he can, he confides the details of what he endures to Maria in a series of post-dated diary letters written when he finds comparative quiet.

12th September

Dear parents,

Six days of fighting on the Somme and there's still no end to it. The artillery thumps down on to our positions, shattering the ground and our nerves with it. I wish the next twelve days were over and I had survived them. So far I've been OK. Thankfully the enemy infantry is useless. We can repel their attack with the help of just a single machine gun and a few rifles. But their

Paul Hub on the Western Front

artillery never stops. They keep pounding us day and night. I really don't know how we're going to survive the next twelve days. We only have our coats, tarpaulin and cooking gear with us. We live like pigs. The cold food doesn't help. My trench coat is several sizes too big now.

Paul Hub's unit is responsible for collecting food from a position behind the lines and distributing it in the trenches. Regularly under fire, it is a dangerous task.

12th September[1]

Dear Maria,

I went with my company to collect our rations. We waited there till 2 a.m. for the porters to bring it up to us. This was the first and last time we had something warm to eat. We carried the soup back in four big pans. But most of the men were so exhausted by the relentless firing that they couldn't be bothered to eat it. They just tried to get some sleep.

Only two of the four soup pans got eaten, the other two went begging, then they were shot to pieces. The men just left them and took cover as quickly as they could. My luck was in: I was in the trench when a shell exploded right beside me, wounding three infantrymen. I got away with shock. Even the shells that came after didn't wound me. But today I can still hear the sound of shells whistling in my ears. On the way back we came under shellfire, as usual.

14th September

Dear Maria

We must have lost 40 per cent of our company today. Many of my men were so exhausted that I couldn't get them to do

---

1 For the sake of clarity, the dates of Paul Hub's letters to Maria refer to the events he describes, as indicated within the letters. They are not the actual dates when the letters were written.

anything. I ordered an NCO to follow me but he threatened to shoot me. I had him arrested. We were then ordered to defend Combles and dig trenches in the open, but it was almost impossible to persuade even a few of the men to come with me. As soon as I got them out of one ditch, they simply disappeared into another. We had managed to collect a few men when the firing restarted and they all disappeared again. There are no trenches here, only craters with waterproof covers pulled over the top. The men knew this and were reluctant to submit themselves to almost certain death. In the end we set out with only six faithful followers. At about 2 a.m. on 15th September we found a hole half a metre deep. My lot covered the waterproofing with straw and thistles. The others did the same. Anything to avoid being seen by the planes.

17th September

Dear parents

I'm more tired now than I've ever been in my whole life. We are constantly under fire. The French attack every evening without fail. My honey jar fell victim to an enemy shell and the rest of my things are mostly shot to bits. But I'm still in one piece.

20th September

My dear Maria,

I had just taken up my position when a heavy mortar hit the wall, burying me and two of my company under the rubble. I can't describe what it felt like to be buried alive under such a mass of earth without being able to move a muscle. Thankfully, my big steel helmet protected my mouth and nose from the earth. Even so, I was having difficulty breathing, but help was at hand. When someone called out asking if there was anyone underneath, we shouted 'Yes!' and they started digging us out right away. They thought they would have to free the others before they could reach me, but in the end they pulled me out at the same time. I felt as if my legs had been chopped off. I sat in the trench curled up in a ball, with my back against the wall and my feet pulled up in front of me, the position I had been buried in. The weight of the earth had pushed my head forward and torn my back muscles.

21st September

Dear parents,

Tomorrow we'll probably be relieved. Many of us are ill. We've done enough on the Somme. My troop (the 8th company) has lost 58 per cent of its original number in the last ten days.

24th September

Dear parents,

Thank God the battle of the Somme is over. We've been resting in Clary since yesterday. We're desperate to wash the Somme off our clothes and our skin. We are slowly becoming human again. We had to march here on foot. Even though I had a light pack, I really felt it. My back was hurting the whole way. Still, I'm pleased to have got away so lightly.

Paul Hub's tour of duty on the Somme is over but he is one of only twenty-three men from his company to emerge alive and without serious injuries. The fighting continues on the Somme until November when the battle finally peters out without a decisive victory but an estimated half a million casualties on both sides.

*

Meanwhile, French and German troops are still locked in combat at Verdun. French fortunes have improved since the Battle of the Somme began which forced the German High Command to split resources between the two major battles. But after seven months of fighting, there is no clear outcome and casualties continue to be heavy on both sides. The French are determined to keep up the pace of the battle until they regain the ground lost to the Germans in their initial attack. At one time or another three-quarters of the French army fights at Verdun.

Recently promoted to captain, Paul Tuffrau arrives at Verdun with his company in September 1916, after months of anticipation. He has been decorated, twice wounded and never far from the front line since he fought in the Battle of the Marne two years earlier. While he remains close to his men, Paul Tuffrau is increasingly critical of the higher ranks and begins to write articles for a magazine published on the home front under the pseudonym Lieutenant E.R.. In the articles he describes the reality of life at the front stripped of military propaganda.

On arrival at Verdun, he finds a 5-kilometre-long front line where 1000 shells have fallen for every square metre. Paul Tuffrau records his first impressions.

25th September, Froideterre

This morning I go on my usual round. De Gislain gives me an introduction to the landscape he now knows like the back of his hand – the blue ridge of the Thiaumont fortification; Douaumont, 1,800 metres away; the wooden stumps which are in fact the Caillette and the Vaux-Chapitre forests. This piece of land, the focus of the entire world, is so small.

27th September

Yesterday evening, at 8.30 p.m., the day's bombardments over, we went on reconnaissance to our position, P. C. Maroc, near Fleury. A lunar landscape, pitted with shell-holes, with one solitary tree, burnt and mangled. We reach the trench, dug out by joining up the shell-holes and it stinks of bogs and decaying corpses. Stagnant water.

28th September

At 10.30 p.m. I go to survey position P. C. 119 near Thiaumont. These plateaux are pounded by shells dropped during the day, but at night they are full of stretcher-bearers bringing back the day's casualties. We walk through battery C. We wade through mud. Craters filled with water reflect the light every time a rocket is fired. The smell of corpses everywhere.

*Two months later Tuffrau is still there. In mid-November the French
regain Fort Douaumont and Fort Vaux in the first counter-offensive
since the battle began. But these are the only major milestones in
what appears to be an interminable tour of duty. While Robert Cude
and Paul Hub were rotated away from the Somme after only a few
weeks, Paul Tuffrau is at the front with only brief periods of rest in
between twenty-four-day tours of duty.*

26th November, Dubois trench

Ah, this sector is in a right mess! The plateau is one great quag-
mire where we slip and fall over repeatedly. This yellow mud
sucks you down till its above the knees. At the Barrault trench I
find men sheltering under the machine gun platform, numb.
The water is a metre high in the sap;[1] useless pieces of wire-
mesh, thrown in to serve as bridges, just float around. It takes me
three and a half hours to do my round and just as long to scrape
the mud off myself. I do at least feel closer to the men, sharing
this common misery and trying to support them a little by showing them that I suffer as much as they do. This morning there
were more friendly faces than usual. When I got back, the
reserve company's workmen were amazed to see me soaked up to
my stomach. 'A bit of mud on your uniform, Sir!' they joked.
And two cooks stopped in the sap, thigh-deep in the mud:
'Reckon we're ready for them, Captain?' At times like these, we
are all in the same boat, laughing at our miserable predicament.

27th November

A close shave this morning. German machine guns had been
jittery all night, and now they spring into action, firing short
bursts at random. We are stranded on the plateau and have to
throw ourselves to the ground into the water-filled craters. Three

---

1 A sap is a trench dug forward into no man's land, the area between the
  opposing front lines.

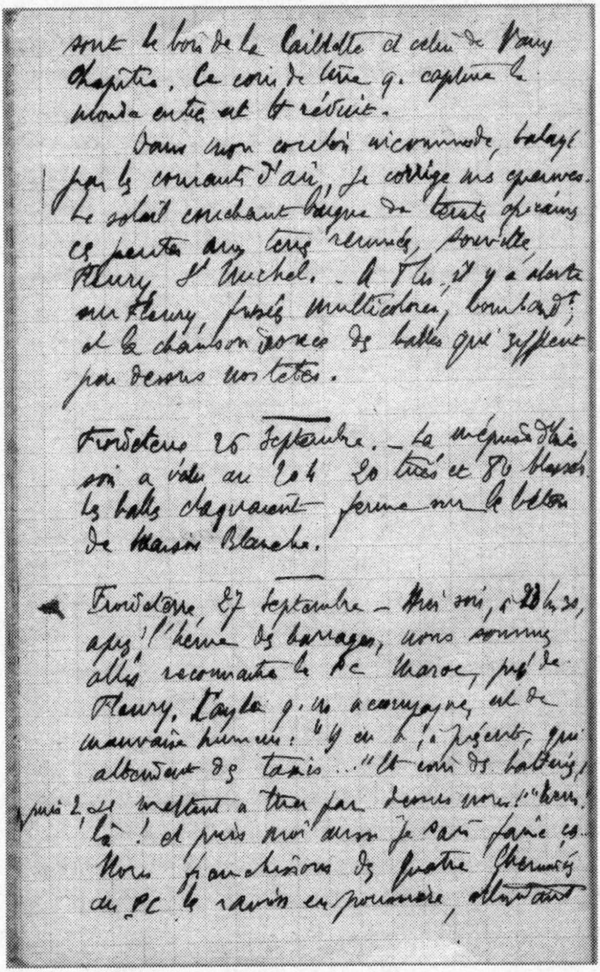
sont le bois de la Caillette et celui de Vaux
Chapitre. Ce coin de terre qui captive le
monde entier est là réuni.
Dans mon couloir incommode, balayé
par les courants d'air, je corrige mes épreuves.
Le soleil couchant baigne de teintes [illegible]
les pentes aux terres remuées, Souville,
Fleury, St Michel. – A l'[illegible], il y a alerte
sur Fleury, fusées multicolores, bombard[illegible],
et la chanson douce des balles qui sifflent
par dessus nos têtes.

Froideterre 26 Septembre. – La [illegible] d'hier
soir a valu au 204 20 tués et 80 blessés
les balles [illegible] fermes sur le béton
de Maison Blanche.

Froideterre, 27 septembre – Hier soir, à 22h30,
après l'heure des barrages, nous sommes
allés reconnaître le PC Maroc, près de
Fleury. [illegible] qui m'accompagne est de
mauvaise humeur: "Il y en a, à présent, qui
attendent des tanks..." Le coin des batteries,
puis [illegible] mettant à terre par dessus nous! "Tiens,
là! et puis moi aussi je sais faire ça."
Nous franchissions les quatre chemins
du PC le ravin en [illegible], attendant

A page from Paul Tuffrau's diary September 1915

machine guns fire at us at the same time. I can see two of them
spitting sparks in the dark on either side of the ravine by the
Camard woods. I give the order to fire back, round for round.

*The French lines keep moving forward. The Battle of Verdun has
been going on for 300 days by now, far longer than any other in the
war. Both sides are being worn down. The Germans have suffered
328,500 casualties and the French 348,300. By Christmas, Tuffrau
has spent three months at Verdun, with brief periods in reserve pro-
viding inadequate rest.*

25th December, Avocourt

At 6 p.m., I leave in the dark and the rain to visit the A-33
trench area, which cannot be reached in daytime. Beaudoin, the
officer commanding, tells me that around three o'clock the Fritz,
250 or 300 metres away, sang them Christmas carols in French,
beautifully. It must have come from the Corne des Vergers.

*After two weeks on leave, Paul Tuffrau returns to the by now frozen
trenches.*

4th February 1917, Charmontois-l'Abbé

It has not been this cold since '93. We leave at night, everyone slip-
ping on the frozen earth. On the plateau, the snow is powdery, like
sugar. It crunches under our shoes without melting. When we get
to Lavoye, in the moonlight, there are no fresh supplies.

At eight we move off again and the men's faces are contorted
by the cold and exhaustion. Red-rimmed eyes, red noses, pale
skin, blue ears, beards hung with icicles. Sweat freezes right away
and looks like snow on the horses' backs and on the men's over-
coats. Our shoes cannot grip on the frozen earth as we march.
Finally, we arrive in Charmontois. The men have to sleep in
barns with broken windows! The conditions are criminal. They
drink in order to keep warm. I am surprised no one gets a cold.

Paul Tuffrau

19th February, Kitchener trench, forest of Nawe

This morning, every face is racked with exhaustion. As for me, I was seized by a strong urge to vomit while walking through the Caurettes forest. I survived thanks to a few drops of mint liqueur. I fell into a shell crater full of water and I got drenched up to my belt. I fell asleep at three in the hot humidity of this wretched sap. These night reliefs are the worst thing about this war.

5th March, Louvemont

The special shells the men call 'shells on wheels' are whizzing by continuously.[1] They explode silently and have no smell but can be deadly. They killed several men yesterday. One of my men refused to put his mask on because he couldn't smell anything. All of a sudden, he was dizzy, foaming at the mouth and his skin went black, then he went rigid and died. On my rounds a little later, I am seized by vertigo. The sentries tell me that the special shells had been dropped here ten minutes earlier.

16th March

We are tired; we all look forward to some leave after the huge amount of exertion since October [1916]. My men are waiting for relief, for the moment when they will leave the firing line, when they'll be able to sleep through the night without having to get up to do chores and wash and change their clothes, which they can only do every twenty-four days here. They no longer have the strength to resist an attack, they haven't even the muscles to throw grenades.

---

1 Shells containing liquid gas. Gas was first used on the Western Front at Ypres in 1915.

French soldiers looking at the dead

The General[1] says to me:
  – Be sure to tell your men we're here for the long haul, so they can start planting lettuce. We'll be staying until October.

I thought he was joking so I replied:
  – In that case, we'd better plant asparagus.
  – This is not a joke you know

Behind his dark lenses, he had the look of a man who will not tolerate dissent easily.

---

1 General Mangin, second in command at Verdun to General Nivelle.

– It is crucial, you understand, that they all know, down to the last private. I will give orders to that effect. We will hold out here until October while the big offensive is launched elsewhere. We will eventually take part in it ourselves, towards the end. But you must expect twenty-four days on the front line and one day of rest, no more.

– Dear God! We've been here eight days and the men, General, are completely exhausted.

– We must redouble our efforts, for the sake of the nation.

And with a bitter smile:

– Other regiments are digging deep – why shouldn't the 246th?

– General, we cannot keep asking the men to do more and more and more again. It is not possible. The sanitary conditions, for example –

– They're not bad.

– They will be dreadful if it starts raining. All of my men have coughs. With the first rains, the division will start melting like sugar in water.

– There is no use debating the point. The 246th must do what is required of it, for the greater good.

Then, with a brief salute, he went back into his well-heated private office where it's easy to avoid the reality and talk of the greater good. As for me, I was stunned by his extraordinary refusal to acknowledge the courage of the men of the 246th.

That night, after hearing this 'heroic' pep-talk, I led my men along the tracks that were horribly muddy and slippery. Some of them were crying with exhaustion and rage.

On 7th April 1917, after more than six months, Paul Tuffrau's unit is transferred from the Verdun area. The two momentous battles of 1916 end indecisively.

A month after Tuffrau and his men are finally released, mutinies

*break out in five towns where French soldiers throw down their arms
and refuse to move forward to the front line. By June half the army
is affected. The leaders are arrested, forty-nine of them shot, the
remainder given clemency. But appeasement is offered to the rest of
the army: better conditions, more leave and more time in reserve.
Tuffrau's 246th is in a quieter sector when the mutinies break out.
Although they are desperate for improved conditions, his men do not
revolt; in fact they are sent in to relieve one of the rebellious divisions.*

*

*German officer Paul Hub writes to his ever-anxious fiancée, Maria,
trying to convince her that he too is out of the worst of it, for now.*

26th April

Darling, again your letters are full of fear and anxiety. You don't
realise how well we are doing right now. You write about blood,
death and horrific battles. But the fighting isn't like that. We are
several kilometres behind the front and are not thinking of death
and the horrors of war. Why do you keep on about it? If fighting
is going on somewhere on the Western Front, it doesn't necessarily mean we are in the thick of it. You see, dearest, your non-stop
fretting is depressing me. Here I am, enjoying some peace in my
nice lodgings full of the joys of spring and there you are at home
worrying. Darling, I understand you and your worries all too well.
But you shouldn't read so much into what they write in the papers.
When you were off skiing, I thought of you happily going up and
down the slopes. If you read about a battle in the newspaper, tell
yourself I am not there. Ninety-nine times out of one hundred
you will be right. So don't grumble unnecessarily. You only make
me nervous. And it makes me so admire my sorely tested parents.

Greetings from your true love,

Paul

*

*In the coming months, Robert Cude is to return to the Somme, Paul
Tuffrau refuses to take up a promotion in order to stay with his men
and Paul Hub joins the lesser-known Second Battle of Verdun.*

Chapter 10

EMPIRES AT WAR

1914–1917

The First World War was fought on a truly global scale, requiring unprecedented resources of manpower and supplies. Distant colonies of the belligerent empires provided millions of tons of food and raw materials for the war effort. Britain's largest colony – India – alone provided nearly 3.7 million tons, including wool and timber, raw silk, beef and tea as well as 70 million rounds of ammunition and 172,815 pack animals and cows.

This was also the first war to involve large-scale troop movements. Thousands of soldiers from around the world joined the European war effort. Volunteers and conscripts, they served as soldiers and labourers, nurses, porters and cooks. British troops included millions of soldiers from across the vast and diverse Empire: 1.4 million Indians, nearly 620,000 Canadians, over 416,000 Australians, more than 200,000 New Zealanders and 136,070 South Africans. They fought across the many fronts of the war, in Palestine and Mesopotamia, in Africa, at Gallipoli and, in increasing numbers, on the Western Front.

The French Empire recruited 600,000 colonial soldiers for its war effort. Throughout the early years of the twentieth century the French government had debated the value of creating a 'force noir' from its African territories to be used for the defence of France. By 1914 French African contingents far exceeded those of any other European nation and at the war's outbreak over 10,000 French-trained African soldiers were immediately transferred from North Africa to the Western Front.

*

Two among the many thousands who travel across the oceans to fight alongside the Europeans are seventeen-year-old Canadian volunteer Winnie McClare, a farmer's son from Nova Scotia and young West African Kande Kamara from Kindia in French Guinea. Winnie frequently writes home to his parents and siblings, detailing his experience, while Kande's account, recorded in 1976,[1] offers a rare insight into an African soldier's experience of the First World War. It is all the more valuable as most African soldiers were illiterate at the time and left few contemporary records of their war.

Kande Kamara was working as a driver in the Guinean capital city, Bamako, when he heard about France's recruitment campaign for its European war. He immediately set off for home, but found his village almost empty, with most men gone into hiding from the army recruiters.[2]

When I arrived home, no one was to be found there, only old people and women. Everybody was in the bush, in the valleys and in the mountains. The only time they would come into town was in the middle of a dark night. I secretly packed all my clothes except for what I was wearing and sneakily brought them to my father's house, because I had already made up my mind to go into the army, even though all of my family were against it. My father told me to go hiding into the bush. [And I told him]

---

1 Kande Kamara's account is based on transcripts of an interview conducted by Joe Opala, 20–24th September 1976 in Bumbuna, Sierra Leone, and translated from the Susu by Abdul Kamara. Tapes and transcripts of Kande Kamara's interview are deposited at the National Archives of Senegal.

2 Melvyn Page p. 5. Traditional African practices, such as a chief's right to the labour of his servants, were misused to obtain men.

Kande Kamara in 1976

I am never going into the bush, because I was no animal. I disobeyed my father, for he thought it was stupid and ridiculous to go to a war I didn't understand and to fight in another country. I was in fact ashamed to see that many children from low houses were going. I felt that, as I was one of the elder children of a chief, it was one of my responsibilities to go to war, if [the white people] needed us. They had already noted down that every slave who went to war would become a chief on return. I was jealous of that and this was one of the reasons I joined the army. I thought it would be insulting to be ruled by a slave when he comes back from war.

I presented myself [to the recruitment office] and said: 'Here I am. A good volunteer.' They said: 'Why are you here?' And I replied: 'I want an army uniform.' The Captain exclaimed, 'That's my man!' I was taken for a medical examination and called 'a good boy'. In the evening I was given a uniform. There was no chance for my mother or father to stop me now, now that I had joined the white man's army. I was given clothes, money and food. In the afternoon I presented myself to my people wearing my army uniform. There was a real uproar, there was hysteria, everybody in the village was alarmed at seeing my uniform.

When Kamara's father comes to visit him at the military barracks, Kande regrets his decision to enlist without his father's blessing.

I said: 'Please forgive me. I'm doing this for the benefit of our house. If I die, I'll die a man. Don't be angry.' I held his feet as I lay on the ground. He placed his hands on my head and said: 'It wasn't your fault, kid, everything's God's will.' He held my hand and prayed to God to guide and protect me. He knew he couldn't be angry, since he'd be angry at the white man. He knew he couldn't fight my decision because he'd be fighting the white man, so all he could do was wish me luck and pray for me.

Few Africans dare openly to go against the white man's will.[1] Many recruits are attracted by the promise of free meals, a uniform and pay and are often misled about the potential dangers they face. Kande, who joins the war as a volunteer, spends the next few months adjusting to military routine at a local training camp in Guinea.

*

Like Kande Kamara, Canadian Winnie McClare is also determined to volunteer for war, being so keen that he lies about his age. After several months of initial military training with the Halifax Rifles in Canada, Winnie writes to his mother asking for her permission to join the overseas forces. His own spelling and punctuation are retained.

22nd July 1915, Mac Nabs Is, Halifax

Dear Mamma,

Just a line to let you know I am well and there is an urgent call out for more men, men, men, and my name is going in for the 40th Regt. Last Friday there was a Capt. (I forget the name) from the front here and he said that the men at the [front] are happy as can be. He made a long speech, told us how they live and everything about them. Said they had a Jolly time. All I need is you concent.

Your loveing Son,
Winnie

His mother agrees, but it will take another year of training before Winnie's regiment finally gets underway to England. By now, Winnie wonders if he might have missed all the action on the Western Front.

---

1 In some cases the conscription drive sparked off rebellions (in Nyasaland in 1915, in Mozambique in 1917) though these were primarily fuelled by colonial concerns.

Winthrop (Winnie) McClare in 1914

2nd July 1916

My Dear Mother,

We are not sure of the sailing date but expect it is thursday next. I would like to go home, but I am afraid there is no chance . . . I tryed hard to get home today, I tryed every livery stable in Halifax, but could[n't] get a horse to save my neck.

I haven't much news to write, but I want to say one thing: I signed over $20.00 a month to you and I want all of it put in the bank unless you need it bad. You know that I will need it after the war. By the look of things now, I will never see the front. Yesterdays papers were very faverable.

With love to all,

Your loveing Son,

Winnie.

H.M.S. *Empress of Britain* **At Sea**

19th July 1916

Dear Dad,

Just a few lines to tell you that we are going fine. The weather has been lovely, no seas at all.

Nobody in our bunch has been sick yet, but most of us felt a little wrong in the pit of our stomacks, but it only lasted a little while.

There is an Awfull bunch of men on this ship, about [censored]. It is getting to be a tiresome voyage and will be more so before we get over.

I am writing this on deck and somebody pointed out a whale. It is a long way of and we can just see him jump out of the water and fall back again with a splash.

I left a watch at a jewelry store to be fixed and I would like you to get it and send it to me. The name of the place is Cogwells on Barrington St. by the parade.

We are going to have emergency drill in a few minutes, so I

will have to go below. We carry our life belts with us all the time.
We sling our hammocks right over the tables and go to sleep. It
was hard work the first night.

Well, it is beginning to rain again. So I will close and write my
address from London. So Good bye.

With Love from

Your Son,

Winnie

P.S. We received word that we could not saw two much in the
letters we send. P.W. McC.

*

*Like Winnie McClare, Kande Kamara travels to Europe by boat.
His journey from Conakry to Bordeaux takes six terrifying days
and nights.*

Some of us were vomiting for the smell of the ship and the oil was
too unbearable. Some cried like women, or wept like little babies.
Some people were saying, 'If this ship wants, it can sink, we're
going to die anyway, so who gives a damn.' Men were beating
their hands against the ship, yelling and screaming. A rumour
went round that we were not coming back, but would be sold as
slaves instead. Some people were trying out their ju-ju charms to
help them return home if they were kept [overseas]. Some used
their cowrie shells, throwing them on the floor to gamble and see
if they could bring them good luck, if they could be saved by
some miraculous charm. Others were singing songs and telling
fairy tales to keep themselves occupied with something else besides
war.

*After a tumultuous journey, Kande Kamara lands in France where
he spends the next nine months training at a segregated military
camp for African soldiers on the outskirts of Bordeaux. As Kande
and his fellow soldiers march through a French town for the first
time, they try to get a glimpse of their white hosts.*

When we arrived we were sent for parades. The people were roaring [as we walked past]. But if you turned left or right to look at them, you were slapped and you actually saw the fire of hell.

We were not used to white people yet. In fact we were afraid of them. We never went anywhere apart from parades. I went to Bordeaux to fight. I never went there to go look for a white woman, like some people were whispering amongst themselves. I never went to Bordeaux to stare at tall buildings; [or] gaze at spectacular sites, even though I admired every little bit that I did see. I went to Bordeaux strictly to train how to get at the enemy, who I was told was a very, very bad enemy.

I had what I wanted to eat, I had cigarettes, I had pocket money, I had clothes, I had everything a man needs for good life. We were doing exercises to understand the tactics of war. If they gave you an order – whatever it was, [if you were told to lie down in] shit, snakes, scorpions, lizards, chameleons, anything – you had do it because that was the order.

While Kande is able to make the adjustment to the army rules, some of his fellow soldiers find most ingenious ways to escape the harsh discipline and punishing military routine.

The only way to get to town was by sneaking out of camp. There were some white women who had mattresses and beds and invited you to their bedrooms. In fact they tried to keep you there. They gave you clothes, money and everything. When the inspector came, he never saw you, because you were hiding under the bed or under the bed covers of that beautiful lady. That's how some soldiers got left behind. None of them went back to Africa.

Kande Kamara had more understanding of the French language than most other African recruits, having served as a house boy for a French colonial official before the war. Yet even he had little understanding of why and what he was fighting for in this war.

We black African soldiers were very sorrowful about the white man's war. There was never any soldier in the camp who knew why we were fighting. There was no time to think about it. I didn't really care who was right – whether it was the French or the Germans – I went to fight with the French army and that was all I knew. The reason for war was never disclosed to any soldier. They didn't tell us how they got into the war. We just fought and fought until we got exhausted and died. Day and night, we fought, killed ourselves, the enemies and everybody else. All we were interested in were the orders – where to fight, when to open fire and who to shoot down. And that was all we obeyed. The white people would joke and chat and play with their enemies. They never fired a shot until the enemy raised a red flag. That was the double standard we saw in that war. If it were us, blacks, when we fight an enemy, we kill him, or he kills us and [we fight] until the time both sides decide to end the war.

Kande Kamara goes into battle imbued with the idea that the German nation hates the black race.[1] *French propaganda seeks to provide explanations why the black soldiers are fighting. Kande Kamara explains how he understood it.*

Because of the colour of our skin, the Germans said that we were shoes. The only people they respected and feared were white. We were black so we were nothing. We fought them because they have been calling us this bad name. There could never be a man in the world who wouldn't get hurt when he was

---

1 They could certainly use racist German propaganda such as this German account in an American *Current History* magazine from 1917, describing black soldiers as 'strong, wild fellows, their log-like, fat, black sculls wrapped in pieces of dirty rags. Showing their grinning teeth like panthers, with their bellies drawn in and their necks stretched forward. Some with bayonets on their rifles. Many armed only with knives. Monsters all, in their confused hatred . . . The black cloud halted, wavered, closed its ranks – and rolled nearer and nearer, irresistible, crushing, devastating.' (p. 8, Melvyn Page).

insulted. It hurt every black man. They actually underestimated us and disgraced and dishonoured us.

Unsure of any specific geographical locations or dates, Kande Kamara remembers a typical day of warfare:

We were going to the war bush. We didn't know where. We were just looking for the enemy, wherever he was hidden, trying to find out where the German was. You dug trenches and you hid there until the enemy advanced towards you.

You had to dig your own gutter [trench], no one would do it for you. You were given all the tools in your kit: iron picks on your chest, shovels and the pick-axes tied to your backpack. I tried to dig a small hole to hide my whole body. Once you know you've got your own hole in your own trench and that you'll be saved, you can sleep and snore.

Once you are in your gutter, you are ready to go. If there are some enemies far away and they are shooting, you are given a command and all of you shoot together. You hear the command from the Captain, you hear the sound of the guns going bbbbbbbbbbbbbbbbbb-swish, and if you stand there and the bullets are coming, you lie down. Then the second group shoots, and the third . . . You can't just shoot as you want to. You have to take it easy. You have to wait for the Captain's command.

Then they give this command, one-two, one-two, one-two, they give us the order to stand up. They tell us where the enemy is. And so we get out of our gutters, stumbling with hunger and thirst and we follow the rest of our allies.

African soldiers have less experience and understanding of modern warfare than their European counterparts and their casualty rates are higher. Unaware of shellshock, a new concept for all soldiers at the time, Kande Kamara watches his fellows turn deaf and dumb, never quite sure whether their condition is real or faked.

Some people would put glue on their tongues just to make them go funny. And there were some people who all of a sudden turned mute, or went deaf and dumb and never spoke. Yet previously, just two months before the incident, they were talking and doing the same things as everyone else. These were all excuses, these were all things so that they could go home to their country. It was because the war was tough. People were dying, people were frightened, some people collapsed and pretended to faint and the doctor would inspect them all over, and when he picked them up, [this soldier] would pretend he were dead.

A devout Muslim, Kande Kamara felt led and protected by his faith.

Coming from the background I came from, which was Muslim oriented, the only thing you thought about was Allah, death and life. So when the people next to you were already dead, those behind you were dead and those in front of you were dead you started thinking: 'Is it God, is it me, is it somebody else?' Whatever we thought was dedicated to the God Almighty alone. And all who were saved went forward to fight.

The Lord Almighty, I believed in Him so strongly that he would never let me be wounded. The Lord would never let me be hit because I was from a ruling house and ruling houses have their own charms.

Shielded by Allah, or through sheer luck, Kande Kamara survived the war intact but compared its profound effect to a ritual of sexual initiation.

To be a soldier during those days was like being circumcised. There were a lot of things you never knew before. It was only once you graduated from the circumcision bush, that you understood a lot of things. That's the same as experiencing warfare through being a soldier.

*

While Kande Kamara's war began earlier, Winnie McClare does not arrive in south-east England from Canada until July 1916. He shares his immediate impressions with his father.

Lower Dibgate Camp
30th July 1916

Dear Dad.

I am writing just a few lines to tell you what a country this is. It is the most perfect place I have ever seen, tho I have not seen many. We came thru about 500 miles of it and it was all farms and citys. There were not very many citys to see on our route, but I enjoyed looking at the farms. They are all marked off with hedges and there isn't a foot of land that isn't put under cultivated. Even the sides of the railroads tracks are gardens growing all kinds of vegitables. I have not seen one poor farm house here yet. All the houses are made of brick. It is all brick here, except in these camps and it is canvas.

So Good bye from

Your Son, Winnie

Once again, Winnie is to go into training and won't see action for months. He writes home about his diverse experiences.

Upper Dibgate Camp
23th August 1916

Dear Mother,

I think it is about time I wrote a letter to you. If you ever forget my address or don't know where I am, be sure and address all letters to Army Post Office, London; and have my name and number, for they would never find me without the number, which is #488944.

We are being drilled pretty hard, and I expect to be through with the drill part of the training and get shooting and bayenet fighting and bombing. When we finish that, I will be ready for the front. It may not be long now. There are men going from this Batt. every week in drafts.

There is all kinds of clubs here for the soldiers. We get good meals here, the finest I have seen in the army yet.

I have not been able to get a pass to London yet, but will as soon as we pass the most part of the drill. It is a pass that the King gives all Canadian soldiers, and is a six-day pass. Norman Black and I are going together. He is that fellow from Windsor that was my bunk mate at McNabs Island.

Loveingly,
Winnie

6th October 1916

My dear Helen

You must be having great time this fall. Your letters sound like it.

Herbert [Winnie's younger brother] is the one that ought to go to school, if anyone should. I wish every day that I had more schooling, and if I ever get back to Canada, I am going to go to school again. A fellow can't get along in this world unless he knows something, and I know nothing so far.

Don't you think I ought to take a course in penmanship? I am an awfull writter. I am not improving in writing, but I can write an awful lot faster than I could before I came to England. That is some improvement as I used to be so slow.

With love to all.

Your loveing brother,
Winnie

Excited by Winnie's tales of soldiering in England, his fifteen-year-old brother, Herbert, is desperate to volunteer. On request from their mother, Winnie writes back to Herbert.

Winnie McClare's letter to his sister Helen, 6th October 1916

6th November 1916, Upper Dibgate

Dear Herbert.

Look here, Kid. Take a tip from me an stop wanting to enlist.
You could do nothing but go in the home guards and stay there
awhile, and it would be a deuce of a awhile. You hold your horses
awhile and go to school every day, and by the time you are seventeen you can get out and enlist.

Don't be afraid that the war will be over by then, because if you ask me, it is going to last some time after 1920. So be a good boy and stay on the farm for a while, and go to school every day you possibly can, as that is the best thing you can ever do. I am haveing a pretty good time just now, but I don't know how long it is going to last. Most of the men here are not near as well off as I am by a long sight.

Well, old boy, I must close now hoping to hear from you soon.
Your Loveing Brother,
Winnie

20th November 1916

Dear Dad.

I saw most of the sights in London. I saw Buckingham Palace. Went through the Tower of London and went to Madame Tussaud's Wax works, and that is one of the most interesting place I went to. It had the figures in wax of all the famous men in the world.

The worst of London is the girls that run around the streets there. The Strand is the worst place for them that I ever saw. They will come up to you, that is, after about nine oclock, and they will take you by the arm and want you to go home with them and stay all night with them.

I have not had much experience with them, but it is an awfull temtation when they act like that. An awfull lot of fellow that go to London come back in bad shape and are sent to the V.D. hospitals. There is one V.D. hospital near here that has six hundred men in it. It is a shame that the fellows can't keep away from it.

Well, Dad, I will have to knock off now as I have to go to work again. I am in the mens mess serveing out grub and washing up the dishes.

Hopeing this will find you all Jake, as they say here.
Your Loveing Son,
Winnie

On 6th February 1917, having spent six months training in England, Winnie is to sail to France, one of thousands of fellow recruits going out to reinforce the depleted 24th Victoria Rifles of Canada. He writes to his sister from his first trench position.

Feb 1917, Somewhere in France

Dear Sis,

As I have nothing to do this afternoon, I thot that I would write you another letter. It is raining to beat the band out now and muddy as it is almost possible for it to be.

My boots and puttees, almost up to my knees, are covered with mud, and my greatcoat is the same up to my waist. Oh, this is a lovely place, I guess not . . .

With Love to all.

Your Loveing brother,

Winnie.

P.S. Excuse pencil please. My fountain pen has dryed up like myself. P.W.M.

Despite the bad weather and discomforts of trench life, Winnie is soon upbeat again and shares his latest news with sister Helen.

Somewhere in France

29th March 1917

My Dear Sister,

I am writing to you again this week, and I may say I have few things to say that may interest you. I will first remark upon the weather. It is rotten. It has been raining hard all day and all last night.

Next, I am well and hope that you and all the rest at home are the same.

Now, over with all that. I will tell you a little secret, and, as it is a secret, I know you will not say anything to the others around there. Well, I have been writing to a girl in Liverpool, England, but I never saw her – as I got her ad from Norman Black. He had been writing to a girl there that he knew and his friends friend wanted somebody to write to, so you see that.

Well, this Girls name is Miss Dollie Parkin, and I wrote and told her of you and she thot that she would like to write to you. She is a very interesting corespondent and writes very interesting letters.

I have said that I have never seen her or even a photo of her, so all I can say is what I heard from others and that is that she is not awfully pretty but has a very cheerful tounge and is witty.

I think that you would like to correspond with her. I have been writing to two or three girls. I wrote to Minnie and Aunt Winnie today, and the girl I met in Hove I write to when I feel like it. I guess that is a good thing that I like writing . . .

Well, Girlie, I guess that I will close now, as I have a book to change at the Y.M.C.A. library. So Good Bye.

With Love to All.

Your Loveing Brother,

Winnie

In the first days of April 1917, Winnie's battalion is transferred to Vimy Ridge, a 476-feet high French upland near Arras where a fresh Allied offensive is planned. Canadian troops are charged with piercing German defence lines at the top of the ridge while the British will attempt to simultaneously break through the German lines five miles to the south.

On 8th April 1917 Winnie McClare enters the front-line trenches at Vimy Ridge for the first time. The next morning, on Easter Monday, the joint Allied offensive begins. Canadian forces fight their way to the top, capturing the previously impenetrable German defences. They gain a total of 4,500 yards of German-held ground at the cost of 3,598 men dead and 7,000 wounded. The British also succeed in overrunning the German lines at Arras. Winnie McClare gets away with a slight injury, snatching a rare moment to write home.

16th April, 1917 France

My dear Mother.

I can only write a short letter this time, but hope I will be able to do so soon. I have not written a letter for over a week an a half as I have been in the trenches for 9 days, and it is impossible to write up there.

You have no doubt heard before this of the big advance of the Canadians and the capture of Vimy Ridge. I was in the whole of that battle and it was Hell. I got a small splinter of shrapnel through the fleshy part of my shoulder. It was very slight and I went through it all with it. It was some battle and I am glad to say that I was through it, as it will be one of the biggest things in Canadian history.

We are out for a few days rest, and, believe me, we need it. I don't know how Roy and Lyle came through it. I have not seen them yet but expect to soon.

Well, Mother, if you can, please send me some socks when you can and anything else you care to send in the line of eats.

I got about all my mail last night. There was 21 letter and the parcel of gum and the family H. Thank you very much for them.

Well, Mother Dear, please don't do any worrying as it does no good. But remember me in your prayer. I know you do that, and it helps me a lot.

Well, Mother, I will close now. Give my love to all.

I remain

As Ever

Your Loveing Son,

Winnie.

This is Winnie's last letter home. On 5th May 1917, within a month of his arrival at the front line, Private Percy Winthrop McClare, is killed, aged nineteen. Winnie has no known grave, one of thirty-one soldiers killed and wounded that day in a German attack near the French village of Acheville, a few miles east of Vimy Ridge. Just as

Winnie had predicted, the success at Vimy Ridge will go down in history as Canada's finest victory in the First World War and a significant victory for the Western Front, making a dent of four miles in a ten-mile-long strip of German front line.

Though African units were segregated from European ones for most of the war, Guinean soldier Kande Kamara recalled noticing a gradual shift towards equality: 'At the beginning of the war, the white people were always in the front line, but when we got to understand them and when they started trusting us that changed. At the very end of the war, we were all mixed, because by then everyone knew their mind and their heart and no one was afraid of colour except for the innocents.' Kande returned home in 1919. An estimated 30,000, or nearly one in four of 135,000 French colonial soldiers from Africa died fighting in Europe.

Chapter 11

THE WAR AT SEA

September 1914– December 1917

The gap between expectation and reality was as great in the war at sea as in the war on land. The arms race in the decade before 1914 was dominated by rivalry over the construction of Dreadnoughts: fast, big-gunned, heavily armoured battleships. Germany had thirteen and was building seven more. Austria-Hungary had three, America ten, Britain twenty. When Britain went to war, her people were led to believe that much of the fighting would be done at sea, where her naval superiority would guarantee a swift victory. Yet the war at sea did not turn out as expected.

Britain used her ships and position to close off the North Sea, imposing an ever-tighter naval blockade on Germany, denying her food and raw material imports. For the most part, Germany kept her larger ships in harbour. The set-piece Battle of Jutland in 1916 was an exception, but though British losses were marginally greater, the result was that Germany's High Seas Fleet returned to its harbours and stayed there, preserved nearly intact as a negotiating counter for the war's end. Instead, at sea Germany would exploit the stealth and surprise afforded by a new and almost untried weapon: the submarine.

The sharpest minds in the Admiralties of both sides had long foreseen that submarines, fast patrol boats, mines and torpedoes could well dominate in the coming conflict. By striking at merchant ships, the submarine might also have a role in economic warfare, although one British admiral was horrified at the thought: 'Submarines are underhand, unfair and damned un-English. As for U-Boats attacking civilian ships, it is impossible and unthinkable. If they do, their captured crews should be hanged as pirates.' Not all Britain's admirals were as short-sighted. Admiral Jackie Fisher realised 'the submarine is the coming type of war vessel for sea fighting. It means that the whole foundation of our traditional naval strategy has broken down!'

Two days into the war, Germany unleashed ten of its U-Boats into the North Sea to hunt down the British fleet. One of them, U-21, made her way to the Firth of Forth, where the British cruiser HMS Pathfinder *was leaving Rosyth naval base in Scotland. U-21 sunk her with a single torpedo and a new era in naval warfare had dawned. In time, Germany would operate a policy of 'all-out' submarine warfare, in which neither tiny merchant vessels nor mighty ocean liners would be safe. The campaign would have a crucial impact on the conduct and progress of the war.*

*

U-Boat service was not a popular naval career choice before the war. German naval officer Johannes Spiess considered his hopes of a successful rise through the ranks on one of Germany's new destroyers were all but ruined when in 1912, aged thirty, he was assigned to serve as a Watch Officer on U-9. A first generation U-Boat, the U-9 ran on a sour-smelling Korting engine and was likened to a 'damp coffin'. All Spiess's worst fears seemed confirmed during an introductory tour of U-9, despite the enthusiasm of his captain, Otto Weddigen, one of the admiring pioneers of the submarine.

A certain degree of 'finesse' was required to be able to live at all in the officers' quarters. The Watch Officer's bunk was too small to allow you to lie on your back. You were forced to lie on one side and then, being wedged in between the bulkhead to the right and the clothes-press on the left, to hold fast against the movements of the boat in the seaway. The occupant of the berth could not sleep with his feet stretched right out, as there was an electrical fuse-box aft in the cabin directly overhead. At times the cover of this box was sprung and it was easily possible to cause an electric short circuit by touching it with your feet.

The cooking problem was not solved at that time since both the electric heating coil and the bake-oven short-circuited every time an attempt was made to use them. Instead meals were always prepared on deck. We had a small gasoline stove for this purpose. It had the particular advantage of being serviceable even in a high wind.

From a hygienic standpoint the sleeping arrangements left much to be desired; we awoke in the morning with considerable mucous in our heads and frequently with so-called 'oil-head'. All of the moisture in the air condensed on the steel hull plates, and had a very disconcerting way of dropping and spraying on your face with every movement of the vessel. Efforts were made to prevent this by covering our faces with rain cloths or rubber sheets. It was just like a damp cellar. In one small corner of the central station there was a toilet separated by a curtain. After seeing this arrangement, I understood why the officer I replaced had recommended the use of opium before all cruises which were to last over twelve hours.

Johannes Spiess managed to overcome his initial misgivings, however, finding there were compensations to living inside the 'steel shark'.

It is an exciting moment when one stands for the first time in the conning tower and notes through the thick glass how the deck becomes gradually covered with water and the boat slowly sinks. In the clear seawater, when the sun is shining, the silvery air bubbles sparkle all over the boat's hull and rise as in an aquarium. At times when the boat was lying still on the bottom of the sea we could observe fish swimming close by the ports of our conning tower attracted to it by the electric light which was shining through.

Officers' mess on U9 with (from right to left) Otto Weddigen, Otto Weddigen's brother, Johannes Spiess, engineer.

Six weeks into the war, U-9 is sent on its first patrol mission in the North Sea. After a few days' cruising off the Dutch coast, early in the morning of 22nd September 1914, Johannes Spiess is on watch duty in the conning tower.

Through my prismatic glasses I noticed a small masthead coming into view. It looked like the mast of a warship. Could this be the first sight of the enemy? Weddigen came immediately up to the conning tower and gave the order to submerge. Shortly after, the seas closed over us.

Our tension changed to cheerful excitement when [captain] Weddigen called out: 'There are three light cruisers with four stacks.' From now on, we worked in the boat with the greatest nervous energy. The periscope was only run out for seconds while in the vicinity of the English in order not to betray our presence. The great question was: will we be able to get clear

after the shot and how will the torpedo explosion affect our
own boat?

At 7.20 the order came: 'Periscope out. First tube stand by.'

Everyone in the boat was counting seconds.

'First tube fire. Periscope in!'

I pressed the firing button with my right hand and withdrew
the periscope with my left, while shouting through the voice
tube: 'First tube fired!'

What is going to happen next? As I fired, I had the feeling
that it was all over for us. Even I have very much overestimated
the effect that a torpedo explosion close by could have on us. I
observed the depth indicator to see we did not come up to the
surface as a result of the explosion, holding on to the periscope
with both hands. I was only a beginner.

Next, we heard a full blow, followed by a clear crash. Could
that be the torpedo hit? Below me in the boat three cheers broke
out and we in the conning tower joined in spontaneously.
Nothing could be seen as we were at a depth of 15 metres.

As soon as we realised our boat was still intact, Weddigen
brought us to periscope depth to observe what was happening on
the torpedoed cruiser. For a few brief moments of what was my
first glimpse at the enemy through the periscope, I noticed their
stern was considerably low down in the water. White smoke was
pouring out of their four funnels, the bow stem was somewhat
out of water and lifeboats had been lowered. The cruiser – it was
HMS *Aboukir* – turned slowly over to one side and disappeared
under the waves.

At 7.30 a.m. U-9 *fatally damages the British cruiser* Aboukir. *The
crews of the other two British cruisers in the vicinity,* Cressy *and*
Hogue, *are asked to help the crew of* Aboukir *to abandon ship,
thus they become sitting targets for U-9. Two further torpedo
attacks follow, and within one hour all three British cruisers are
sunk.*

The young crew of U-9 were overjoyed with their first triumph. The German Admiralty takes note, keen to expand on their success, and places orders for new U-Boats. Britain is in shock: 1,400 men – many of them young cadets – have died in a single submarine attack. To limit potential damage, the Royal Navy immediately withdraws many of its ships out of U-Boat range to remote naval bases at Loch na Keal in Scotland and Lough Swilly in Ireland.

Using less important vessels, Britain continues to implement its naval blockade. Cargo destined for Germany, including all neutral merchant shipping, is now monitored by Britain's agents from the moment it leaves the docks or is inspected by Allied patrols at sea, with much of it being seized. By January 1915, German and Austro-Hungarian shipping is effectively immobilised, with nearly 3 million tons of cargo arrested in neutral ports and 405,000 tons captured at sea. Shortages of essential raw materials contribute to severe deficit of weapons and ammunition, required in increasing quantities for the Western Front. Food rationing, enforced by the Central Powers within weeks of the British blockade, hits the home front first, lead-ing to considerable civilian hardship and discontent.

*

By the spring of 1916, millions of civilians in Austria-Hungary and Germany are suffering from acute food shortages. One of them is German schoolgirl Piete Kuhr. Now fourteen years old and still living with her grandma and brother Willi in Schneidemühl in East Prussia, Piete is now in charge of running the house and queuing for food, while her grandma tends the wounded at the local Red Cross station. On return from one of her daily shopping trips, Piete records what she has seen.

15th March 1916

What a to-do in town today! There was a whole crowd of women in front of the baker's shop chattering excitedly and waving their bread cards. They were abusing the baker and blaming the bakeries for all the shortages. Then along came a policeman who

Piete Kuhr and her kitten

tried to calm the crowd. The policeman – I know him, and he's a horrible man, very bad manners – grabbed a fat woman who was carrying a milk can. She fell down and there was pandemonium. The fat woman got back on her feet, raised her milk can and smashed it into the policeman's face. Then all the women jumped on the policeman. The baker saved the day by opening his shop. The mob stormed inside. I heard them shouting for a long time. Bread! Give us bread! Our children need something to eat!

2nd June

The women are all at work in munitions factories, because the men are nearly all at the front. When the women come home in the evening, they are too tired to look after the children. This is bad when the children are small. The bigger ones try to help with the housework. Grandma says that we women are an 'Emergency Force'. Many women and girls sell their lovely long hair to provide money for the Fatherland. 100 grams of hair fetches 2 marks. The hair is used for military purposes.[1]

German civilians are paid for such contributions during this war. A Ministry for Ersatz Materials was set up in Berlin in 1914 to develop substitute materials for military production due to the shortages of raw materials and supplies inflicted by the British naval blockade. Piete herself seems no longer much interested in patriotic gestures but is increasingly drawn in a different direction.

7th August

The soldiers speak to me differently now because I wear full-length skirts and have my hair done up. Sometimes I am called upon to provide 'tea-time music' when my classmate's big sister invites a few lieutenants and their girlfriends for coffee.

---

1 During the First World War, human hair was used as substitute for rubber and leather belts in industrial machinery.

Yesterday I met a young air force officer on the stairs. He said hello and asked whether I was 'one of the party'. I said no. I was just the pianist. He laughed and said – 'Oh, that's a pity.' 'Why a pity?' I asked. But he just laughed and disappeared into the room.

Piete regularly corresponds with her mother who still lives apart from the rest of the family in Berlin. On 4th September 1916 she writes:

Darling Mummy! I no longer share most people's enthusiasm for war. I think about the dying soldiers, not just Germans, but also French, English, Russian, Italian, Serbian and I don't know who else. They might come home crippled. I'm worried that Willi will be called up one day. Have you enough bread to eat? We are all right but food is getting scarcer all the time.

*

While Piete has all but lost the patriotic fervour she had at the outset of the war, young German naval officer Johannes Spiess is enjoying the challenge of hunting enemy ships at sea. In 1916 his success is rewarded by an Iron Cross first class for taking U-9 into the heart of British waters, the Dogger Bank, and sinking Northward Ho, Coquet, Progress, Hector, Bob *and* Straton *and the steamers* Don *and* Queen Wilhelmina, *all in one day.*

In April 1916 America, affected by some of the sinkings by U-Boats, issues an ultimatum. If Germany does not scale down its indiscriminate attacks on shipping, America is likely to enter the war. Germany's resultant drawing back from all-out war at sea affects Johannes Spiess, recently promoted to captain and given charge of his own submarine, the old-fashioned and hard to manoeuvre U-19. In September 1916, he is sent on his first independent mission, this time to inflict damage on Russian merchant shipping in the Baltic Sea.

12th September 1916

An eventful day. As usual in this operations zone we submerged during the day and waited like a crocodile for our victim. At 2.30 p.m. the duty watch officer called me to the conning tower. There was a long convoy in sight.

'Both engines full speed ahead!' Intermittent glimpses through the periscope showed eight transports of different sizes steaming in a line, but in our haste we could not determine whether they were escorted or not. In great expectation, I stood on one foot and then on the other. Would we be too late?

Ten minutes after the first sighting, we were in attack position for the leading ship. It was a typical grey Russian steamer of 1,500 tons. I let this one pass, since a much larger ship with four masts was following on astern. At 2.41 the bow tube was fired with a torpedo set for a shallow run. 'Hard astarboard!' I shouted for a stern shot at the rear of the ship . . . Brmmmmmms . . . Hit!

When I got the periscope above water again, I saw the transports all lying criss-cross. I made a new approach and at 3 p.m. fired right past one of the steamers. Whether he avoided our torpedo after sighting the clearly visible track I don't know. Most enemy ships immediately took flight, though a few held their positions.

At 3.25 I had two ships in line dead ahead and fired. I could distinctly follow the track of the bubbles as one torpedo struck the damaged ship in the engine room, while the other one missed. This victim had number '28' on the side and was called 'Elizabeth' (4,444 tons).

Our U-Boat came up to the surface while turning, because our horizontal steering rudders did not function properly. Immediately, someone started firing at us. Shortly thereafter, I noticed the bow wave of a destroyer approaching us and we got out of his way by diving.

We observed the subsequent course of events from a safe

position. Number 28 sank deeper and deeper into the water until only smoke stacks, masts and bridges were above the surface, while its crew abandoned ship. At 7.52 a half-flotilla of destroyers came out in line and cruised around nearby on zigzag courses. This procedure is known as 'submarine chasing'. We were very pleased each time with their nice appearance, which did not disturb us at all. After fifteen and a half hours of submerged cruising we came to the surface in the dark to recharge our batteries. We took a photograph of the vessel with our new periscope photographing device.

It's a wonderful feeling when one has overcome all obstacles and feels like a pike in a fish pond. To this was added the sporting expectation of further naval success and the wonderful fresh air of a quiet summer evening.

*

Although German submarine attacks led by enthusiastic young officers like Johannes Spiess are successful in disrupting the flow of Allied supplies, they can do little to break the British blockade of Germany's own shores, the effect of which Piete Kuhr continues to record.

10th October

If only we had a bit more to eat! Bread and flour are so scarce, and it is no better with any other sort of food. There was a wonderful smell in the house recently when we came home from school. With a mysterious look on her face, Grandma placed a stewed bird with jacket potatoes on the table. It tasted wonderful. Grandma smiled when we'd eaten it all up: 'Guess what you have been eating!' 'A partridge!' cried Willi. 'A young pigeon!' I said. 'A crow,' said Grandma. 'A farmer from Colmar sold it to me.'

26th October

Yesterday a lieutenant in a pilot's uniform greeted me in Posener Strasse. I turned bright red. It was the young lieutenant I met on the stairs at my friend's sister's coffee party. He said: 'You are the young lady who plays the piano so nicely, aren't you?' Then he introduced himself: 'My name is Werner Waldecker and I come from Bielefeld.' I was struck dumb and just looked at him. I must have seemed utterly stupid. I never know what to say at times like this. I was so annoyed with myself afterwards, I could have died. It didn't seem to bother him, however. He smiled and said he would like to have an éclair with me sometime in Fliegner's. They have enormous éclairs at Fliegner's and the whipped cream tastes nearly as good as real cream.[1] We talked about flying and Lieutenant Waldecker told me that he flies a Fokker. When we parted he kissed my hand and asked whether he might hope to see me again. 'Not likely!' I said. 'Pity!' he said again with a little smile.

2nd November

All we ever do is eat turnips, or queue for bread so we can have mustard or marjoram sandwiches. All the bigger girls walk up and down Posener Strasse between four and five o'clock in the afternoon; they go 'courting' with the grammar-school boys and lieutenants. I must confess, dear diary, that Willi and I have started 'courting' too, and frankly we find it great fun. Yesterday I met Lieutenant Waldecker. He was walking arm-in-arm with two 'ladies'. He bowed politely and gave me a military salute. I nodded coolly; however, I went beetroot red again.

Piete and Willi manage to have fun even during what became known as the 'Turnip Winter' of 1916–17, the harshest of the war. As another wartime Christmas approaches, Germany is gripped by civilian discontent. Food riots spread across the country and morale deteriorates. Having toned down submarine warfare for fear of America's reaction to the sinking of neutral shipping, the German High Command now pins its hopes on a dramatic naval breakthrough.

---

1 While rationing applied to daily supplies, some luxury goods were available.

23rd December

The third war-time Christmas. German Admiralty wants to promote the so-called 'Total U-Boat War' round the whole world as
a giant protective fence against Allied attacks. No one talks about
peace any more. On Christmas Eve we shall have turnip and
potato purée with horsemeat balls and mustard sauce. Willi and
I fetch our mother from the station today. We've heated our place
as much as we could so that Mummy doesn't freeze. We've been
warming up her bed with hot water-bottles since this morning.

*Their mother's return is as thrilling an occasion as ever, though
much seems to have changed since last year.*

25th December

It seems that Mummy doesn't love me as much as she used to.
She asked me if I still kept up my war diary. I was afraid she
wanted to read it; then she would read all the nonsense about
Werner Waldecker. Luckily, she only said 'Hm!' I know my
mother has always loved Willi better than me, but I am
Grandma's favourite. We never talk about our love for each
other, but we know it in our hearts. Mummy thinks I have
become as thin as a rake, but who has not lost weight in this war?
Willi's legs are like sticks. We queue for one loaf of bread.

*Lieutenant Waldecker, the pilot Piete had last encountered three
months ago, is back in Schneidemühl after a tour of duty.*

19th February 1917

Greta Dalüge and Trude Jakobi called for me today to go skating.
I landed on my bottom and slid for at least three yards, when
someone shouted 'Hello, young lady!' and there he was, skating
up towards me – Lieutenant Werner Waldecker! 'I've had
enough, I want to go home.' I said. 'Oh no you don't, first we
have to go and have éclairs at Fliegner's!' It was nearly dark

when we got to Fliegner's. I suddenly felt incredibly happy. Lieutenant Waldecker found a corner table and hung my skates next to his. I told him about Mummy. I asked whether he liked being in the Flying Corps. He took one of my plaits in his hand and untwisted it a bit so that the hair fell between his fingers. 'Such wonderful hair! I should like to see it all undone. May I one day?' I said that I really must go home now. He brought me to the door of our house. In the hallway he was suddenly going to kiss me, but it struck me that all the lieutenants kiss the girls they take home. So I quickly said, 'Good-bye' and ran up the steps. Of course I wanted to let Lieutenant Waldecker kiss me. Very much so! I really was a goose – God, what a goose!

Lieutenant Waldecker will soon have to return to his unit, leaving Piete uncertain she will ever see him again.

*

Severe shortages at the front and civilian discontent at home threaten Germany's ability to sustain the war. From 1st February 1917 the German Admiralty lifts all restrictions on submarine warfare, first introduced in 1915 under pressure from the United States. Despite the implication that the United States may enter the war in retaliation, the German Government hopes success at sea will help it achieve a swift overall victory. Two days later, the United States severs relations with Germany and will eventually join the war on the Allied side. However, in the short term, the unrestricted U-Boat campaign is a success. In April 1917 Britain alone loses over 800,000 tons of shipping and British civilians are in turn forced to tighten their belts.

The lifting of all restrictions is welcome news for U-Boat Captain Johannes Spiess, who now returns to raid the North Sea. In May 1917, after several days waiting in ambush on an Allied shipping route between England and Norway, Spiess finally spots his prey.

It was practically dead calm, the sea was like a mirror and the cruising conditions very pleasant. They were steaming in a

perfect line: a manoeuvre which we had believed impossible for
merchant ships, particularly as they were of different sizes. Every
ten minutes the detachment changed course 20 degrees, following the movements of the leading ship. As a screen, four escort
vessels were disposed fan-shaped ahead, while two destroyers
zigzagged on the flanks.

I was compelled to show my periscope at times, to avoid the
danger of collision and observe the course of the convoy. For this
I stopped both engines and gave the order 'periscope out', until
it just broke the surface. With the help of the helmsman, I
grasped the periscope handle and gave a sharp turn for a quick
look all around. This required tremendous physical exertion;
although I took my coat off before starting, I broke out in such
profuse perspiration that I had to dry off afterwards.
Furthermore, the nervous strain was terrific.

The patrol had been successfully passed, and our U-19 now
had to prepare for firing. Shortly before the shot, the convoy
changed course. At 9.04 p.m. I had the target in my cross-hairs[1]
and was clear of the destroyer. I ordered: 'Second tube fire!' and
immediately thereafter: 'Dive quickly to extreme depth!'

While the U-19 was obeying its horizontal rudders, we listened for the torpedo explosion, but nothing happened. Damn,
missed. Then, suddenly: Brrrmmms! . . . An explosion shook
our whole boat. This was my first depth charge,[2] and I was
somewhat frightened. I only began breathing easier once the
report came from below: 'All clear in the boat.'

We listened apprehensively: would they drop any more of
these unpleasant things on our head? Had an oil slick been left
behind that would betray our presence on the surface? Exactly 15
minutes later another explosion occurred, this time considerably
further away from the boat.

---

1 Cross hairs are a marking inside a periscope, enabling the captain to aim at
   the target.
2 A depth charge was a highly explosive underwater bomb, designed by the
   British during the First World War to combat the U-Boats.

One hour later we very cautiously came up to periscope depth. It was rather dark. In the distance I saw the smoke clouds of the departing convoy. Too bad, it would have been so nice.

The game of cat and mouse at sea isn't as easy as it used to be due to the introduction of a convoy system for all Allied shipping: for protection merchant boats are now travelling in groups, flanked by fully armed battleships and destroyers.

*

Like Johannes Spiess, when the war at sea intensified in early 1917, twenty-year-old British officer Robert Goldrich was fast-tracked to First Lieutenant and given charge of his own vessel. Until now, the young midshipman had been waiting for promotion on board HMS Thunderer *in the Royal Naval Reserve. But for one day of excitement during the Battle of Jutland, Goldrich has had a quiet and pretty dull time waiting for big naval battles that fail to materialise.*

Now an officer in charge of the sloop Poppy, *Robert Goldrich deals with the daily U-Boat alerts in the North Sea. On 27th March 1917,* Poppy *sails out to rescue the crew of yet another U-Boat victim, SS* Holdgate. *He finds the perpetrator still loitering at the scene.*

27th March 1917

A ship reported having seen another fellow torpedoed off Shelligs', so proceed there at full speed. Sighted her at 10.30 a.m., steering all over the shop. A square hole about 20 feet by 16 lets in insufficient water to put her down by the head a bit. Sighted the crew in two lifeboats under sail and picked them up. While I was aft, 'Action' was sounded and I dived to the bridge to find a submarine panic on. I sighted the Fritz U-Boat 8,000 yards off, high up out of water. I did not see him soon enough and only got as far as 'Control', but did not get a round off. I was very sick about it, 'cos she must have been watching us. We noted her course and steamed full speed for a point over her and dropped a DC [depth charge], but without sending up the Fritz as we hoped.

Zigzagged in the vicinity of SS *Holdgate* waiting for assistance before trying to take her in tow. We towed her stern first until 9.15 when the tow parted. At 9.30 Clough said: 'She's going'. She appeared to me to break into three – the engine and boiler rooms sinking first and funnel going over the side.

We did our best for twenty-seven survivors amongst whom was a passenger whose 2nd 'Submarining' this was. The Fritz had taken the captain out of the lifeboat when it was a long way from the abandoned ship and then dived immediately.[1]

The survivors saw she [the U-Boat] was beautifully clean and looked as if she had just come off the docks. The three or four Huns were clad in a kind of khaki and were big-limbed fellows, clean-looking and well-fed. I expect they have just arrived if they were clean-shaven, 'cos I don't shave on this racket and I don't suppose they do!

28th March, Patrol

Just before midnight we had a panic and went to Action Stations. Moore saw an explosion and we headed towards it. I saw a track in the water going at a good speed and it seemed to me that the submarine 'shunted' right across our bow nut, a moment later I saw her again on the beam for about three seconds and so did Clough. I only got an impression of about 30 feet of smooth black hull in the water rushing by at a good speed.

The adversary Goldrich has glimpsed is not unlike the U-19 submarine commanded by Captain Johannes Spiess. Spiess's stubborn and persistent stalking of Allied convoys pays off handsomely once more on 24th May 1917.

During the afternoon smoke clouds were sighted. I made out three large steamers in a convoy, coming directly towards us without

---

1 British captain is taken away for interrogation, while the crew is left unscathed.

steering zigzag courses. I ordered a quick dive. I moved slowly to meet the convoy, turned sharply ahead of them on to a course for firing and was fortunate enough to arrive in position just as the flank destroyer turned away on its zigzag course. The sea was slightly ruffled so my periscope was not easily noticed. At 2.42 the stern tube was fired. I remained at periscope depth and was able to see a tremendous fountain of water rising majestically near the forward stack of the ship. 'Hit! Quick! Dive to greater depth!'

We heard the propeller noises of the destroyers approaching us at high speed on the surface, now the depth charges surely must follow. Yet all was quiet . . . nothing followed. The English were not in position.

The sinking of the steamer occupied about two hours, the surface of the water was strewn with parts of the wreckage.

Robert Goldrich and his crew aboard Poppy *have spent the summer of 1917 racing to the scenes of U-Boat attacks. All too often they arrive only in time to see the diving U-Boat and witness the slow sinking of its victim.*

21st July 1917

About 9.40 a.m. we were able to see a big submarine on the port bow of the merchant vessel, but she dived shortly afterwards, well before we were within range. After circling round the ship – which was on fire aft and had several large holes from gunfire – we stopped and picked up the survivors. The ship was meanwhile getting lower and lower and it was apparent that she was 'gone in'. At 10.30 a.m. she turned over on her portside and sank slowly, seeming to pause for a moment just below the surface, as though reluctant to leave the sunlight for the darkness of the deep sea. One of the first things to come to the surface was a kind of calcium light, which burnt vividly amongst the floating coal dust and wreckage like a funeral pyre on the surface of the water.

A remarkable point was the way her boats floated, right way up, as she left the surface for ever without a ripple. In the next twenty minutes wreckage kept coming to the surface, shooting high into the air before it fell. The crew, twenty-five souls in all, told us their tale. They were chased from about 4.30 a.m. until 7.30 a.m. by a submarine. The sub closed in and hit the *Romillies* several times after which the captain obeyed the Fritz's order to stop and abandon ship. The sub then fired about seventeen rounds at the *Romillies* at a range of about 300 yards. The sub came alongside the boat and took the captain prisoner. They then dived promptly and were seen no more. The submarine's crew were very dirty and vicious looking. Her captain was young and wore one stripe on his arm.

On 6th August 1917 Goldrich and his crew seem to have finally caught up with one of the elusive German U-Boats.

6th August

At 11.45 we had another stint. The blow MacIntyre hoisted the red flag and the Medina dropped a DC [depth charge] on what turned out to be a whale! The whale was injured and went 'bugs'. It caused very considerable excitement by leaping out of the water and seemed unable to dive. We passed within a quarter of a mile and I should estimate the length as 25–30 feet.

A few days after this false alert, Poppy *has a collision and goes ashore for maintenance when Robert gets a much-needed break. He had recently turned twenty-one and noted on his birthday: 'The health is good. The spirits are good and the powers of seduction are at a maximum.' A week later he is back home in London, determined to spend as much of his leave as he can in female company but first he visits his father.*

14th August, on leave

Hit London a bit late . . . Awakened the Old Man who was delighted to see me and had breakfast.

In the evening saw the 'Maid of the Mountains' [show] with Dad and Uncle Gem and after supper sallied forth and spent the night with a rather revolting wench.

15th August, Brighton

Dad rang up and as I was not there tumbled that I had been 'on the batter'. He said nix but thought a lot. Journeyed down to Brighton and met up with [the rest of] the family. In the evening had a look at the seafront, meeting one 'Nancy', a lady and a very finely built girl. Did her a good turn on the beach and so home to bed very well pleased with Brighton.

16th August, Brighton

Took the Old Lady and party out to tea as well as Marjorie's friend Margaret B. Had a fairly amusing p.m. with Margaret, a talented Yiddish girl but well chaperoned by a Mother of the Hindenburg type.

In the evening looked for Nancy but got hooked by an Old Cow of 40 or 400, or maybe more and was doomed to talk spiritualistic shit until midnight and even permitted to call tomorrow. That is the worst of attacking the eternal problem too sober.

17th August, Brighton

Called on the 'Old Cow' in Montpelier Rd in hopes of getting something else. Nix and developed so big a mould that was unable to clash successfully on that front.

18th August, Brighton

Determined not to be out-distanced by my hoodoo, I called on the Ramages for tea and took Eileen out to dinner and to a show at the Hip[1] called High Explosive. I dined well and got rather

---

1 Hippodrome Theatre.

'canned' before the bar closed, but had a fair to middling evening.

19th August, Brighton

Was introduced to Phyllis Monheman on the Pier and had the pleasure (?) of putting pennies in slot machines for the party and afterwards partaking of a somewhat rowdy tea. Tried to get a little honourable advancement from one Vera who turned out to be an 'ice maiden', so checked my hand in early.

20th August, Brighton

Telegraphed to Moore and to Clough to find out if there is any hope of an extension of leave. Took Mother to 'Pygmalion' on the West Pier this evening. I did not behave very well 'cos I spotted a female I had my eyes on yesterday and felt I was wasting the evening.

21st August, Brighton

On the pier this p.m. with Hunt and made arrangements to meet a rather charming girl at 7 p.m. to which end I equipped myself with a dozen 'sixpennies'. She failed me – damn her eyes! So I took a very nice girl to dinner and spent a respectable evening until 11 p.m. when I fell across a little damsel whose name I forget and retired to 75 Middle Street with her. It appears she is of decent parentage of Russian extraction and ran away from home with an army officer. He is in France and allots her the shekels. Only seventeen and a half, a very pretty kid with beautiful eyes and mouth and teeth and short (11″) black hair. A very worthy bedfellow!

After this eventful series of brief encounters during his leave, Lieutenant Goldrich returns to his ship on 1st September 1917.

*

In Schneidemühl, Piete Kuhr's romance with pilot Lieutenant Waldecker has a little more time to develop, as he returns from his most recent tour of duty.

8th September 1917

I have been out with Lieutenant Waldecker, Lieutenant Leverenz and my friend Trude in the forest. First we had coffee at the 'Little Castle in the Forest' and then we walked over the Sandweg to the village of Küddowtal and on to Königsblick. Werner Waldecker put his arm round my shoulders and gave me a quick kiss on the nose. I said nothing. Lieutenant Leverenz raised a warning finger and said in fun, 'Now then – she's underage!' But Lieutenant Waldecker drew me to one side, smiling, so for a time we were walking by ourselves. He kept bending forward and looking at me so lovingly. We held each other's hand. He kissed me in different places – my plaits, my forehead, my shoulder, every single finger of my left hand. By now we were deep in the forest of Königsblick. I suddenly stopped and whispered, 'Quiet! A deer!' Lieutenant Leverenz and Trude appeared; I couldn't believe they hadn't seen the deer. We returned home on the little railway between Königsblick and Schneidemühl. When we parted at the stairs to our house, Werner Waldecker whispered in my ear, 'I love you!' I looked at him but all I could say was, 'Thank you!' Then I jumped for joy.

10th September

I wonder whether the war has perhaps some meaning? Otherwise God wouldn't allow it to last so long. It has become a sort of permanent fixture; you can no longer remember properly what it was like in peace time. We hardly think about the war now. Nothing more is said about it at school, except perhaps when another friend or relative has been killed. What really interests us girls are the boys from the grammar school and of course the officers on Posener Strasse. Everyone is trying to get hold of food. We have new potatoes in the cellar. Some turnips too. Very little bread and fat, though.

There follows a big gap in Piete's diary. She resumes writing to share terrible news.

2nd December

When I entered the classroom, Greta Dalüge and Trude Jakobi were parting from each other. They had shocked faces and were quite embarrassed. I asked, 'What's the matter?' Trude Jakobi stammered, 'Don't you know? Werner Waldecker has crashed.' 'Dead?' 'Yes. Dead. He was going to go over to Bielefeld tomorrow. To his mother.' All she knew was that Waldecker had taken off from the airfield that morning and had crashed soon afterwards. I picture his face, his flashing eyes, the wisps of fair hair. Is all that shattered, broken to bits, smeared with blood, his skull in pieces? What am I to do now? How can I hide my feelings from all the people, from Grandma, Willi, Androwski, my friends?

Piete then writes nothing more significant in her journal until Christmas.

23rd December

I spend most of my free time queuing up at the shops. Grandma has sewn a piece of horse cloth into my coat as a lining. But she can't sew a lining into my shoes; I have chilblains on most of my toes. Well, never mind. At least we have a little Christmas tree. And wartime gingerbread, and macaroons. And on Christmas Eve there will be carp.

*

Over 2,000 British naval and merchant ships were torpedoed by U-Boats between 1914 and 1918. Overall, the Allies lost 11 million tons of shipping in the war at sea, of which 8 million tons was lost by the British. U-Boats accounted for 6.5 million tons of sunk British shipping, with the rest lost to mines and surface action. Despite the grave impact of submarine warfare on the British war economy, Germany's gamble on a swift naval victory did not pay off.

However, the British naval blockade was a strategic success. Food shortages in Germany became so acute that by the end of the war three-quarters of a million German civilians had died from starvation. Civilian discontent eventually resulted in strikes at home and naval mutinies at the front.

Both Johannes Spiess and Robert Goldrich continued to hunt and patrol at sea for the rest of the war. Robert Goldrich remained on the Poppy until the end of the war. In 1918 Johannes Spiess was awarded the 'Knight of the Hohenzollern House Order' and given charge of a brand-new luxury submarine, U-153. He was not to use it against the Allies, however. U-153's first and last target in this war were to be Germany's own mutinous ships during the Kiel naval mutiny in November 1918.

Chapter 12

IN CAPTIVITY

June 1916–August 1918

Over eight million men were incarcerated as prisoners of war in camps scattered across Europe and beyond, in Siberia, Turkey Mesopotamia and parts of Africa. More than half were taken prisoner on the Eastern Front. Although there were differences across the host nations in the mortality rates and conditions, all the major belligerents adhered to the provisions regulating the treatment of prisoners of war laid out in the 1907 Hague Convention, which stated that all prisoners of war had to be treated humanely. It also stipulated that the signatory countries should send relief to their imprisoned soldiers in the form of food parcels and clothing. While Austria-Hungary and Russia made modest provisions, Germany and Britain were more generous.

What made the most difference to the treatment of a POW was rank. At the time these differences were taken for granted and considered acceptable. According to an additional wartime agreement, an ordinary soldier was entitled to five square metres of space, one blanket, one sack filled with straw or wood shavings as well as bathing and laundry facilities. Captors were permitted to make soldiers work to pay for their own maintenance costs. An officer, on the other hand, was entitled to three times as much space and a list of

*comparative luxuries: a standard issue mattress, a pillow, a blanket,
a chair, a stool, a trunk, dishes, glasses, a hand towel and a bucket.
He was also allowed the service of an orderly to attend to his needs.
Unlike rank and file prisoners, officers were exempt from all manual
work and paid a monthly salary to be reimbursed by their own government after the war.*

*

*Twenty-eight-year-old British captain Douglas Lyall Grant, Duggie
to his friends and family, is captured and sent to an officers' camp in
Germany in 1916. A Londoner of Scottish parentage, ex-public
schoolboy, Lyall Grant has served in France since 1914 and in 1916 is
working as an embarkation officer in Boulogne. On 1st June 1916 his
first diary entry describes what happens when he sets off across the
Channel to return to his job in France after a few weeks' leave as the
only passenger on a small plane.*

2nd June 1916

All the best captives write a diary, so what more fitting than that
I should keep one. Whether it will be allowed or not remains to
be seen.

Well, little did I think on leaving home yesterday morning
that by seven I should be in German hands. For one reason and
another we were unable to leave Farnborough until after lunch,
when we set off in a 200 hp Rolls Royce, the pilot being one who
had never been to France before and whose career there as a free
man certainly proved to be a short one.

I enjoyed every moment of the flight across the Channel at
7,000 feet and in fourteen minutes. We passed over Boulogne
and I could distinctly see the Quai where the gods have apparently decreed that I shall work no more.

*The pilot loses his way. An hour later their plane comes under fire.
Thinking they are under attack from their own gunners, the pilot
dives to show he is also British but he dives so steeply that the engine
gives out.*

As we neared the ground I could see that he was making for a more or less clear field below. To reach this we had to avoid some telegraph poles but after crashing through the wires, when my face was saved by the gun mounted in front of me, we struck a post and turned to land upon our nose. I was thrown clear and escaped with a shaking, and got up cursing our gunners to receive the surprise of my life in finding ourselves surrounded by Boches.

Lyall Grant soon finds himself in the company of English-speaking German officers and he is taken off for some polite questioning at the local headquarters based in a French château. That evening he arrives in his barracks where he finds himself suddenly alone.

Today has been one of the hardest, a continual fight against depression. I never knew that a heart could be so heavy and it mustn't be carried on the sleeve. To my guards I appear the most cheery of mortals and greet them all in French, but to myself I'm in the depths of despair. Solitude was never pleasing to me, and when one has nothing to read, nothing to see, and nothing to do but think of 'this time a week ago!' and the like, it takes all one's time to keep back an ever-rising lump and I never realised before how nearly mental sickness could make one physically sick.

Duggie Lyall Grant continues to fight the onset of depression over the following week as he waits for his transfer to a camp in Germany to bring him into contact with fellow officers once more.

*

French officer Victor Guilhem-Ducleon went into hiding with five of his men when their regiment was overrun during heavy fighting in Belgium three weeks into the war. They found refuge with a Belgian family in the German occupied village of Graide. The six men hide in an old mine shaft under the family's pigsty, nine square metres of underground space with two small openings letting in some daylight. They are occasionally able to visit the family at home using a specially dug tunnel. Its exit, disguised by a sheet of metal covered

Douglas Lyall Grant

with a layer of turf, is by the family's back door. Four years into his self-imposed captivity, Victor Guilhem-Ducleon starts keeping a diary in which he is careful not to name the family for fear of reprisals.

30th June 1918

My mind is going numb. I write to try to curb the numbness. Admittedly, I live like an animal here, but until now (except for the first year) I had managed to cope with it. Now though, I can feel myself sinking slowly. How can I pull myself out of it again? Well! I'm going to try to get into the habit of writing a few lines in this notebook every day. Thus, I will force myself to do some thinking in order to cover a bit of paper with ink. So I get started. Why didn't I do this earlier? Because I worry that a detailed diary would only serve to expose the people who have helped me.

And who do I address it to? Oh! No need to think about it: it is to you my dear wife and to you my dear parents that I am going to write. This way, every day I will come alive a little in your company. In fact, I already do: every morning and evening; and I think of you quite often during the day too. From now on, I will write down what is on my mind.

For the last few days, our food rations have been somewhat reduced. We eat what we have and that's not much. Still, this morning we had apples, soup, salad and a little (oh! So very little) slice of bread. It must be said this is more than we had during the best winter days. Even so, we complained that there wasn't enough to eat. The force of habit! You will probably remember that people used to accuse me of being a fusspot. Is that what I was like, dear parents? If I think about it, I do believe that this nasty side of my personality has grown. Here, I have my little routine: at this time, I do this, at that time, I do that. If I am disturbed, I bear a grudge against the intruder for some time. I must stop all this moaning.

In the absence of any external routine, Victor Guilhem-Ducleon creates one and imposes it on his five soldiers in an attempt to keep them all sane. He learns some new crafts from their host family and occupies the men with activities from hairdressing and knitting to carpentry and shoe repairs.

*

Over the border in German Westphalia near the village of Gütersloh is a transit centre for officers to which Duggie Lyall Grant is transferred after his capture. Duggie slips into the daily schedule with relative ease.

11th June 1916

I have, as usual, landed on my feet and am in a room with excellent fellows who have invited me to join a mess that they have with one or two others as the weekly ration here would only last an ordinary being for a day and living on it is out of the question.

12th June

I've spent most of the day looking round and in the afternoon had a game of soccer by way of a little exercise. It is very like being back at school again. Everyone, all nationalities, messes in the same building and all meals are run in two relays, but we act more or less on our own. Instead of breakfasting at 7.15 we get up at 8.00, attend roll call at 8.30, and then four of us breakfast quietly in the restaurant at 9.15. We're supposed to lunch at 11.30, but stroll in at 1.00 and have a light lunch from the food parcels of the members of the mess, all of which are pooled. Tea is taken in the restaurant at 4.30 except on Sundays and Wednesdays when we tea in our room, and dinner at 7.30 chiefly consisting of parcel contents again. Lights are out at 10.30 but silence does not necessarily reign! We are allowed one hot bath per week.

14th June

I must say that this camp has come as a very pleasant surprise to me, being infinitely more comfortable than I had anticipated. This afternoon I played my first game of hockey, and at night I was invited to pay a visit to the Russian quarters by some Russian Guards officers that I've got to know. This is usually a dangerous undertaking as their capacity for strange mixtures is enormous, but I had been warned and tasted warily. They are good fellows and those who don't speak English speak French. Most of their names appear to end in '-off'. They also appear to be all musical and all good artists. In fact there is an abundance of talent of all sorts in this camp.

16th June

The sale of all wine and beer has been stopped for a week because yesterday somebody succeeded in getting an Austrian flag and hoisted it half-mast to the great sickness of the Boche.

18th June

Being Sunday foreign languages were given a miss[1] and in the morning I attended a church service held in a loft and taken by a Canadian padre. A German was present to see that the time was not utilised in making preparations for escape. The whole place is surrounded by two fences of barbed wire, but I do not think these would prove difficult to escape.

Duggie Lyall Grant never seriously considers escaping himself but records the frequent attempts, both foiled and successful, made by his fellow officers. Relatively comfortable in his new surroundings, Duggie never mentions any desire to resume fighting.

20th June

The chief event today was the removal of the ban on wine and beer, and to celebrate the occasion, coupled with the fact that tomorrow will be the anniversary of my wedding, our room gave a 'beer'. This takes the place of giving a dinner here and one asks just a select few to discuss the affairs of nations and sing a song or two.

1st July

Dominion Day, which was celebrated by the Canadians by a game of baseball in the morning and a dinner at night, both

---

1 Officers taught each other foreign languages in classes held in the camp.

very noisy entertainments. The French lesson got a miss for tennis and in the afternoon I watched our Hockey Team defeat the Russians' 1st by 15–12, the 12 being their handicap.

3rd July

This afternoon, in the company of thirty-nine others, I went for a walk. This is a new idea, mutual arrangement between British, French and German Governments, by which officers give their parole not to escape while out walking, and in return no guard is sent with them but only one man as a guide. We have parole cards which we sign and give up on our return. We go out in batches of forty twice a week. The crops looked to be good but we saw practically no men and certainly no young ones, while the ladies of the district must be noted more for their rotundity than their beauty.

*

It is only in his mind that Victor Guilhem-Ducleon can be transported beyond the walls of his confinement. His companions are now getting on so badly that two of them will not talk to the other three.

2nd July 1918

It pains me not to be able to serve my dear country when so many others are selflessly giving their lives for her. In addition, I am surrounded by people who do not understand me and with whom I have to battle constantly. Oh! What terrible days these are! Horrible nights when I dream I am back in the family home and all the chairs are empty. I imagine all kinds of suffering.

We must be brave Mum, be brave, Anick.

Victor married Anick three months before the outbreak of war so they have spent most of their married life apart.

4th July

Whenever I think of my family, of my parents and parents-in-law, I almost invariably picture them sitting at the dinner table. I enjoyed my food then, but it's not the gastronomic pleasure that I remember, even though I am totally deprived of it. No, it seems to me that it was only around the table that our families gathered together; we chatted and shared the day's news. I still have these family scenes in my mind: Mum serving everyone, Dad pouring the wine. I can always picture Dad savouring the cheese, then rolling his cigarette. And you, my dear friend, you were there, next to me. Alas! It all seems so far away.

5th July

Today is my birthday. What a sad day! All I can think about is everybody over there and particularly of Mum and Dad. My poor parents, this 5th July used to be cause for celebration. Now you have tears in your eyes when you think of me, your son who is so far away and you have no news of him whatsoever.

7th July

For two days now, I have had an additional problem, or rather an old one that has got worse. Our stomachs are almost empty and this brings with it a kind of craziness, which increases my unhappiness a great deal. We have abandoned trench warfare to fight in 'no man's land', territory under no one's control. The result is constant skirmishes. We argue endlessly. Luckily we exchange only words. We have yet to resort to physical violence, but I am far from being above that.

I have some depressing observations about Man. He is best studied when under pressure and it seems to me, and I say so with great sadness, that three-quarters of a man is his stomach and that all his higher faculties can be measured by the fullness or otherwise of his stomach.

8th July

Gloomy day, but I have managed to do quite a bit of work. I'm sure you must remember that I never liked anyone 'rummaging through' my things. I always complained when my corner of the attic was tidied up. I am still the same. Everybody here just helps himself to my tools, my books I've been lent and sometimes even to what little tobacco I have. This infuriates me. They could just ask me for things if they want them. Politeness simply does not exist here.

10th July

I have just realised, my poor friends, that this diary is full of complaints. Nevertheless, reading this will make you realise that I have accepted my lot and that there is courage in me still. Can these lines help me bear all my sorrows? Sometimes you need a sympathetic ear. As none is available, this diary will have to do just as well.

11th July

I must thank you, my dear parents, for teaching me to use my hands when I was young. How terrible my life here would be without any work! Dividing my time between manual work and reading helps the time to pass more easily. Yes, a thousand thank yous for teaching me not to be too clumsy.

*

For Duggie Lyall Grant, six weeks into his captivity, a new sporting season begins.

10th July 1916

Cricket started today.

11th July

Very stiff after yesterday's bowling, but put in two hours work on the new tennis courts and an hour at the nets.

12th July

We have now been forbidden to shout at football matches, which is sad as half the fun is the barracking. The reason given is that the people of Gütersloh complained that it was not seemly while Germany was passing through such a trying time! They apparently fail to recognise that from a life and death point of view Britain is also having her share of trials, but anyhow, as the village is two miles away it must have been 'some' shouting.

14th July

This being a French fête no one did any work. The Boche had told the French that they were not to celebrate it, with the result that they did so to a man, ably assisted by many of their allies. They started off with the 'Marseillaise' at morning 'appel' and from that minute never looked back. Most of them lunched in the restaurant and all the allied national anthems were sung frequently and loving speeches freely exchanged. I made one in French!!

*

On the same day two years later the French fête has a detrimental effect on Victor Guilhem-Ducleon, stuck as he is in Graide.

14th July 1918

Today is the 'fête nationale' in France. Alas, I so wish I was on the other side of the front line! If I were on my own I would get myself captured and thus get out of this thieves' den without anyone having to bear the consequences – but there are several of us. What would happen? We have to carry on as before. God! Dear God! Get me out of here.

15th July

Of all the deprivations, of the bodily and spiritual hardships, none can equal the absence of the person you hold dearest. Having no information whatsoever, not knowing where you are or what situation you are in, not being able to communicate, even by mail: all this makes for unbearable suffering. It is the same for you, my dear friend, with the added burden of knowing that I am in a dangerous situation and of being surrounded with objects that are reminiscent of our old life. Your sorrow is then deeper than mine, but be brave, Anick, and have faith in God's mercy.

*

Duggie Lyall Grant, who is also married, is allowed to write two let-ters and four postcards a month.

20th July 1916

Received my first letter from home. Tremendous joy.

29th July

Hot and dusty and another day of loafing. On 'appel' the Boche reminded us that we were POWs and under martial law. Why I don't know, as we were hardly likely to forget it with two rows of barbed wire and a string of sentries all around.

2nd August

In the morning our mess had two Russians to breakfast. The meal provided by the Germans consisted of one thin slice of black bread and some washy coffee. Our menu for our guests was fruit and cream, porridge, fish, sausages, bacon, tomatoes, various potted meats and game, toast, butter, jam and mar-malade – all from parcels of course.

*

Alexei Zyikov, a Russian soldier from Moscow, was captured in Russian Poland in 1915 and is now held in Marienburg POW camp in north-eastern Germany. In common with most Russian prisoners, he receives no food parcels from his government. In January 1916, eleven months into his captivity, Alexei writes the first of his irreg-ular diary entries.

27th January 1916

Hunger does not give you a moment's peace and you are always dreaming of bread: good Russian bread! There is consternation in my soul when I watch people hurling themselves after a piece of bread and a spoonful of soup. We have to work pretty hard too, to the shouts and beatings of the guards, the mocking of the German public. We work from dawn till dusk, sweat mingling with blood; we curse the blows of the rifle butts; I find myself thinking about ending it all, such are the torments of my life in captivity!

On Sunday we did no work but stood around outside our huts under the gaze of the Germans with their wives and children, full of curiosity and hate watching us from their windows and from the street. And, it was wonderful, they could see that we were people too and they began to come a little closer. But then some of the little German children began hurling stones at us. We complained to our escort. But he only laughed, and I thought, is it just that Germans are cruel?

If someone had said to me, 'One day you're going to eat soup made from dirty potatoes', or 'You're going to fight over a swede', I would have said 'What nonsense!' But nothing surprises me here – like today, I saw a soldier rummaging in a rubbish pit, picking out potato and swede peelings and eating them slowly to make them last. The hunger is dreadful: you feel it constantly, day and night. You have to forget who you once were and what you've become.

Our people resent the fact that the French, Belgians and English live so well and are not forced to work. They don't go about hungry like we do. They boast to us that their governments send them bread and parcels from home. But we, Russians, get nothing: our punishment for fighting badly. Or, perhaps, Mother Russia has forgotten about us.

Dear God, it is so bitterly shameful and offensive watching Russian soldiers scramble after scraps. When they begin shoving and fighting over them, the guards just point at them, laugh and say 'That's a Rus for you! Ivan eats whatever he's thrown!' But what can you do? How can you force your stomach not to ask for food? If only they fed us a little better. There's no way we can survive on this watery stuff. Water in the morning, water at lunch and dinner, and half a piece of bread a day. No sugar and no tea.

28th January

We have become very skilled at finding things to eat here, even if we have to take a beating to pay for them. The Belgians won't eat their rations if they've gone bad and they're forbidden to give them to other prisoners, but some of our lads manage to sneak through the barbed wire and get some of their bread from them. It's fine if the Germans don't notice. But if they spot you, you're done for. They beat you about the face and back till you're bruised and no longer feel hungry. Then there are those of us who eat potato peel: they take it out of the pit, wash it and boil it, eat it and say how delicious it is. Some consider it the greatest happiness to snatch food from the tub where the Germans throw their leftovers. There's such a crush to get these scraps! But this is how we survive the hunger and just about manage to stay on our feet. Such is our life here in Germany. The Germans look on and laugh while we endure it in silence. There is no one to complain to.

Russian prisoners in a German POW camp

5th February

We are woken at 4 a.m. have our breakfast and go to work. We demolish houses, churches and cemeteries to dig new quarries with rich deposits of iron ore. They make money from the mines so they put us to work, removing corpses from their resting places and displacing people from their homes. The work is very hard: you shovel the ore on to little carts, drive a pick axe through it and so on day in, day out, your legs and arms get very tired. Get back from work, have dinner and go to sleep.

8th February

We have been prisoners for a year now and nothing good has come from this time in captivity.

*

The Russian officers in Duggie Lyall Grant's camp enjoy a privileged life in captivity which bears little resemblance to the wartime experience of Zyikov or their sorely tested compatriots back home.

7th August 1916

Tennis today with two Russians, one of whom owns a little place in Russia, about half the size of France, and wants me to go there after the war for some bear hunting. He also says that he is coming to England to see me – I'll be able to show him round the back garden!

Soon afterwards Lyall Grant is moved to Crefeld Camp north of Düsseldorf, thirty miles from the Dutch border. He compares the two camps on arrival.

26th August

On the whole I put my money on Gütersloh, principally because of the games. Here one can only get tennis and fives, but the latter club is full, with a big waiting list. There are some fifteen tennis courts so one can play more than at the other camp. There is a loft which is used as a gym and where single-sticks and fencing can be pursued, and now a boxing class has been started which I intend joining.

The food here is very much better and there is one large dining hall and two smaller ones, also better, but there is nothing that really takes the place of the Gütersloh restaurant. There is a bar and a small room with a coffee bar where one is waited upon by two buxom damsels. The dry canteen is far and away better and things not on sale there can be ordered from the town.

Last but not least the Germans here are far and away nicer that those we have just left, all obliging and polite, and everyone agrees that the commandant is one of the best. Summing up, one might say that if one is keen on exercise and games, go to Gütersloh; if not, then come here. Personally give me London.

*

In his underground refuge Victor Guilhem-Ducleon draws his own conclusions about the way he reacts to his present circumstances.

26th August 1918

Some people always seem to have a smile on their face and manage to make light of their troubles. Others always look as if they have a heavy weight on their shoulders. I think I am one of the latter.

1st September

For the second time in a few days someone told me that I have got terribly thin. Why is this? There are so many possible causes I do not know which one to blame. Is this the end? If it is, then I ask you, God, to forgive my sins and to lessen the suffering of those whom I hold dear, my family and my country.

*

Duggie Lyall Grant, well fed on parcels from home, approaches the final rehearsal for his part in the Crefeld show.

9th October 1916

Started very violent exercise today, chiefly with a view to reducing my figure. It consisted of boxing, skipping, dancing and lying on my back waving my legs in the air. It remains to be seen what the result will be, probably more stoutness.

23rd October

The first night of the show and apparently I made the other artists laugh too much as I was told that I must only spread myself at certain periods. The whole thing went well.

28th October

The last night proved to be a howling success. It was attended by the camp commandant and one Erasmus, who is a doctor of the Kaiser's. I caused huge joy by making a wooden parrot lay an egg, which, when I squeezed it, burst and proved to be full of flour.

Three months on and Lyall Grant is still at Crefeld. In the camp at large there are an increasing number of escape bids, many of them successful.

28th January 1917

Renewed joy in the morning when it was discovered that two Russians had escaped last night. We wish them all the best of luck and a rapid journey over the frontier. The method of their escape was particularly cunning. Each day Russian orderlies wheel out barrels of refuse to a ground nearby where the pigs are kept. Today two of these barrels had refuse on the top but Russians underneath.

*

For Alexei Zyikov there is little chance of escape. This too is a privilege largely reserved for officers with more time on their hands.

11th April 1916

It is Easter Day. We got up at 7, washed, sang our prayers and sat down to break our fast. What with? With the following – two days before Easter, we were sent one loaf of bread each and an eighth of tobacco, on top of that after a great deal of effort we procured one egg and a bottle of beer each, at 20 pfennigs a piece. I am bored, sad and depressed. We ate up our food and I thought of my family and friends, breaking their fast on this Holy Day. Are they thinking of me? My thoughts are with them every minute of every day.

18th April

The Easter week passed and we were saddened to have to work all the way through it. Everyone is getting letters from Russia, except me. I did get one letter and that made me much happier. I can't help thinking all my loved ones have died. Or perhaps they are just too busy to write? Maybe I really have no mother or father and am now a poor orphan? I look round at the other prisoners: one's got a letter from his wife and children, another has one from his parents and siblings and I haven't received any-thing from anyone. Why did I lead such a debauched life? Why did I not cherish my family and friends? I don't know. I loved adventure and now I am paying for it. I feel very sad. Must I really die like this, fruitlessly, with nothing worth repenting of?

*

Duggie Lyall Grant has now been in captivity for exactly eight months.

1st February 1917

Eight months today. One of the recent arrivals confided to a serious-looking prisoner that he was sure that everyone here was mad because they were always laughing and apparently didn't realise that there was a war going on! Perhaps, though, we are mad.

Duggie Lyall Grant spent another year in two further camps before his release. Under a new agreement for the repatriation of long-serving prisoners, in April 1918 he managed to get himself and his diary out. The diary made it across the border to neutral Holland sewn into the waistband of his kilt and the rest hidden in the bag of his bagpipes. He did not resume writing it after his transfer to Holland where he sits out the rest of the war.

Victor Guilhem-Ducleon would wait patiently in Graide for liberation.

Alexei Zyikov made increasingly rare entries in his diary which stopped altogether in 1917. Perhaps he succumbed to starvation or disease like many thousands of POWs or maybe he took his own life, a way out he had already contemplated in his diary. No one knows what became of him. The diary itself was found by a Russian soldier in Germany during the Second World War.

Chapter 13

THE BROWN SHIRT AND
THE RED COMMISSAR

March 1916–March 1918

By the beginning of 1916 the Eastern Front had stabilised to Germany's advantage after the chaotic Russian retreat of the preceding summer. By the time the Central Powers stopped advancing in September 1915, the Russian army was reduced to a third of its fighting strength and Lithuania, Russian Poland, parts of Belarus and the Ukraine were under German occupation. Inside Russia unrest grew among soldiers and civilians alike with desertions and malingering at the front and strikes and food riots at home. In reaction to the crisis, Tsar Nicholas II assumed supreme command of the army and moved to the military headquarters in rural Russia. This move left the Tsarina and her confidant Grigory Rasputin to wield their influence in Petrograd. Political and bureaucratic chaos ensued. Meanwhile at the front, the ranks of the army had to be replenished if Russia was to launch any further offensives.

The German Chief of the General Staff, Erich von Falkenhayn, asserted: 'The Russian Army has been so weakened by the blows it has suffered that Russia need not be seriously considered a danger in the foreseeable future.' Free to concentrate on the Western Front, he launched his bid for victory with the Battle of Verdun in February 1916. By mid-March the battle remained inconclusive and Kaiser

Wilhelm grew pessimistic, saying 'One must never utter it, nor shall I admit it to Falkenhayn, but this war will not end with a great victory.' Public morale deteriorated as economic hardships grew and the long promised victory failed to materialise.

*

Two future adherents of Nazism and Communism keep a record of their wartime experience. One, Rudolf Hess, is a founding member of the National Socialist Party in 1920, the other, Dimitry Oskin, will join the Bolsheviks and become a Red Commissar after the Russian Revolution. During the war both are keen soldiers with high aspirations. Meanwhile Russian soldier Vasily Mishnin remains neither keen nor ambitious. He is still working as a clerk at a field hospital behind the front line.

Rudolf Hess volunteered enthusiastically for military service in August 1914 and joins the 1st Bavarian Infantry Regiment. After some basic training he is sent to Hardicourt, near the Somme. The following year he spends a few months at an officer's training course back in Germany but otherwise remains on the Western Front. Rudolf corresponds regularly with his parents in the small town of Reicholdsgrün, in the Fichtel mountains north of Munich. His patriotic mother, Klara, responds with equal regularity to these letters. In March 1916 Rudolf is in a local field hospital, sick with a cold after his latest tour of front-line duty in the Artois. Klara writes to him while on a visit to the local city of Gera.

20th March 1916, Gera

Dear Rudi,

What should we believe now? The city air seems to breed more pessimism than our fresh mountain air. They won't manage to change my mood though and I have a cheery certainty in our victory; slowly but surely we will progress.

   Your Mother

21st March

Dear Rudi,

Many thanks for your card. I am particularly pleased that your words show so much faith in our success. That is what I feel, despite all the defeatists who do not believe in our progress I remain rock steady.

Your Mother

30th March

Dear Mother,

Thank you for your dear words. It is really comforting to know that at least you have as much faith in these matters as we do out here. Back home (in Germany) people are complaining about days without meat. Here they only get meat every two weeks. They live off rice, potatoes and bits of salami. Grass cuttings are cooked as a vegetable. We could go without so much more before we have to live like this. And this is all nothing compared to what the soldiers are going through. Oh, they don't know what a sin they are committing, these beer table gossippers and whingeing coffee sippers! They should be silent. We have to keep fighting back home and in the field. The people here at the front are having a much worse time of it and they are not starving. Warm greetings to you, father and Gretel,

Your son Rudi

While still recuperating, Rudolf writes home about an incident which distracts him from the hospital routine.

21st March 1916, Western Front

Dear parents,

There is a medical orderly here, an elderly man, who says he can tell your character from the shape of your skull. After feeling my head he concluded the following:

Good sense of colour, particularly colours in nature; great

love of nature in general. I spend as much time outdoors as I can and do a lot of sport (true).

Good at maths, technology, not so good at languages (true, according to my school reports).

Sense of place. Find my way around an unfamiliar town quickly (not true, at least not in towns, true in the countryside).

Good humoured, gentle, great sympathy for animals. (true) I can get worked up about the smallest canary locked up in a cage.

Very sharp and quick to grasp things (true). (Recently I was on a machine gun course, I understood everything long before the officers and sergeants. The artillery course was the same.)

Suited to military life. Trustworthy.

Good judgement. Good at comparing and evaluating things. (true)

Religious but without adhering a particular creed or form of worship, like going to church. (true!)

Everyone I have told about this is astonished.

Rudi

12th April, Reicholdsgrün

Dear Rudi,

Your cousin, Rudi Münch, has finally been made an officer, so there is great rejoicing in the family. We even drank the new wine in honour of the occasion. We are very sorry that you are still waiting to become an officer. But there is still enough time for that later, your rest in the hospital must come first. Does it really take that long to recover from a cold? You must be more poorly than you have let on.

Mother

After weeks in hospital Hess finally returns to normal duty in time for his regiment to be sent to Verdun. At last, he is participating in a major battle.

15th June, Bad Homburg

Dear Parents,

None of us thought I'd be back in Germany so quickly. I hadn't been in the trench for five minutes when I received my wound. I was furious of course. I have been waiting to join an attack since the beginning of the war. That's the only reason I went into the infantry. When I finally see some action, after enduring all that artillery fire, I get wounded. People are saying it was the finest moment of their whole war. We moved forward 700 metres. My wound is not serious and it doesn't hurt.

23rd June

Dear Parents,

I made inquiries about my transfer to a military hospital today. They said it was unlikely to get approved because my injuries are so minor. Needless to say, I would really like to come home. Anyway, I'll tell you how I got injured. We arrived at the trench. Some artillery shots were falling short [into our own lines]. We normally use flares of a certain colour to signal a shortfall, so I ran to the shelter to fetch a flare-gun and fire some off immediately, so that the artillery would realise their silly mistake. I'd almost reached the shelter when there was a tremendous thump. Another of our 21 centimetre shells had landed beside me in the trench, filling the air with earth and smoke. I felt two sharp blows to my hand and upper arm. I'd been hit by shrapnel. At first I thought I was more seriously wounded, but then I realised that it was only my arm. I sat down in a dugout and took off my coat to inspect the damage. A man from my platoon came to help me. I could move my arm and fingers, so my bones and tendons were all right. The man, a big country lad, patched me up with bandages that we all carry in our packs, which are nice and clean. I was wondering whether I could still take part in the attack, when I suddenly felt dizzy and realised that by the time the battle began, which was still five hours away, I would be too weak. So I rested for a while then went back to the rear with two other wounded men. I was overjoyed to get my post, including your parcel of milk and socks.

*

Future Bolshevik Commissar Dmitry Oskin is a young Russian peasant quickly promoted from soldier to officer as most of the Russian career officers are dead or out of action by early 1915. Dmitry comes from the village of Yepifan in the Tula region south of Moscow. A year before the war broke out, aged twenty-one, he volunteered for service in the infantry. By June 1915 Dmitry Oskin is in command of his own platoon. His division is caught up in the rapid Russian retreat from the German and Austro-Hungarian forces who have just retaken Przemyśl in Galicia. They have taken Austrian prisoners and Dmitry orders one of his men, Poliakov, to examine their belongings. The poorly equipped Russians are in need of any booty. They are in luck, as Oskin records.

June 1915

After subjecting a prisoner's flask to a thorough inspection, Poliakov found it contained not water, but rum. All of the Austrians' flasks were immediately confiscated and brought to me. I gave each of my soldiers a swig of rum, like a 'benevolent commander'. I didn't forget our warrant officer Khanchev either, I sent a full flask up to his dugout. After a stiff drink, my soldiers were in a heroic mood. 'If only the Austrians would advance,' they kept saying. Their wish was soon granted: I was handing out the last of the rum when a new Austrian line appeared in front of our trenches. Poliakov, Tartar Gabidullin and many others dashed at the Austrians without even waiting for my command. I noticed, however, that they focused mainly on enemy soldiers who had these by now very familiar flasks slung over their shoulders. Those taken from our new prisoners were all brought to me. I shared them out in cupfuls amongst the soldiers and sent another flask up to Khanchev in his dugout.

A break allowed us to finish off the rum we had seized in the battle. However, after all the excitement it made me sleepy. I wanted to stretch my legs. Fighting off the drowsiness, I set off to see Khanchev, thinking to myself that he would probably still have a small supply of rum left from the two flasks I had sent him. Instead of going through the trench as usual, I took a short cut, straight across the field.

I had not gone ten paces when someone hit me very hard on my knee, with what felt like a truncheon. I looked round in alarm, but there was no one to be seen. I then realised that I'd been hit by a bullet. Then my right leg went from under me. I tried to keep going forwards but collapsed into a trench instead.

A medical orderly was called to take a look. He said a bullet had gone through my knee. The pain was bearable, but my whole leg was going somewhat numb. The orderly bandaged it up. I fell asleep from exhaustion or perhaps from all the rum I had drunk.

Dmitry spends July in a Moscow hospital while his leg heals. A year on, in the summer of 1916, he takes part in one of the offensives made at the same time as Anglo-French offensives on the Somme. The plan is to pull the Central Powers in different directions and though the main offensive takes place to the north with little discernible gain, in Dmitry's sector the Russian attack is overwhelmingly successful. It will become known as the Brusilov Offensive after its overall commander, General Brusilov. In forty-eight hours the Russian troops break through fifty miles of the Austro-Hungarian line. Dmitry describes his part in the subsequent fighting.

July 1916

Right on top of the Austrian trenches. Scattered machine-gun fire whizzing all around, shells fall like hailstones. We dive for cover. My soldiers are losing their nerve. Some are trying to retreat. I have to threaten a few flinching cowards with my gun. After about an hour, the shooting subsides. Seizing our chance opportunity, we race towards the barbed wire at full tilt. Luckily, there are some holes in it.

During the night of 13 July we receive the order to advance again. Bloody idiots. The Austrians will have reinforced their positions by now.

This time we met fierce resistance. For the first time in this whole war, there was a bayonet fight in our trenches. The Austrians fought tenaciously. Our soldiers, too, attacked the Austrians in a frenzy until they retreated into the forest, where it wasn't so easy for us to use our bayonets. The battle became so vicious that our soldiers started using spades to split Austrians' skulls. This hand-to-hand fighting went on for at least two hours. Only nightfall stopped the butchery.

At dawn, seeing no movement from the Austrian side, we began to survey the forest cautiously. A horrific scene emerged before our very eyes: piles of Russian corpses in front of our trenches, and just as many Austrian dead behind them.

*

The Brusilov Offensive continues but by the end of August reaches the limits of its westward advance into Austria-Hungary.

Meanwhile Russian Poland remains firmly under German control. So much so that before the end of the year Germany will declare Poland a kingdom with Warsaw as its capital, albeit without granting it any political independence. Vasily Mishnin, whose impeccable handwriting secured him a job as a clerk and rescued him from his terror of front line duty, is still working at the field hospital. Pushed back from Warsaw in the headlong retreat of the previous summer, the hospital is with Russian troops in Belarus. War weary and dejected, Vasily continues to write his diary making frequent references to his wife, Nyura, and young son, Vasily, whom he longs to rejoin back home in Penza.

13th October 1916, Steberaki Village

I finally got a letter from Nyura today. I was madly happy. My hands were shaking. But as soon as I read it I felt like my whole head was on fire. Shurka and my two young cousins have all been taken to the front. What can we do, when will all this end? They keep sending more and more people to the front.

14th October

I feel sad. The young lads are dancing and playing the harmonica while I sit here on my own. For me there's no joy, no happiness in anything, only Nyura's letters bring relief. The officers are partying like crazy and their festivities often end in a fight.

19th October

I got up early this morning and washed all my underwear and pillowcases. I know the ropes now, and I'm quick about it. I have to look after myself, or God knows what I'll turn into.

I went out into the field at night. It was so quiet and warm I wanted to shout out to the whole world – enough blood! But what am I worth, and what are we all worth? My head full of this, tears poured from my eyes.

A week later Vasily is preparing to go home on leave.

27th October

We sold our trousers today, my mate Ostry and I, for two roubles seventy-five kopeks. We need money for the road. Our bosses are jolly again today, drinking wine. I don't know why they are so cheerful. I can't sleep. All I can do is think about home.

30th October

At 5 a.m. I found a good space in the train's mail carriage. At 5.20 we're off. The third bell is sounding as I write these words. My heart is beating so – and we're off. I feel as if I am nearly home, this train goes directly to Penza. We pass Tula in the evening and Ryazhsk at night.

Vasily Mishnin on leave

31st October

At 9.30 in the morning I am back in Penza. I hire a horse and cart for one rouble and two minutes later I am with my family. We can't stop crying. All is well at home and my son is growing well, praised be the Lord. I spent all day at home. I am so happy I cannot describe it in words.

1st November

I wake up in the morning and I feel such joy in my heart. My son is already at me: 'Daddy, get up!' I spent all day at home playing with Vasya.

3rd November

A holiday, the Day of Our Lady of Kazan. I sleep in. Nyura has been up for ages, all the pies are ready and we have tea.

13th November

What a beautiful life, what joy, as if there was no war. I get up late, I make toys for Vasyusha out of boxes.

I feel merry and content, I want to talk about it all, but I've no words for it. I persuade Nyura to go and see the dentist, because she is suffering so much, my dear one.

24th November

The day of parting. The last day is gone and I get ready to go where no one's waiting for me, where nobody wants me, where I am a stranger. Nyura is crying and I can't talk enough to my sonny-boy. And time is running out fast.

4th December

It's a clear day and there's a good frost, but my heart is cold. How could I not be worried and anxious after reading the letter I received from Nyura today. She is suffering for herself and for me, my poor little one. She is pregnant again and all on her own.

She has so many worries she says she would be sinning if she went to see the midwife.[1] My poor Nyura, you never imagined when you married me that you would suffer like this? But it isn't my fault that we've been given so little time to live together.

I am out of my wits. What if something has happened to her, please save her, dear Lord. I love her with all my soul and I worship her. No, take these thoughts away from me, dear Lord, let my poor one be healthy and let this problem be the last one, never ever to be repeated. And what if she dies? No, no, I cannot write any further, I have no strength left, my head is spinning, I am shaking, what have I written, it is not necessary. Please forgive me, dear Nyurochka, you are suffering now and I am pouring salt on the wound. Please forgive me I have no more strength to write to you. Good-bye, I am kissing you, you and only you alone.

Forever yours, your beloved Vasyusha.

On the last day of the year, Vasily confides his New Year thoughts to his diary.

31st December

Last day of this year and God willing, it will never return. Let such a year as this die for ever and never come back. How I'd love something new, to cheer my soul and make my heart and soul clean and bright again. I want to be happy. Instead, there are tears in my eyes. Oh Lord, what is this and when will this end?

This is the end of the hateful year, 1916 – let it disappear into oblivion, for ever.

*

Hundreds of miles south of Vasily Mishnin's position at the other end of the Eastern Front is Romania. Towards the end of August, after months of indecision about whether to join the war, Romania sides with those who offer the most. In this case the Allies, who agree

---

1 To have an abortion.

to trade land in return for Romanian soldiers. Rudolf Hess, now recovered from the shrapnel injury he received at Verdun, is sent to fight the Russians in Romania. Finally seeing some action, Rudolf writes home.

27th December 1916, South Eastern Front

Dear Parents,

Yesterday was the best day of the whole war; the first proper attack I've fought in. The Russians were sitting tight in their well-prepared position. Our artillery shelled them for a few hours and then the Bavarian, Prussian and Austrian troops bombarded the village. From where I stood I could see the whole division. I watched the defence lines at the front until it was our turn to attack. When the Russians peeked out of the trenches to fire, we shot at them from behind the ridge. We were aiming at their heads from 100 paces away. I saw some of them sink to the ground after I'd fired and later, when we went into the enemy trenches, I found their bodies shot through the head. Next, we advanced through the village and attacked the Russians as they retreated.

   Yours,
   Rudi

Elsewhere peace attempts are being made. American President Woodrow Wilson, not yet willing to engage American troops, had tried briefly to initiate peace negotiations between all the warring parties back in November, but to no avail. Parallel peace proposals put forward by Germany's Chancellor, Bethman Hollweg, foundered just as quickly, rejected by the Allies as too unspecific. With both her sons now fighting for Germany, Klara Hess shares her thoughts about the peace proposals with Rudolf.

22nd January 1917, Reicholdsgrün

Dear Rudi,

When I heard about the peace agreement, I felt dejected rather than relieved. I fear we are settling for too little, after all the blood our nation has spilt. Of course I know that an armistice would mean your safe return, my sons, but your future and that of the Fatherland would be built on shaky foundations. Thank God the German Michael[1] has finally had the guts to stand firm until our rights to water and land have been secured. We shall fight on, even if it means hard times ahead of us. Why give in at the time when we have been winning victories? Deceit and lies will not bring victory. It would be cowardly of us to worry about you. Instead we should be proud that through our sons we are fighting for the salvation of the Fatherland.

God be with you, dear son!

30th January

Dear Parents,

My warmest congratulations on your silver wedding anniversary! May you enjoy many more years of health and happiness together. I know your celebrations will be quieter than usual as your eldest children are not with you. However, you should take comfort in the thought that they are serving a great cause, doing their duty as Germans. Our schooldays were over all too soon. But these years of war have not been a waste. They have made me stronger and more independent, they have toughened my character. I hope that this shall be proven in years to come.

*

In a by now recurrent pattern Germany tries again to lure Russia out of the war and initiates secret peace negotiations. Russia sticks by its agreement to conclude no separate peace and the talks founder at a secret meeting between representatives of both countries in neutral Stockholm at the end of 1916. In January 1917 news of discontented rumblings reaches Dmitry Oskin who is enjoying a brief spell in reserve behind the Russian lines.

---

1 Patron saint of Germany.

January 1917

The men are starting to look human again, they can cut their hair, shave, put on clean underwear and mend their clothes and clean their guns. The officers spend all day drinking and playing cards. They get their batmen to get self-distilled vodka from the rear or buy up triple-strength eau de cologne which does just as well.

There is nothing to read, just some old newspapers. But Borov got hold of a whole pile of new editions. They accuse the Government of greed, indecision and secret negotiations with the Germans. We read all this in secret. Zemlianitsky says: 'It's time to finish off this war, brothers!'

Fresh reinforcements keep on coming, mainly Ukrainians. On their first day lunch arrives. It's lentils. The first ones to try the soup throw their mess-tins on the ground: 'A pig would turn her snout up at this!' [they say] One of the soldiers raises his mess-tin and pours uncooked lentils on to the ground: 'This isn't food – it's some pellets. The Austrians are feeding us bullets in battle, now our own side wants to fill us up with them! We're not having this!' – 'Yes, to hell with this!' shout others. An incredible uproar breaks out, some soldiers throw the cook out of his field kitchen, others pour the contents of his pots on to the ground.

In the end, I am told to split up the new arrivals between different companies and warn their commanders to keep an eye on them.

Dmitry then goes on leave. Soon after, on 8th March, discontent back in Petrograd spills out on to the streets. When the Petrograd garrison refuses to disperse the demonstrators by force, order deteriorates and mutiny turns into revolution. Just a week after the initial demonstration the Tsar abdicates. Russia is still at war but now in the hands of the newly created Provisional Government. The news travels quickly to the field hospital at Gorodok in Belarus where it rouses Vasily Mishnin from his sedate life behind the lines.

15th–16th March 1917, Gorodok

Rumours are flying round, saying there's chaos in Petrograd and elsewhere. The Duma's been dissolved, but the deputies are refusing to stand down. Tsar Nicholas has abdicated it seems and the entire government has been arrested. My God, what is Russia going through. It sounds like a revolution. But it's all quiet here tonight.

17th March

We really are living in troubled and frightening times. What's happening back home is completely extraordinary. Our whole government has been replaced by the left-wingers and imprisoned in the St Peter and St Paul Fortress. Tsar Nicholas II has abdicated and Mikhail Aleksandrovich is in power. Of course, this affects all of us and is momentous. The chief doctor read out the telegram, then he shouted 'hurrah', though you could tell he wasn't entirely happy. God in Heaven, it's like a miracle of miracles, it all happened so quickly. But that Semenovsky Regiment, defenders of the old regime, they've had it now. I wonder what's for dinner at the St Peter and St Paul Fortress? Stale bread and soldiers soup, I guess. Let those bastards have their fill of it!

19th–20th March

Such joy, such anxiety that I can't get on with the work. I want to convince all the doubters that these developments are good news and that things will get better for us now. Good Lord, it's so great that Tsar Nicholas and the autocracy no longer exist! Down with all that rubbish, down with all that is old, wicked and loathsome. This is the dawn of a great new Russia, happy and joyful. We soldiers are free men, we are all equal, we are all citizens of Great Russia now!

21st–22nd March

It's important that none of it can be reversed. The police are being arrested, their weapons are taken away from them. Please God let it be like this for ever. What joy, what an unprecedented change. I want to save the newspapers. They're already collector's items. One edition of the 'Russian Word' has sold for 10,000 roubles.

*

News of the revolution puts fear into Klara Hess who hopes that such ideas can be prevented from taking hold in Germany.

19th March 1917, Reicholdsgrün

Dear Rudi,

The revolution in Russia and the possible consequences cannot be ignored. But the reports so far are so contradictory that nobody can get a sense of what is really going on. Here the priests are forcing the farmers to distribute out their food stocks. We must share resources and be sure to keep the towns and cities supplied. I don't like the taste of black market food anyway. And I'm too patriotic to get fat at someone else's expense.

Rudolf Hess himself is more concerned about his long-awaited promotion.

30th March, South Eastern Front

Dear Parents,

My commission papers arrived ages ago. But paper alone won't change anything. There are enough officers in the regiment at the moment. I had mixed feelings today when I read in the papers that six of my comrades have already been made officers. I wasn't because I switched to a different regiment. Sometimes it is really hard to write more about it: I mustn't get angry! At least they want to make me an acting officer.

Two months later, Rudolf does report back to his parents about the extraordinary changes behind the Russian lines.

19th May

Dear Parents,

Yesterday we saw heavy fighting but only amongst the Russians themselves. A Russian officer came over and gave himself up. He spoke perfect German. He was born in Baden but is a Russian citizen. He told us that whole battles are going on behind their lines. Their officers are shooting at each other and the soldiers are doing the same. He found it all too ridiculous. They can all get lost as far as he's concerned. We invited him to eat with us and he thanked us. He ate well and drank plenty of tea before going off.[1] There was a lot of noise coming from the Russian side yesterday. They were fighting each other in the trenches. We also heard shots coming from their infantry but they were firing at their own rear. Charming!

*

A telegram reaches Dmitry Oskin's Tarnopol sector of the Russian front giving notice that An All Union Congress of Peasant Deputies is to be convened in Petrograd. Each division is to send one elected Deputy as a representative, giving ordinary people a new voice after centuries of autocratic Tsarist rule. Dmitry is elected as one of the deputies for the 11th Army. He arrives at Petrograd's opera house where the Congress is taking place and later describes the scene.

May 1917

The foyer was full of stands selling revolutionary books and brochures, each one with a different banner: 'Party of people's freedom', 'Party of people's socialists', 'Party of social revolutionaries', 'Party of social-democrats'.

At every stall I approached, they immediately asked me which

---

1 To give himself up as a POW.

party I belonged to. On hearing I did not belong to any, they invited me to join theirs straight away. 'I'll wait,' I laughed – 'just give me a chance to get used to all this.'

'There is no party better than ours!' – each of them said.

In the end I got fed up with them. It was like being at some market where everyone tries to force you to buy things you don't need.

Once the Congress convenes it goes on for days. Of the 781 delegates only 100 are members of the radical Bolshevik party led by Vladimir Ilyich Lenin. The Bolsheviks, and Lenin in particular, are calling for an end to Russia's participation in the war. Dmitry remains cautiously unaffiliated.

June 1917

On 8th June it was my turn to speak. I arrived in time to take up my place in the sixth row, right opposite the presidium. Leader of the party of Social Democrat Bolsheviks Mr Lenin asked to be allowed to speak out of turn as he was so busy that today was the only day he could speak.

– Let him speak, let him – shouted the hall.

Lenin came up to the rostrum with swift steps. He was short, stocky and balding with a high forehead and sparkling eyes. The hall resounded with applause. He waited for it to die down. Then he began, speaking in plain language that we, simple peasants, could relate to. He said: 'The main point is that land should be taken immediately from the landowners and given to the peasants without compensation. All ownership of land is to be eliminated.' The hall listened attentively but suspiciously. I couldn't concentrate on the words of Lenin's speech but sat staring at him, trying to figure out whether the rumours going round about him being a German spy could be true.

Didn't look like it.

When I approached the rostrum I looked around. On seeing thousands of eyes fixed on me I was so scared my knees began to shake. Me, an army lieutenant, was terrified to speak in front of such a large crowd. It is easier to take part in a bayonet attack than to speak at a congress. But I had to do it:

'Comrades,' I began – 'soldier-peasants of the 11th Army have authorised me to declare . . .'

'Louder, louder, can't hear!' – came from all sides.

'Soldier-peasants have authorised me' – I shouted in a thin sharp voice.

And then I read out my speech:

'We, the soldier-peasants demand that the land be immediately decreed common property. That it is immediately taken from the landowners and given to local land committees. Only the immediate implementation of this measure will reassure the army, sitting with rifles in their hands in faraway trenches.'

A burst of applause.

I wanted to carry on but Avksentiev rang the bell and looked over at me: 'Your time is up.'

*

The radical Bolsheviks call for an end to all hostilities at the meeting in Petrograd, but Kerensky and his Provisional Government want to continue with the war, even planning a new offensive. Despite the revolution nothing much seems to have changed for Vasily Mishnin.

16th June 1917, Gorodok

Today is a special day. I sent a parcel to my dear Nyura, ten pounds of sugar. I am very pleased about this. Meanwhile, we received a telegram that tomorrow we are leaving Gorodok for the front line.

1st July

There are rumours of a new offensive on the south-western front and there are already prisoners from there. The soldiers here are all on edge, preparing for battle. But some regiments are not leaving their positions and refusing to join the advance.

10th July

The bells are ringing and people are cheering. Something has happened. I think our soldiers have broken through the enemy lines and are advancing with the battle-cry 'For liberty – forward!' It is raining and cold. I'm in a terrible mood.

22nd July, Gorky

There is heavy fighting and the 1st Siberian Corps are under attack. Many have been taken prisoner by the Germans. I went to Belitsa and saw the new English super-weapons. A steam engine, that moves without tracks.[1] A remarkable invention. That's what the Germans and English are fighting with. The morale is good. There are lots of casualties.

28th July

All the efforts of the 1st Siberian Corps have been in vain. The 10th Corps didn't leave their trench, didn't even move into the empty German ones, so the southern front has collapsed. The atmosphere everywhere is really grim. We've heard that Kerensky might come here to say something to us.

3rd August

A new life begins at home, it's a boy, Yevgeny. I got a letter from home saying Nyura has given birth and is doing well. I am glad it's a boy.

An anxious night, there are planes overhead, and anti-aircraft fire. Too scared to sleep, I am shaking all over.

*

Hundreds of miles to the south in Romania, Rudolf Hess is in hospital again.

---

1 Tanks.

10th August, South Eastern Front

Dear Parents,

Injury no.3, again not serious, but it will take a while to heal. A bullet went clean through my left shoulder and came out of my back. It missed the bone. Alfred[1] has a few small shell shards in his face, and is in a military hospital somewhere, otherwise he is well.

    from your loving son

    Rudi. (The bullet was from a low calibre Russian infantry pistol. I have a hearty appetite.)

Rudolf uses his time in hospital to change the direction of his military career. He wants to try another branch of the army which is calling for new recruits.

26th August, Reicholdsgrün

Dear Rudi,

We were surprised to hear that you have joined the flying corps.[2] I cannot say that we are happy about it, but we are glad your sincerest wish has been granted. I can quite understand the attraction of being a pilot and since you are strong, have great presence of mind, and the necessary composure, you are well suited to this difficult, dangerous work. It would be cowardly of us to try and prevent you from serving the Fatherland with this most powerful weapon.

*

While Rudolf plans for future days of glory in the sky, the Eastern Front is in mounting disarray. On 19th July at the Tarnopol Front between Russia and Austria-Hungary, Russian soldiers and officers free when faced with a mild counter-offensive by German and

---

1 Rudolf's younger brother.
2 Still a part of the army, there was no separate air force in Germany at this time.

Austro-Hungarian troops. Dmitry Oskin returns from his Congress in Petrograd to find an unstoppable retreat underway.

September 1917

'Where is our Headquarters?' Museus[1] screamed in anger as he saw the last of the 11th regiment walk past.

'In Kiev, or perhaps in Moscow,' replied the soldiers sarcastically.

'The bastards, the swines,' fumed Museus. 'Where are they running to? Why are they running? The Germans have only broken through on one tiny strip of land. One company would have been enough to send them packing. What a disgrace!'

'See what all this revolutionising does!' Museus keeps ranting on.

And our troops, it has to be said, are retreating so fast, there's no stopping them. 'It's all the Bolsheviks' fault,' say the officers. 'They are undermining the front. It's all their fault we are retreating. Those German hire-hands! The spies!'

The chaos is stupefying. The rear is seized with panic. All divisional and army officers serving at the front have disappeared without a trace. The field telegraph and post office have vanished.

*

Political duties call again and Dmitry, in his capacity as a Peasant Soldier Deputy, returns to Petrograd to get money for cultural-educational work at the front.

Vasily Mishnin remains with the field hospital in Poland hoping for peace at any price.

5th September, Ustron Forest

The weather is foul, cold and wet, and on top of that there is the news that Riga has fallen to the Germans. We are beside ourselves with worry. It seems all is lost. Worrying rumours abound about a retreat. They say we are giving up Minsk, Kiev, Odessa

---

1 The commanding officer.

and everything right up to Moscow, but there is still no sign of peace. I am in a rotten mood and the troops even more so. Peace is all we want, that's all.

9th November

I just don't understand what is going on, why there is no news from Nyura still. Not a moment of peace. My head is swimming with all kinds of weird thoughts. There hasn't been a gap like

A page from Vasily Mishnin's letter to his wife, Nyura, 17th December 1917

this between the letters during this entire war. Why now, when the war seems to be coming to an end?

*

On the road between Petrograd and the front Dmitry Oskin finds he is out of touch at a critical moment. Lenin and the Bolsheviks have seized control of Petrograd in the year's second revolution.

November 1917

Stunning news: the provisional government has been over-thrown, the Union of the People's Commissariat has been formed, with Lenin at its head. All the telegraph wires are buzzing with news about this new revolution, about the leaders of the Union of Workers, Soldiers and Peasant delegates and the decrees of the new Bolshevik government. All land is to be trans-ferred to the people immediately.

Will the Bolsheviks hold on to power? Will they manage to bring peace? What do I think about the revolution? Do I sym-pathise with the Bolsheviks? Their slogans are the slogans of the workers. Their demands are the demands of the soldiers.

To the front! The front will follow the Bolsheviks, no doubt!

*

One of Lenin's first decrees as leader of the newly empowered Bolshevik party declares an informal armistice. The formal treaty will be signed after weeks of negotiation.

For Vasily Mishnin, desperate to return home, the end cannot come soon enough.

2nd December, St Prudyi

The truce has been agreed. The older men are going home first.

17th December

My dear and lovely Nyurusha, Vasyania and Zhenichka,
I am sending you my most heartfelt greetings and, most impor-tantly, wishing you to remain healthy and patient until this war ends, although it is really over even now. The Armistice has

already been agreed. We are living under conditions of peace already, everything is quiet and the aeroplanes no longer circle overhead. I am very nearly home despite this unknown delay.

My dear Nyurochka, with God's blessing I am still alive and healthy. I am feeling very well. The only drawback is that I think it will be a long time before my year, 1908, will be demobilised and can head home. The men of 1902 have been demobilised already and the men of 1903 leave on the 10th. And then come 1905, 1906, 1907 and then it will be my year's turn and 'toot-toot' I will be able to come home.

My dear and lovely Nyurochka, did you receive my parcels? Did everything arrive safely? Did nothing go off? I was particularly worried about the herring. Please write to me about this, my darling, I would so like to know. My dearest, how I long to be with you. I promised to return by the end of January but I think it will be the end of February before we can be sure to see each other.

Eternally yours

V. Mishnin

14th January 1918

The last year of this awful war, the last year of separation – how much time we have spent apart.

7th February

We are ready to leave. All they give us to eat for a long journey home is a few rusks. The road is same as ever, except there are soldiers everywhere. 8th–11th February we were on the road non-stop. A two-day journey has taken five days and nights.

11th February, Penza

At nine in the evening I am already home. The end of this accursed war.

Vasily Mishnin is finally home with his Nyura and their two young sons. All fighting ceases on the Eastern Front, from the Baltic to the Black Sea.

On 3rd March 1918, Russia and Germany sign the Treaty of Brest-Litovsk, to the dismay of America and the Allies who boycotted the negotiations, which led to the separate peace settlement. While Russia agrees to give up all claims to the land and people invaded by Germany in the sweeping advance of 1915, American President Wilson proposes a radical fourteen-point plan for a peace without conquests and annexations. But neither the Allies nor the Central Powers are ready for Wilson to broker the peace. The end of hostilities in the east releases Germany to send forty-four additional divisions to the Western Front.

Rudolf Hess, who spent the rest of 1917 in hospital recovering from his third injury of the war, is finally made an officer in October. In January 1918 he starts his pilot's training in Munich where his mother, Klara, writes to him.

12th February

Dear Rudi,

The first I heard of the peace with Russia was at 11 this morning, when a station official announced the news. It was such a great relief. We had already resigned ourselves to the idea that the peace talks would collapse and the negotiators would go their separate ways, having failed once again to reach an agreement. But peace has come sooner than expected, thank God. Perhaps now we will be spared a dreadful bloodbath in the west. The prisoners will be ecstatic that they are free at last. I hope we have enough vehicles to get rid of the damned POWs and bring food in for our own people.

Rudolf, however, seems more concerned with his own hoped-for part in the war.

Rudolf Hess as a pilot on the Western Front

23rd February, Munich

Dear Parents,

I've just met a pilot I know. He said it is out of the question that I might still make it to the front. The war will be over by then. All this aimless drifting is awful!

3rd March

Dear Father,

I simply had to write and tell you that today I flew for the first time ever! I was granted a test flight a few days back and today the weather was finally clear and calm enough to go ahead with it. At 6.20 I drove to Schleissheim, where I was given a fur coat and knee high boots and a crash helmet with goggles. My head was wrapped up in wool, leaving only my nose free. The plane was in the hands of a good pilot. At 8.20 he hit the accelerator, the engine was running at full power, throwing stones and earth into the air. The plane sped across the ground a short distance, then climbed into the air and suddenly we were flying. We'd left the airfield behind in no time and were high above the villages, fields and streets. Everything seemed to shrink. The world lay below us like children's toys. I imagined that we were the only living souls in the whole world and we were flying away on a giant bird.

*

Rudolf Hess flew over the front line of a battlefield for the first time a week before the end of the war, on 3rd November 1918.

Vasily Mishnin was finally able to settle down and enjoy family life at home. He safeguarded this quiet life successfully, keeping his head down throughout the tumultuous changes the revolution brought to Penza.

But neither Oskin nor Hess laid down their arms with the war's end – each went on to fight for their respective causes in their own countries, one with the Bolsheviks, the other for the National Socialist Party.

Chapter 14

THE FINAL PUSH

December 1917–August 1918

On 26th April 1917 America declared war on Germany after nearly three years of neutrality. President Wilson made his decision reluctantly. Two recent developments compounded the gradual shift towards war: the German declaration of unrestricted submarine warfare in February 1917; and the interception of a telegram which revealed Germany's hopes that Mexico would side with the Central Powers and invade the United States.

For two years, President Wilson had attempted to play a mediating role between the opposed coalitions but neither side was willing to negotiate. Now, as the leader of a belligerent power, he intended to broker the peace once his army had helped to bring the war to an end. As he wrote to his closest advisor Colonel House: 'England and France have not the same views with regard to peace that we have by any means. When the war is over we can force them to our way of thinking because by that time they will, among other things, be financially in our hands.' America joined the war as an associate power, with an army that in April 1917 consisted of only 287,000 officers and men. Within two months more than 9 million men registered for the first draft, although only 2 million of them would ever become part of the American Expeditionary Force in France. The pressure

*was on to equip and train the new troops in time to help bring victory
to the Allies.*

*German First Quartermaster General Ludendorff calculated
that, despite America's entry into the war, its largely untrained
Expeditionary Force would not be ready for combat for at least
another year. At the end of 1917, prospects were good for Germany
on many fronts. The Austro-Hungarians had beaten back the Italian
army 80 miles; the Russian Bolshevik leader, Vladimir Ilyich Lenin,
had decreed a temporary armistice aiming to take Soviet Russia out
of the war; peace negotiations were underway with Romania; and
Serbia remained under German occupation. General Ludendorff
would have to act quickly to secure victory by launching a major new
offensive on the Western Front. 'The Last Card', as it was referred
to by the German High Command, would be Germany's final bid to
break through Allied lines before the arrival of American troops
from across the Atlantic.*

*

*In December 1917 American recruit John Clark starts his training as
a Second Lieutenant in the US Field Artillery at Valdahan in France
20 miles from the Swiss border. John Clark initially enlisted with the
US Medical Corps working as a guard, porter and kitchen assistant
at US Base Hospital 15 in Chaumont, 70 miles from Verdun.
Surrounded by men in uniform, he finds his job does not match the
ideals with which he set off for France and applies for a transfer to the
artillery. This decision is made with some regrets as it means he must
part company with Red Cross nurse Emma Marie Zangler, whom he
describes as 'the belle of the ball'. They first met back in July while
travelling on a liner which took the new staff of Base Hospital 15 to
France. While John merely mentions meeting 'Miss Zangler' in his
diary, Emma Marie records talking to 'Jack Clark – dandy boy –
against the rules of course'. Despite strict orders forbidding communication between nurses and enlisted men, they engineer a few evening
meals out in Chaumont, a number of strolls and some trips to the
cinema before John Clark makes his decision to transfer. At Christmas
he interrupts his training course and travels overnight to Paris in*

order to snatch a few more hours with Emma Marie. By New Year John is back in his barracks near the Swiss border.

31st December 1917

I am writing now during the last few minutes of the old year – 1917 – the year of my life which has undoubtedly been the most eventful and full of significance. Four years ago, it loomed ahead as the time when my collegiate career would come to an end. It did – somewhat abruptly as it turned out. And I expected that in the fall I should be starting what would be destined as my life-work in the 'wideworld'. Then came war and I found myself

John D. Clark

crossing the sea to the Old World – another dream realized prematurely though under unforeseen circumstances. The same reasons which led me over here in the first place influenced me to change to the artillery. What that portends is still a mystery, perhaps the end of this adventure of life – but I hope not, for in the latest revelation of the old year has been the meaning of true love, which I want to continue. So wishing for the best but ready for what comes. Here's to the New Year – 1918.

*

The enthusiasm with which John Clark looks forward to the new year, his first year of combat, differs markedly from the outlook of schoolchildren Piete Kuhr and Yves Congar, who have spent three years of their lives at war.

Yves Congar, now thirteen, still lives under German occupation in his home town of Sedan in north-eastern France. His diary now runs to four notebooks, the second ending with his description of flouting the law and pinching potatoes in September 1915 and it continues to be his record of the war against the 'Boches'. His two brothers, Pierre and Robert, now nineteen and seventeen, have for the last year been forced to work for the occupying troops.

21st December 1917

At long last there's butter, flour and chocolate in the house. But not much of it: only two small squares of chocolate each! It has been so long, it brings back memories of breakfasts before the war. We are having a hard time. It is very cold, which increases your appetite. My older brothers go to work in thick boots to keep their feet warm. But we have faith in France and God, and comfort ourselves with the thought that over in Germany they are almost as unhappy as we are. There is famine in all the big cities: Berlin, Dresden and Bavaria; I hope they all die!

24th December

Very cold: 12 degrees! There are icy patches on the Meuse and its banks are frozen. It is snowing, as it should at Christmas. But there will be no midnight mass and no big party. Then again, even if we're not celebrating Christmas Eve properly, at least we have what feels like a banquet: waffles, cocoa . . . what a treat, it's great! Unforgettable! The whole family sings until 10 p.m. and Tere keeps interrupting to offer us more waffles!

25th December

Christmas again . . . Oh dear!

*

Fifteen-year-old Piete Kuhr is at home in Schneidemühl on the now quiet Eastern Front. Only days before Piete's former friend and admirer pilot Lieutenant Waldecker died in a plane crash. Her mother, back home from her singing school in Berlin, joins Piete, her grandma and her brother Willi in their usual Christmas festivities.

25th December

I wasn't looking forward to Christmas. All the church-going and the singing reminding me of everything again, and I would be unable to stop crying. Then Grandma said that she had thought of something special as a Christmas present for me. I could take dancing lessons with Herr Kleinschmidt – she had already arranged it.

'Because you seem so gloomy,' said Mummy, laughing.

I was overjoyed.

'I would really rather be a dancer than a singer,' I exclaimed.

'I thought you might like to take over my singing school one day,' said Mummy. 'When have I ever seen you do a graceful pirouette?'

'Never,' I answered, and everybody laughed. Willi performed a comic ballet dance for us, until he tripped and nearly knocked over the Christmas tree.

*

In Sedan, Yves's school lessons continue between Christmas and New Year.

28th December

Snow and a cold wind! We had our regular maths test today and the classroom was dead silent. All of a sudden Mr Laroche, the headteacher, came in and read out an order saying that Turenne College and all the other schools have to go and sweep the snow from the streets! There is chaos, noise and laughter. Soon afterwards you could see the apprentice sweepers under the watchful eyes of their teachers, having left maths a long way behind them, not sweeping very hard but having fun, as new snow settled behind them.

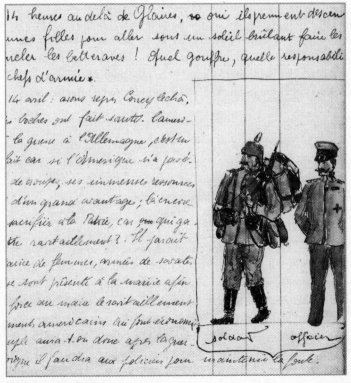

Yves Congar's diary

31st December

Mme Guichard has died, like so many of the old people do nowadays. The students are still clearing the snow. It's the last day of the year – time for us to make a wish.

This is mine: 'May the war end, the hard times be over and may France, with peace in her heart, turn once more to God and enjoy a prosperous victory, Amen.'

1st January 1918

Another year! We are all so weary. I would like to give up everything, my diary and everything else and just stretch out and sleep and not wake up until the war is over! Heaven!

In the morning we exchange presents. Then at 4 p.m., following our wartime custom, we go to Mr and Mrs Qinchez's. Topics of conversation include the herring rations, and the hostages the Boches are planning to take, men and women alike. Everybody here is worried, we're unlikely to be affected. We are calm about it.

The Germans have a practice of taking civilians from occupied Belgium and France as hostages to guarantee compliance from the local populations. Thousands of French and Belgian civilians are sent to camps far behind the German lines.

4th January

Bitterly cold. I went into town to do some sweeping but we got sent home. On my way back I meet H. Facquier who tells me that hostages will be taken in Fond de Givonne. On the list are Mr Girard, Mr Facquier and Mr Congar! The news is confirmed in the evening. Dad reads out the names: 27 men and 33 women. We are quite calm, because we do not believe they will leave. They are allowed 50 kgs of luggage but Dad will only take a suitcase and a bag.

6th January

Time is flying by. We eat our last meal together and drink a toast to the hostages' return. The afternoon passes by without incidents; then it's finally time for goodbyes and we hug each other, perhaps for the last time. Now I am really upset – it hurts, and I feel like crying. Dad wants to go to the station with his boys only. We set off, they walk a bit ahead of me. I stare at the houses, my face turned away from the passers-by. I bite my lips and screw up my eyes. From time to time I make an effort, walk a bit quicker and look around, but I can't keep it up. A few people offer us their sympathy. As we walk through town, everybody turns to look at us.

There is a crowd in front of the petrol station. Dad takes us aside and says: 'I think I'll be back, but it's as well to be prepared. If I don't come back, Pierre, I want you to have the desk that is in Marie's[1] room; Robert, you have the mantelpiece ornament; Mimi can have the chest of drawers in the office and you, Vonet, you can have Uncle Victor's watch. I love you all very much. Think of me and burn all the papers I told you to. Adieu.'

We wait for ages. Eventually, we go back home. The first reaction I have is loneliness. In the gloomy kitchen two women sit reading: Tere and Mimi. Yes, from now on the house is going to feel so empty, especially to begin with.

*

In a desperate attempt to boost the number of soldiers available to fight in the forthcoming German offensive on the Western Front, troops are being called up at a rate of 58,000 trained and 21,000 untrained men per month. Piete's brother Willi, now eighteen, has already tried every available means of dodging the draft.

---

1 Yves' fifteen-year-old sister, Marie Louise, called Mimi by the family.

1st February

Willi got his call-up papers! Pleading 'water on the knee' and 'muscular weakness of the heart as a result of scarlet fever' won't work any more. The staff doctor declared him fit for military service. Willi was furious. He said that he and other recruits were examined stark naked in the ice-cold barracks. The doctor just pressed his stomach and listened to his lungs, that was it. 'Sound as an ox,' he declared.

Will spat and said, 'What a twat! He just wants fresh cannon fodder for Emperor Wilhelm!'

'Just let Uncle Bruno hear that – or Mummy,' I said. 'To them "the German nation" is still everything. Fall with a cheer for the Fatherland, and you will die as a hero in their eyes.'

I don't want any more soldiers to die. Millions are dead – and for what? For whose benefit?

We must just make sure that there is never another war in the future. We must never again fall for the nonsense peddled by the older generation. Our parents and relatives have used up all their money, jewellery and valuables buying war bonds. Grandma supports us with a few marks paid in rent by the poor people who live in our house on Berliner Platz. They are even poorer than we are and some can hardly afford the rent any more. About ten people are cooped up there in two miserable rooms. I think I would rather die. But that is not the answer. It's better to live. Definitely.

*

On the same day, in Sedan, Yves finally gets some news.

1st February

We have heard from Dad! We are so happy. They travelled for five days and six nights with no rest at all. For meals they had a bowl of German soup (dirty water in other words) in the morning and a cup of coffee in the evening. That's it! Dad is travelling with 600 others. His postcard is not very reassuring. Though we were glad to get some news of him, we are still sad and worried.

13th February

It's Pierre's nineteenth birthday today and I will soon be fourteen! They say the Germans are preparing for a big offensive. Maybe the last. Someone rang the doorbell today and I went to open the door but Mme Olivier had already done so. Tere was in the kitchen and, thinking it was a refugee looking for lodgings, she shouted, 'Who is it?' 'It's a Boche', I replied, at which Weinberg (I have since learnt his name and jump when I hear it) looked at me angrily, asked my name, and age and said, 'I will teach you to respect the Germans!' He is as prickly as a hedgehog. The bastard took over our entire first floor, including the dining room. We got so worked up, we even thought of moving.

22nd February

I am officially a criminal! I have to go before court martial. Today we got the summons: Mr Congar must present himself in front of a judge at such and such an hour. Robert thought it was for him but it turned out it was me who was summoned. I remembered one word: it was to do with Weinberg! So I went, and tried one office after another, finally arriving at the right one. A Boche, sorry, a German, (I don't want to be a criminal) came up and grabbed me by the collar:

– What have you done?

– I don't know.

But after some more of this I admitted that I used the word 'Boche'. Oh and that this has caused great offence.

– But I didn't mean to offend anyone.

– Yes, you did.

– No, I didn't.

– It offends the German army. Go and stand in the corner.

In the corner, for the first time in my life! Not long afterwards I am summoned again:

– You caused great offence.

Yves Congar's identity card from 1917

– I didn't realise at the time but now I do.

– Where did you learn this word?

– In the streets.

– Do you go to school?

– To college.

– You were a schoolboy but now you are criminal. Follow me. We go into a small stuffy room.

– You caused great offence.

– I didn't mean to do anything wrong.

– Do it again and you will get two years in prison, you little sod. Now off you go.

And I left very quickly.

*

In Schneidemühl, Piete finds a new distraction from the war.

1st March

The dancing lessons take place in Bromberg in a long, ugly hall that smells of beer. But what does that matter? It is wonderful. If only we had decent partners! But the good dancers have been called up and the younger ones are shy clumsy boys who have to be cajoled into it. Not every girl has a partner, so I stand in for a male dancer. The girls prefer to dance with me and I pretend that I am Lieutenant Joan von Yellenic dancing with beautiful, elegant ladies at a big regimental ball.

I have bought myself a hardback notebook, in which I write down every dance step and every command. I asked [Herr Kleinschmidt] if he would give me private ballet lessons. But he said he was only qualified to teach ballroom dancing. I was very disappointed, especially when he said I was too old for proper ballet lessons; I should have started at the age of five or six. I said that I had already worked out dances for the stage and had decided to take ballet lessons secretly in Berlin as well as singing lessons. In the end he said he would show me the first position. Herr Kleinschmidt now always finds a few minutes during the lesson to take me through the five ballet positions. I practise at home every chance I get. I nearly pulled a muscle, which made Willi laugh himself sick.

17th March

Grandma, Fräulein Ella Gumprecht, Frau Schönfeld and Aunt Otter are racking their brains about what I should wear for my confirmation. I need two dresses: one for the day of the public examination in the church and one for the actual confirmation. I am dreading it, my brother Gil[1] even more so.

Yesterday Grandma and Frau Schönfeld went into town and after a long search bought an incredible piece of material; it looks just like those silky-shiny sweets with stripes right through them. The colours! Red with white and green.

'Oh God!' sighed Willi.

Grandma said resignedly that I could wear Aunt Louise Otter's old black silk skirt if it was taken in a bit. I was furious and ran into the yard to call for Gretel and go for a walk with her. That evening by lamplight began the great sewing operation for the confirmation dress. Grandma had sacrificed a brown and green curtain from the trunk in the attic; it became a confirmation dress, with a narrow black braid for a hem.

18th March

Willi has to join up. He will train to be in the Flying Corps and is assigned to the 75th Fighter Squadron. When he left my heart was like a lump of clay. Will turned round and said, 'Adieu, dear sister!' To make him laugh, I shouted: 'Adieu is a foreign word!'

Then I quickly called after him: 'Come home on leave soon!'

I call my brother Gil now, because he likes the name so much. He doesn't want to be called Wilhelm like the Emperor any more, he wants to sound like a Mexican. There is a revolution in Mexico and Gil has pinned the photographs of all the Mexican

---

1 Piete's new nickname for her brother Willi is Gil.

heroes above his bed. To think that someone like this is now a German recruit!

Palm Sunday, 1918

We were confirmed today in the town church. It was a sunny day. I wore the curtain dress with the black braid. We girls had little posies in our hair. Gretel's mother had cut the myrtle from her own window box. I wore lovely shoes with tiny heels, which Grandma had magically conjured up. They were a perfect fit. Grandma and Frau Schönfeld looked at each other and smiled, but Fräulein Ella Gumprecht burst out laughing, the silly goose. Mummy had not been given leave from the office and Gil of course had no leave.

For the first time we were allowed to take communion. But, diary, I had expected to be deeply moved. Instead, all I could think of was the toilet; I was dying for a pee. It was dreadful. I was really frightened it might happen in the church. I hardly know how I got home.

2nd April

We had a dancing-school ball. I wore the pink blouse from examination day and Aunt Louise Otter's black skirt, with Grandma's little black shoes, which had made Fräulein Ella Gumprecht laugh so much. Connie and I had barely begun walking arm in arm down the street when a group of boys were pointing at my shoes and grinning. To my horror, more and more boys joined the group, doubled up with laughter: 'Just look at them! Coffin shoes! Coffin shoes!'

Connie suddenly grabbed me and whispered, 'You have to change your shoes! They are the kind people wear in their coffin.'

I nearly collapsed. That was why the horrible Fräulein Gumprecht had laughed so much! Connie and I ran back to our house as quickly as we could; I took the shoes off at once. Grandma was working in the kitchen when I burst in like a bomb and hurled the shoes at her. She was quite calm.

'Calm down,' she said. 'You wanted to have nice shoes for confirmation day. Where was I to get hold of any? Then it occurred to me that I could enquire at the undertaker's. I thought no one would recognise them as coffin shoes if you wore them with your confirmation clothes. And they only cost three marks. So I bought them.'

I hurled the shoes in the coal bin. Then I put on my old buckled shoes and rushed out with Connie. I was so embarrassed.

*

That summer in Sedan, Yves, a devout Catholic like the rest of his family, also prepares for a religious ceremony.

2nd June

All the hay is in, the weather is beautiful – all the preparations are complete. I am so excited I jump up and down all afternoon. Finally, everything is ready. There is a huge crowd (700–800 people) from all the parishes. Lots of young girls in their veils, boys and men. This is the order of the procession: first the children in the choir, then the rest of the children, then the little girls throwing flowers in front of the Sacrament carried by Father Drouart. The Sacred Sacrament is escorted by the young: young France, young French believers, Catholic France. Their most beautiful motto is 'Catholic and French for ever', the France of the future! At the end there is a huge crowd of people praying together. 'Oh Lord! So many prayers rise up to you, so many prayers for relatives, friends, for our beloved France! May it be free of the barbarian's yoke.'

The procession is beautiful, the most beautiful ever. The priest is delighted, our only regret is that Papa was not there to see it, we are all thinking of him and wish he were with us.

20th June

Sometimes I thought about giving up this diary, but now I'm glad I haven't. I want the feelings I have when I write these lines to spread through all France. Let everyone know from these entries written day by day what occupation really means. I will never stop loving my country, never!

*

Meanwhile, Germany's bid for victory, 'Operation Michael', is already underway on the Western Front. It starts at 4 a.m. on 21st March 1918 at a weak point on the Allied line at the River Ancre just south of Cambrai. After a dramatic six-day German advance pushing the British back forty miles, the place slackens. German casualties are considerable and a third of the artillery has broken down or been destroyed. Food and new supplies of ammunition do not reach the front line fast enough and German soldiers resort to plundering the abandoned British supplies.

Twenty-six-year-old German Paul Hub is taking part in 'Operation Michael'. He is now an officer in the 247th Infantry Regiment and is advancing through familiar territory on the Somme. He writes to his fiancée, Maria Thumm.

5th April 1918, East of Albert, Ancre Somme area

My dear Maria,

The 247th were the first to cross the Ancre. If only the artillery had made it too. If it wasn't for the terrible state of the roads we could have advanced twenty kilometres further. We have suffered quite heavy losses. Twenty of our officers are down, five of them dead. We have been sitting in the same spot for eight days now. I slept from eight in the evening till four the next day and felt much better afterwards. We lie piled on top of each other like sardines to keep warm! We wouldn't have put up with these conditions in the trenches, but in a war of movement anything goes. We will be setting off again soon. I get tired of lying around doing nothing. Hopefully, I will be fine just like before.

See, your dream where you saw me wounded was just that – a dream. Sometimes when I see the lightly wounded going home, I think that I would gladly swap places with them, if only to see you again. But you know, it's great to take part in this kind of war of movement. When we move on we always come across civilians. That's when we find booty. The English tins of meat are fantastic compared to ours. And English sugar tastes so good! Unfortunately, we've finished the English cigarettes and biscuits!

9th April

We are now just east of Albert. We put up our tents yesterday in the pouring rain. We don't like all this waiting around. We like our mobile war but wish it were 100 times more demanding. But of course we can't rush. The terrain is more difficult in this godforsaken part of the Somme. I am sending you all my letters today. If anything happens to me, I don't want them to fall into strangers' hands. The loot we found on our forward march was only military gear. I might have got myself a good pair of boots at Pozières station, but by the time I got there the only ones left were all too big. Maybe I'll have better luck next time. In future we'll have to put guards around the buildings we're about to loot. Let me know if there's anything you'd like, I would be very happy to get something for you.

15th April

My dear Maria,

Perhaps I'll get some news from you today. We feel so abandoned here. We can't go very far because we are now surrounded on all sides. The first few days we went pigeon-hunting. I shot some too. They taste delicious. There were many sheep here, but the Prussians ate them all. Some of our infantrymen said that dog tastes just as good and brought one in. Of course it's all a matter of taste. Sometimes I go out foraging, but I'm not very good at it. One of my men found a pound of soap today. I have put three large pieces of soap and a bundle of string in a parcel for you. I don't know when I'll get to send it. But you do need this kind of thing, don't you?

16th April

Dear Maria,

What bliss it will be to go home! It will soon be four years since I became homeless, moving from one ditch to another, dirty and crawling with lice, dead tired and so bored that I don't know what to do with myself. You can only imagine, how I long for ordinary family life.

We have a few days of rest. Perhaps we'll be able to change our clothes. I have found four lice since I've been here. I hope that plague won't start again!

29th April

Yesterday I lay down on my mattress just to have a bit of rest. When I woke up it was 12.30 the next afternoon. I slept through the evening meal and a heavy exchange of fire. I heard nothing.

Do you know a place where you could have some leather gloves made? I have cut up an English leather jacket. I will send the pieces of leather home. I think it could make a good pair of gloves. I am not very well equipped any more. I have to make the best of every opportunity I get and be very careful with what I have. If only we could send our parcels. Unfortunately, there is no post collection at the moment.

5th May, Cournay

There's nothing left standing here. Just the ruins of one house. The trees are all stumps. But every night from what's left of the wood you can hear the nightingales sing! It's so beautiful! Just imagine, in the middle of the battlefield, nightingales. Just a few kilometres away, one shell after another, nonstop shooting. My dear friend Lutz from Plochingen is dead. Hit by a bullet, killed instantly. We buried him yesterday. I felt very sad as I threw earth on his grave. The musicians played 'The Song of a Good Comrade'. Another of my closest friends is in his grave! He was the most dashing officer in the regiment.

Paul Hub's friend is just one of half a million German casualties in the first six weeks of 'Operation Michael', which has reached the limits of its advance. Paul now goes home on leave and finally marries his fiancée, Maria, on 11th June 1918 in their home village of Stetten near Stuttgart.

*

American officer John Clark has not seen his sweetheart, Red Cross nurse Emma Marie Zangler, since January. Trained to use the 75mm field guns, he joins the 2nd Division of the American Expeditionary Force in April, assigned to B Battery of the 15th Field Artillery. By the beginning of June the German army is once again within 56 miles of Paris – a repeat of September 1914.

In an unprecedented move, the French general Ferdinand Foch has been made generalissimo, in overall charge of the previously separately commanded Allied troops, in the hope that tightening the coalition will help rebuff the German advance. Foch then puts pressure on American President Wilson to deliver new troops faster to give him the superiority in manpower he needs to launch a series of surprise counterattacks.

In June 1918, John Clark is with the 2nd Division of the AEF as it moves forward to help the French stop the German advance on Château Thierry, west of Rheims.

25th June

Since writing last, I have seen and experienced more of the war than in all the previous months put together. Just six months ago tonight it was – Xmas night – that I stopped in the middle of the tanks course and bade farewell to Emma Marie and Paris. It seems as if I never would get a 'permission'.[1]

2nd July

A second service stripe due today, marking the completion of a year in the AEF. As the popular saying goes – 'It's a great life if

---

1 'permission' – French for leave.

you don't weaken.' The weakenings are liable to be sudden; but if the coming year is as lucky as the one just past I shall have nothing to complain of.

Celebrated yesterday with a successful attack on Vaux. Both artillery and infantry did splendid work and we advanced our line a kilometer, took 500 Boche prisoners and a considerable number of machine guns. Their counterattacks were checked and 150 more prisoners taken. More glory for the Second Division!

4th July

Night before last, when I was on the guns, the Boche tried to 'come-back' with intense artillery fire, so that we were kept busy discouraging them. It sent a thrill through me. On all sides was the noise of guns – the booming of the 'heavies' mingled with the sharp crack of the '75s'. Flashes lit up the sky, and the gunners sweat as they laid the pieces on the twinkling lights which served as aiming points and others prepared the shells and shoved them into the breech. But no one complains of this work for all believe it is more blessed to give than to receive.

8th July

Together with the First Division, ours has been commended in general orders by the Commander-in-Chief. I believe it is planned to make these two divisions 'shock troops'.

17th July

'Shock troops' we are, I guess; for on the evening of the 14th we received orders to pack and move out. We travelled for two days and nights with practically no sleep or food – drivers went to sleep in the saddle, falling forward on their horses' necks. Last night we finally pulled in, finding ourselves in the Villers-Cotteret sector where the French have been making some successful local attacks recently. All indications are that we shall participate in a grand attack. The roads are choked with troops, ammunition and supplies. During the night and this morning I saw a large number of tanks going forward. They certainly look formidable as they slide along, giving an impression of invincibility. The large ones have '75s' protruding from the fronts of them. Also saw a battalion of motorized '75s'. It made me envious when I thought of the way we hiked. The troops which have been massed here are the best of the French army. That we are joining them is a sign that we have gained some prestige – I received orders last night and am now attached to brigade headquarters as a liaison officer for our regiment. I hope the assignment is only temporary for I prefer to be with the battery.

19th July

A birthday in the battlefield. At 4.35 yesterday morning the attack was launched! It came as a surprise to the enemy who is still retreating before the onslaughts of our troops. Supported by artillery and tanks, the infantry 'went over' and gained all its normal objectives successfully, tho they have suffered heavy losses. Stretcher-bearers and ambulances have not been able to reach all the wounded, many died last night lying out in the cold. It is now open warfare, movement being carried on irrespective of whether it is day or night. Our batteries are lined up in the open, firing with practically no concealment, tho enemy planes are thick overhead. The French cavalry – lancers – attacked early this morning, also armoured motorcars and the tanks. It is all like a great cinema, constantly changing, constantly moving. Cars, trucks, men, horses, aeroplanes – all in a jumble. It seems almost impossible to write of them coherently. It is just reported that we have crossed the Soissons–Château Thierry road. That means another forward move for us – we average about 12 hours in a place. More guns and camions coming up and more camions loaded with wounded going back. Up to date, several thousand German prisoners have been taken. I've averaged almost three hours sleep in each twenty-four for the past

five nights and am still going strong. 9 p.m. This day now drawing toward its close. Our division, which went into action
yesterday morning at practically full strength, has lost half its
men. The battle is not nearly over. We have gained from ten to
fifteen kilometers in depth but the Boche have now had time to
recover to some extent. It is sad to see the wounded in the hospital, but not nearly so gruesome as on the field where both dead
and wounded are strewn about covered with blood. I am just
beginning to realize what war really is.

*The joint French and American defence described by John Clark
ultimately succeeds on 18th July in rebuffing the final advance by the
German forces. It is dubbed the Second Battle of the Marne. The
Allies use new tactics and technology, including large numbers of
planes and light tanks. They have a plentiful supply of arms and are
boosted by the support of American Troops. The first Allied advance
of 1918 begins.*

30th July

I was right. I was only beginning to see what war really is. At the
end of the third day of attack, the division was relieved but at the
last minute it was found that the artillery was needed, so we
remained in line. Outside of the enemy fire, it was a terrific
strain on our men, for we were firing night and day – on a couple
of occasions, for ten hours without any intermission. We spent
our spare time burying the infantry dead which were scattered all
around us. It was gruesome work, for the bodies had been lying
on the battlefield for two, three or more days. On the crest just
before us were light 'tanks' which had been shattered by German
shellfire. They were most gruesome of all, for the charred bodies
of their crews were still in or scattered about them. All in all, we
were glad when our relief came on the 26th. We are now resting
in a small village near Meaux, but entrain for the Toul sector day
after tomorrow.

*

British private Robert Cude has served as a messenger with the East Kent Regiment, the 'Buffs', in or near the Somme area for three years. He is one of only eight messengers out of thirty from his battalion to have survived the British retreat during 'Operation Michael'. After months on the defensive, in August 1918 his regiment is finally preparing to counterattack.

2nd August

News is to hand that at last Jerry has found it too hot for him, and is anxious to get back a bit, for a breather. Now it is a case of he who laughs last, laughs longest. It is believed that he has evacuated Albert.

5th August

Rain continues until this afternoon, and things are rapidly nearing a head, for the guns and transport that pass every night is simply astounding. It must be the deciding battle of the war, for neither side can go on supplying men and munitions in the gigantic numbers that is to take part in the next one. It is to be a terrific slam this next one.

8th August

Early morning we move off across to see Jerry. I reach the first dugout in advance of the others and find the inmate waiting for me. He offered no opposition. The sum total of my haul consists of cigs, cigars, biscuits, sweets, hat, stick, gloves, revolver, one of the smallest that I have ever seen, and last, but not least, a small pocket camera. We carry on almost into Mariancourt which place is alive with German troops.

That day, 8th August 1918, General Rawlinson's British army, supported by French divisions, 400 tanks, 1,800 planes and strong artillery, breaks through the German line at Amiens. First Quartermaster General Erich von Ludendorff will call this the Black Day of the German army. The Allied tanks play a crucial

Paul and Maria's wedding, 11th June 1918

*role in the closing battles of the war. Germany had underesti-
mated their importance and has only 45 tanks while the Allies have
3,500.*

*

*Paul Hub returns to the Somme after his leave during which he
finally married Maria. He is now positioned near Amiens where
German forces are rapidly losing the ground they gained during the
dramatic advance in March and April.*

9th August, Somme

Dear little wife,

Yesterday started with an enemy barrage followed by a ground
attack shortly afterwards. We only lost a small amount of
ground. It sounds like it's really bad south of the Somme. I hope
it doesn't get too terrible here. Our neighbouring division has
lost most of their ground. The shooting went on all day. We
were forced out of our lovely position in the most horrible
manner. But then the night was unexpectedly quiet.

11th August

We have fought brilliantly in the last three days. Our losses are
heavy, like the last time on the Somme. But the enemy hasn't
made much ground. Their gains are all down to their tanks. We
can't do anything against them! The armour plating is stronger
than on the old ones. Our M6s have no effect whatsoever. To the
left of us it looks even worse. We desperately need reinforcements. We just need to hold our nerve and everything will be all
right. I will write more when we're out of this mess. Please let my
parents know how I am and send my best wishes.

16th August

Dear Maria,

Two days without news from my little wife. How would you
feel if I left you for so long without news! We have lost our
forward positions and need to dig new trenches. For this we

urgently need lots of new materials. Everyone is in a rush, and everywhere I go the men are saying, 'Lieutenant Hub, Lieutenant Hub, we need to do this and this and this . . . ' They think I am a magician! I try my best, but I can only do one thing at a time. Tommy hadn't attacked for a few days, not here anyway. The day before the attack I reluctantly had to take over command, because my own commander stayed behind at Mons. If I allowed myself to think of the losses we have suffered I would have gone crazy by now. I will see how it goes. Hopefully we can grind our way out of defeat.

The last letter from my father was so full of praise for you. I hope you are not too shocked by this! You know I am always delighted when my little wife is praised, but it must not cost you your health!

17th–18th August

I almost forgot to write to you today. That has never happened before. I usually find some quiet time for you. I'm always uneasy when I can't, because I really don't want anything to come between us. This afternoon I realised that I could write you a quick note when the food arrived, so as not to leave you without news. We were shot at today, unfortunately one of my men was killed, torn apart by a direct hit. The shooting is really horrible, sometimes just one constant bombardment. The barracks shake. I think of how peacefully you sleep in your beds back home.

I must send this letter tonight. Last night was very noisy. There were constant explosions around the barracks and more shooting this morning when one of our men went too close to Tommy. You seem to be very busy, judging from your letters. My parents must be so happy to have your help. Please remember what I said in my last letter.

These are Paul Hub's last words to Maria, whom he hesitated to marry for almost four years, fearful of turning her into a young widow. They have spent only a few days of their two months of married life together. Within a week of writing this letter Paul dies from shrapnel wounds to his head and leg at Maricourt on the Somme. His parents have lost the third of their four sons.

*

That August, American officer John Clark is granted leave. He uses this opportunity to visit Chaumont, where American Red Cross nurse Emma Marie Zangler is still working at US Base Hospital 15.

Emma Marie Zangler

31st August

The event of the month was my 'permission'. Fortune smiled at last and I received leave among the first in the regiment. Most of the permissionaries answered the call of Nice, Biarritz or Aix-les-Bains – but a much more human and compelling interest drew me back to old Chaumont. Except for a couple of days in Paris and Versailles, I spent all my time in and about Base Number 15. It was good to see all the old bunch, but particularly one with whom I spent each afternoon and evening. Down in Brottes – in our 'winter home' – we were welcomed again by the old lady and there it was that I left my pin with a tentative pledge to Theta Delta Chi. Glorious Days!

*

In Schneidemühl Piete hears news of the Allied advance.

15th August 1918

Germany is nearly finished, diary. We have suffered a terrible defeat. Most of our troops have surrendered to the English. At the station a sergeant said to Grandma, 'Well, Mother, you will soon be able to close the soup kitchen. We are done for, fini, beaten!' When Grandma came home from duty she was very pale. 'Make me a strong coffee, child,' she said. I heated up so many roasted barley-beans that the coffee looked black. It did her good. 'You look as if you are ready to drop as well,' she said. We looked at each other. 'There's nothing wrong with me,' I said.

20th August

The doctor who examined Grandma also listened to my chest and he diagnosed an overstrained heart and something to do with the ribs. I have to stop working in the infant's home 'with immediate effect' and cannot go back until he gives me a clean bill of health.

We must stop playing 'Nurse Martha and Lieutenant von

Yellenic'. I don't want be a soldier any more, still less an officer. Things have changed. There is no point in Gretel and me going on with the same old game – war, casualties, hospital, convalescence, officer's dances and aircraft crashes. Funerals too. Perhaps it is bad that Gretel and I are so happy in spite of everything. When we play 'Nurse Martha and Lieutenant von Yellenic' we forget how terrible life around us really is. Now it must finish. We are no longer children. It's all over.

30th August

It was night-time. No one else was in the house. I covered the camp bed in Gil's room with a cloth and with old sheets and pillows. I made up a life-size dummy – head, chest and everything else, covered it with a black coach-rug to make it look as if there was a body underneath. Then I put Uncle Bruno's old army boots under the rug. I put a dented steel helmet where Lieutenant Yellenic's head was. I placed my uncle's old cavalry sword and a little bunch of dried lilac that Mummy had brought from Norderney where the hands should have been. I made two Iron Crosses, first and second class, out of cardboard and a paper 'Order of Merit' which Lieutenant von Yellenic had been awarded after his 80th 'kill' in his fighter-plane 'Flea'. I laid out these three medals on Grandma's blue velvet pincushion, then I drew the curtains and lit two candles at the head of the corpse. They were only two little stumps really, but as they were stuck in Grandma's tall brass candlesticks they looked a bit like big funeral candles. After all this I shut the door.

Meanwhile, Gretel had dressed up as the mourning 'Nurse Martha'. She wore Grandma's black dress, which we shortened with safety pins, a thin black veil and had a white handkerchief. We pretended the officers and staff of the Schneidemühl Flying Corps were marching to the funeral of their imprudent, but greatly admired hero of the air. I sat down at the piano and played Chopin's 'Funeral March', then I beat a slow-march rhythm on a saucepan covered with a cloth. It sounded just like a drum roll at a military funeral. The procession then made its way from the bedroom through the dining and drawing rooms. I rushed back to the piano to play 'Jesus, my protector and saviour, lives', and Gretel instantly started to cry – they were real tears.

Now came the high point: I opened the double doors. Gretel whispered 'Oh God!' when she saw Lieutenant von Yellenic's corpse in full war regalia in the candlelight, and I must say that it really looked as if there was a dead officer lying there. Nurse Martha sobbed as if her heart was about to break, for she was of course secretly in love with Lieutenant von Yellenic.

I didn't know whether to roar with laughter or cry. I was near to both, but then it suddenly struck me that the whole affair resembled Lieutenant Waldecker's funeral procession. I made a speech about Flight Lieutenant von Yellenic, honouring his 80 'kills' and burst three paper bags which I had blown up.

And so ended the game of Nurse Martha and Joan von Yellenic.

*

British private Robert Cude and American 2nd Lieutenant John Clark continue to advance across France. In the last days of September 1918, after a fifty-six-hour artillery bombardment, the Allied forces break through the Hindenburg Line, a line of defences previously thought impenetrable.

Chapter 15

VICTORY AND DEFEAT

October 1918–March 1919

On 1st October 1918, at a meeting of German Supreme Command, General Ludendorff made a sudden announcement requesting an immediate armistice. With the Central Powers still in control of large swathes of land including Belgium in the west and Poland, Ukraine and the Baltic States in the east, his urgent declaration came as a shock. Desperate counter-proposals included the 'mobilisation of the entire German nation', but it was too late. With Turkey defeated in Palestine and Mesopotamia by the British, Bulgaria newly out of the war and Austria-Hungary's ethnic battalions paralysed by mutinies, Germany faced the prospect of fighting the rest of the war on the Western Front on her own. Her exhausted, hungry and much-depleted regiments were now at a severe disadvantage in confronting the Allied armies reinforced with over a million battle-ready American troops.

Earlier that year in January 1918 American President Woodrow Wilson's Fourteen Points peace proposal was indignantly rejected by Germany. At the time, German leaders believed victory was within their grasp. Now Wilson's proposal suddenly looked very attractive, compared to the terms likely to be put forward by French or British leaders. On 4th October 1918 the Central Powers sent a formal *request to President Wilson proposing to begin peace negotiations. While Wilson negotiated the terms of ceasefire with German representatives, the view in Europe was expressed by British Prime Minister Lloyd George who believed that the only guarantee of a long-lasting peace now was 'the actual military defeat of Germany and the giving to the German people of a real taste of war'.*

With their offer of peace rejected by the Allies, the Central Powers' dwindling armies were ordered to fight on across the Western Front. The Habsburg battalions, plagued with sickness, malnourished and war-weary, gradually began to withdraw from Albania, the Isonzo Front and Serbia. The Allied forces, having crossed the Hindenburg Line in September 1918, were meanwhile rapidly advancing through previously German-occupied France towards Belgium.

*

In these autumn days of 1918, millions of Belgian and French civilians are still living under occupation and waiting for news of the Allied advance. Fourteen-year-old Yves Congar and his family in Sedan in north-eastern France have, like millions of others, endured four long years of hunger, humiliation and fear. With memories of the fighting for Sedan in August 1914 still fresh in his mind, Yves Congar waits impatiently for the news of the Allied progress.

29th September 1918

We are expecting the French troops very soon, any time in fact. Finally, the moment we've been waiting for! It is coming fast; we still fear its arrival a little: evacuation, gas, fire, maybe even death – even though we have lived for this very moment for four years. It's pretty rough, but there is also great excitement of a kind that's hard to describe.

9th October

We heard the sound of artillery and bombs throughout the night. What a racket! My brothers are exhausted with work. They didn't come home till 7.30 because there were so many wagons of ammunitions and equipment coming in from the Front. The station square is chaotic: it is the departure, it is the end.

17th October

The Boches' behaviour in France is scandalous. The loot they are taking back to Germany is unbelievable: they'll have enough to refurbish every one of their towns! But one day soon it will be our turn: we will go there and we will steal, burn and ransack! They had better watch out!

*

Private Robert Cude is among the British troops that crossed the Hindenburg Line at the end of September 1918. He records the scenes that unfold as his regiment enters the newly liberated areas of France.

18th October

Now we reach the area where civilians were left by Jerry. The first place we see them is Serein. A fairly large-sized town which the 54th have taken. Plenty of old civis here, and judging by the look, had not had much to eat for years. I have seldom seen a worse sight. The poor beggars cry at the sight of our chaps. However, it is from the joy of their deliverance. Arrive Elancourt just before dinner and find 281 civis here. Anything that resembles white is prominently displayed outside the houses where the civis are. It is to be remarked that although the surrounding country has been battered with shells, not a shell dropped inside the villages.

20th October

We rest and clean up. Taking over line tomorrow, in front of Le Cateau. Plenty of civis here, however this place has been knocked about very badly, and the sights one meets are horrible in the extreme. Horses, men, and women are lying about in the streets, and in the shops some very tough fights have occurred. Civis live in cellars night and day.

*

On the outskirts of Yves Congar's town of Sedan, the artillery bombardment intensifies by the day. Yves's father is still away, held hostage in Lithuania, far behind the German front line.

22nd October

Last night's artillery bombardment was terrible, deafening. The noise is getting nearer and we have started to take precautions, because if Dad was here, that's what he would do. We often wonder what Dad thinks; he must be worried about us. When will we see him again?

30th October

No one in Sedan wants to leave. We would rather be buried beneath the ruins than on some country road.

31st October

We are about to be engulfed by the blazing furnace of the Front, which is coming nearer and nearer.

*

As October draws to a close, Robert Cude's regiment is moving rapidly across French countryside, daily encountering shattered towns and streams of uprooted civilians caught up in the fighting.

24th October 1918

We move up to a village just behind Robartsart named Bouzies. Rather a decent place and gardens full of vegetables. He [Jerry] shells the place day and night so one does not prowl about for pleasure at any time. Civis are here but are being hurriedly evacuated. Between the hours of 3 and 7 a.m. a steady stream of women, children and infirm men walking down the road with all they can carry, having regard to weight. Dead civis abound, and whether dead or alive, they are a heart-rending spectacle at the best of times. Jerry has not treated them too well. The people are so crushed by Jerry's persistent cruelty, and every little kindness

that we can show to them is too much for them, and the tears roll
down their cheeks. In the houses, the devil has been played by
Jerry. All civis have [been] herded into one room, and practically
all their furniture has been requisitioned, and the remainder of
the house has been the sleeping quarters of the troops. Was there
ever such swines.

29th October

We watch a Jerry aeroplane, up a tremendous height, and
engaged with two of ours. It is all over in a minute or two and the
Jerry dashes to earth. We see one of the airmen fall out, and the
parachute opens, but the other was not so fortunate and he falls
like a stone. We watch him all the way down, and he drops in our
garden. We find that his parachute was on upside down. Serves
him right. He was a magnificent specimen of an officer of the
German army and he must have been 6ft 3in in height. I think
that every bone of his body was broken, for we can roll him up
just like a carpet. He has not a cent on him however, and nothing to identify him with.

*With news coming in that suggests these could be the last days of the
war, Robert records the changing nature of fighting.*

31st October

I note one thing that makes me a little uneasy. This is the fact
that the front is getting very violent. Today news is to hand that
Turkey has been granted the armistice. When Austria caves in,
then Jerry will be fighting us all on his little own. It is the Foret-
de-Mormal. Simultaneously with our attack, four British armies
and two French are making an attack, so that Jerry looks as
though he is in for a rough time of it. Not one of us has the certainty in our own minds, that this is to be the last attack, and
now that we are so near to the finish, we begin to wonder if our
luck, that has brought us right through up to now, will hold out,
and thereby enable us to live and reap the benefits that we have

given up the best years of our life for. The attack opens in dismal weather but it would take more than the weather to make us go down in the mouth now. The village of Englefontaine is soon in our possession. I observe a girl of about twenty years crying bitterly, and I speak to her. It is the old, old story, with the addition that they shot her brother in front of her. Jerry only makes a half-hearted attempt to stop us. This time, I have the chance to observe first hand the expressions of joy from the liberated populace. I have to go through a village that has not been taken yet. It was with extreme care, that I with six men, walk down the main road, with rifles out at the ready. Soon I see quite small children peering out of the doorways at us. I am staggered with the reception that I have received. One house that I visited, after being invited in, was full of girls, aged eighteen to thirty years, and I was embarrassed by the kisses that I had to submit to but I have as much Cognac to drink as I am able to carry for a while.

*

While Robert is already enjoying the first benefits of victory, Yves Congar's town of Sedan, not yet liberated, receives orders from the German Occupational Administration instructing all inhabitants to leave.

2nd November

The town is to be evacuated at 11 o'clock tomorrow. Forced evacuation is the worst of part of war for civilians, who find themselves with no roof over their heads and no food, tossed from one place to another. They want to drive us out so they can pillage or destroy the town. But we will stay, firm and unwavering in our duty and if we have to die, then we will die! Vive la France!

3rd November

Today is spent preparing ourselves, mainly burying things. We bury as much and as deep as we can: first our most precious possessions (jewellery, silverware, souvenirs, diaries, papers, gifts, anything valuable), and the rest, well, we leave it to fate. If we get it back, all well and good; if we don't, it doesn't matter all that much.

Among the most precious possessions Yves buries are his diaries. His five notebooks, where he has meticulously recorded his daily experiences, venting his anger and humiliation and sharing small personal victories, are carefully packed and hidden deep in the ground. Yves's family decide, however, to stay in Sedan. For the next ten days they hide in their cellar during violent artillery exchanges between the German and the Franco-American troops across the River Meuse.

In the early hours of that day, 3rd November 1918, Austria-Hungary signs an armistice, the last of Germany's allies. The day after Yves buries his notebooks in Sedan, 540 miles away in the East Prussian town of Schneidemühl, sixteen-year-old Piete Kuhr is also preparing to part with her diary.

4th November

I shall soon finish my war diary. It will be the last war diary that I write in my life, for there must never be another war, never again. If only they would sign the armistice agreements, for fighting keeps flaring up again. On the South Front the Italians have seized Trieste and are advancing on Innsbruck.[1] They meet with no real resistance any more; the Austro-Hungarian army is said to be in complete disarray.

On this day, 100,000 German sailors mutiny in Kiel harbour, seizing control of all ships and refusing to continue fighting. Over the next few days, revolution flares up across the rest of war-weary Germany.

---

1 The port of Trieste was seized by the Italians only after the Austro-Hungarian surrender on 3rd November 1918.

8th November

Revolution is everywhere. It has just been reported that the Supreme High Command wanted to use front-line troops against the rebel sailors, workers and citizens, but it came to nothing. The soldiers refused to fire. Soldiers all over are gathering together, kissing and embracing. Everyone shouts: 'No more war!' The Bavarian King Ludwig has fled his capital. The revolution is at its height in Munich. Bavaria is no longer a kingdom. Where are Emperor Wilhelm, the Empress, the Crown Prince and the whole family of princes and princesses? Perhaps they are all dead already. I feel as if I am on a merry-go-round spinning faster and faster.

Events in Germany begin to unravel at a giddying pace. The next day, 9th November 1918, Kaiser Wilhelm is told to abdicate by his senior military staff. Within twenty-four hours he is sent into exile in Holland. The same day, Germany is proclaimed a republic with a new socialist Chancellor, while across the nation mutinous troops seize control of German cities and demand an end to the war.

*

Despite spiralling chaos at home, Germany's soldiers continue to fight on the Western Front, having been told their last efforts will determine more favourable terms for the Armistice. Their allies, and some of their foes, are in the meantime beginning to make their way home. With Austria-Hungary out of the war, after three years of occupation Serbia is free again. For Serbian soldier Milorad Marković the war is nearly over. He heads for home – and finishes his record of the war.

7th November 1918

I wondered if I should stop writing this diary. Sometimes it seems stupid to keep writing, but I just can't stop, it has become a habit. It's like having a conversation with your best friend. The time will surely come when I will find much of interest in here. This war will end, many years will pass and many a memory will fade too and then, when I grow old, when the time comes for me to live in the past, if my memory begins to fail me, my dairy will refresh it. When I reread these pages, the faces around me now will be with me again. I will remember fondly all that now seems so tough and gruesome, just as I now remember my boyhood with affection, though I was often hungry.

So here I am – writing again, picking up where I left off. I arrived home at noon on the 19th [1st November][1]. I enter the yard without a care, because I already know everyone is alive. Many of the villagers are gathered in front of the school and the yard. We embrace and kiss, then my family arrives. What happiness, what joy! My children are there, but they don't recognise me! They get scared and run away from me. I spend the 20th and the 21st [2–3 November] at home, and then I have to leave again to return to my unit.

So much has happened during the last few days! Turkey capitulated long ago and now Austria has also. Hungary is an independent republic; so are Poland and Czechoslovakia; Bosnia and Herzegovina have proclaimed the rule of the Kingdom of Serbia, and Croatia has declared the rule of Yugoslavia.[2] Italy has made peace with Austria, prisoners are returning from Austria: Serbs, Russians, Romanians, Italians. They say: 'You can't imagine what it's like over there!' The Hungarians are disarming the Germans; their king has fled to Austria. Our people – the Serbs – decorate their houses with national flags and greet us cheering: 'Long live King Petar!' and 'Great Serbia!' The Hungarians shout it too. Our troops have gone across to Zemun, Kovin and other places. Now we are going to Kličevica. Somewhere near

---

1 Dates in brackets convert Orthodox Julian calendar to Western Gregorian.
2 The former Austro-Hungarian-controlled lands in the Balkans, including Bosnia-Herzegovina, were unified with Serbia. On 29th October 1918 a new sovereign state of Slovenes, Croats and Serbs was declared in Croatia. It signalled the imminent creation of a Yugoslav state.

there we are to mark our new border: it will go through Bela Crkva, Vršac and Temišvar [Timisoara].

With the historical task of marking Serbia's new borders with Romania completed, a jubilant Milorad Marković can now return home to his family for good.

*

British soldier Robert Cude is meanwhile still on the move, facing daily danger in the newly liberated areas of France.

6th November 1918

[During] the night we halt at a village on the bank of the canal, named Sarsegnies. All roads and houses are mined. One has to be careful, where one walks, what one touches and what one knocks against. With all our care, one can hear the explosions all day long. This puts the fear of God himself into us, still, it is the price we have to pay for our advance. It also provides work for the Jerrys that we have caught, and they prove to be good decoys. Where we think that a house is mined, one of the Jerrys has to walk in first, and this frequently saves one or more of our chaps from visiting Kingdom Come, and means that it is one less for us to feed. We have to start mopping up, for all troops available are rushed forward, leaving the mopping-up to chance. Brigade is to clear up from here forward to the line, which is a vague term, to say the least of it, for the line is being constantly advanced.

The Allied advance is approaching the borders of still German-occupied Belgium, where six self-imposed prisoners, French officer Victor Guilhem-Ducleon and his five men, have been hiding since the autumn of 1914. For over four years they have survived first in a grain barn and then inside a disused mineshaft under a pigsty in the Belgian village of Graide, all the while looked after by a compassionate local family. From his dark and cramped underground position Victor peers out and listens obsessively for clues of the Allied progress.

7th November

4 p.m. The cows have left this morning and numerous convoys pass by all day. They say the armistice is very near. The Germans had learnt the news this morning and they were singing and dancing in the office. Lots of villagers came to milk the cows. It is quite sickening to see people who have seven or eight cows of their own take the milk needed by the two poor Italian prisoners who are also trying to milk them. Not all the cows have left yet. I think a lot of them are still here. What a lot of looting in the German army!

10th November

3 p.m. Lots of planes today, apparently. This morning we saw three of them brought down by the German artillery, not far from here. There are fewer convoys than on other days. It is Sunday and we expect the armistice to be signed any moment.

This terrible war is finally going to end, in a few days or maybe even in a few hours. As for me, I am going into the outside world again, a world I have not been part of for four years. How will I fare in it? What effect will it have on me? I think about this a lot today. I feel that people are rather mean and that war has made them even meaner (perhaps because living under brutal occupation, deprived of the bare necessities, makes people revert to barbarism, theft, plundering etc . . .). If I can be reunited with my family, I hope to find a safe haven, a safe place to rest after the storm. But where will I find them? To think that in a few days, a fortnight, a month, I might get some news of them. I have heard nothing for four years – it feels more like four centuries, to be honest!

*

As dawn breaks on the morning of 11th November 1918, the Armistice is signed and peace finally descends on the Western Front. After four years and three months of bitter fighting, countless deaths, misery and devastation, this war is finally over. There are still pockets of fighting in a few distant battlefields: in East Africa, where General Von Lettow-Vorbeck refuses to accept Germany's defeat and in Albania, which fails to receive confirmed news of the war's end. Robert Cude, on the Western Front, describes the last tense hours before the Armistice takes effect.

11th November 1918

At 9 a.m., we are staggered to read the news that, commencing at 11 a.m. today, an armistice will be in force, at Jerry's asking. I am up forward at the time and the lads let off all their ammunition, but at a target every time. The Artillery too do not mean to be saddled with spare shells, and so right up to the minute of the time fixed for the armistice, they are pumping over shells as fast as they can. Jerry must be having a great time, but we get a little back, for Jerry has lost his temper, I suppose, and although I would not miss the sport at any price, I am as nervous as a kitten. If only I can last out the remainder of the time, and this is everyone's prayer. I am awfully sorry for those of our chaps who are killed this morning, mines are still going up. 'Stand fast' was sounded by bugles and our minds were taken back to our training days, so many years ago. With the thoughts of the past come thoughts of those good chaps who were then with us, but have now departed for all time. I have a keen sense of loneliness come over me, for in my four years out here almost, I have missed hundreds of the very best chaps that have ever breathed. Immediately upon the bugles ceasing the call, a steady stream of civis, British prisoners, and prisoners of all nationalities, come across the line to us, and some of the sights are terrible in the extreme. A good many Germans come over, with the idea of fraternising, but meet with the best surprise of their life. The hatred of the Boche is much more pronounced, since the armistice was called. They are taken prisoner, for we shall need them to locate the mines that are still about in their thousands, and there is plenty of work to be done clearing up, and the more done by the prisoners is the less that we shall have to do. Remainder of the day, the German wireless was busy sending out locations of the hidden mines, and on receipt of the news, squads of German prisoners were put to work to dig them up. During the afternoon, the German wireless makes a request of us to observe the terms of the Armistice, as guns of both 1st and 3rd Armies are still firing at points behind the lines. Our reply is 'noted', so we do not waste much words over him. Still, the guns stop.

*

A day after hostilities cease French Captain Paul Tuffrau is heading towards the German-controlled former French province of Alsace-Lorraine, where his war began in the early days of August 1914. Unsure of the Armistice until it's 'in the bag', for he has heard countless rumours before, Tuffrau records the tense hours that lead up to this extraordinary moment.

11th–12th November, Neuviller-sur-Moselle

At long last, Victory is ours! It is a greater triumph than we had ever dreamed of. I get a lump in my throat just thinking about it.

Yesterday we received orders to move on to Neuviller. We marched through the night, first by moonlight, then in a dark fog. There were no convoys on the roads, just dozens of cars full of headquarters staff driving with their headlights on. At night we set up camp at Neuviller. Major himself told me that the armistice was to be signed shortly, but I was still sceptical.

[The next morning] we get up slowly. Newspapers. Davoigneau, more agitated than usual, tells me that some men from the artillery have picked up a message on the wireless in Bayon, saying the Armistice has been signed this morning at 5 o'clock. I still don't dare believe it, but an officer announced the news to the old colonel I am staying with. While I am in his office, a neighbour hands him a copy of the Prefect's message to all mayors: *The armistice was signed at 5 a.m. under the terms imposed by the Allies. Ring the bells.*

Women knock on each other's windows to spread the news. Children run along the road leading to the church; the streets fill up with smiling soldiers; flags appear from every window (they had them ready!). The bells are ringing. Nearly every soldier has tears in his eyes, choked with emotion. The bells of Victory! We are set free by their ringing, they make our hearts swell. There is a joyful buzz in the streets, but it is somewhat muted, not the wild scenes that were feared. There is a lot of dignity, a great calm, a feeling of infinite relief. Every head is dizzy with happiness and thoughts about our families. The bells ring all afternoon. Our feelings are so intense, we don't speak, but everyone is glowing with happiness. This hour is repayment and redemption enough!

In the evening I blew half of my grenades and ammunition on the terrace of the Chateau to make fireworks. The soldiers

French women welcoming the first French soldier to enter Lille

enjoyed it like children (Look! There goes another one, and another! What's going to go off next?!). And the good people of the village said to me: 'So this is how you end a war?'

When I wake up the next morning I think about my family and about all the women of France waking up this morning with a great sense of relief, apart from those left to cry on their own.

*

In occupied Belgium French officer Victor Guilhem-Ducleon, still afraid to leave his underground hideaway, is recording the German soldiers' reactions to the Armistice.

11th November

1.45 p.m. In the last half hour it's been announced that the war ended at 11 o'clock this morning. They tell us the news is posted on all village walls. The Germans are singing, dancing and shouting at the top of their voices. Is this really happening? The Germans have fourteen days to evacuate. We will count the hours during these fourteen days. It was four years ago yesterday that we came down this mine.

12th November

8 o'clock: The Germans are getting rid of everything: files, nails, wire, vices, screws, hammers, forges, cows, horses, etc . . . There is complete mayhem along the tramway tracks. People go and load up their wheelbarrow, then come back to the village then go back down straight away. Papers, registers, books etc . . . They are burning the lot (the Germans in the office fuel their stove with their accounts every morning). What does all this mean? On top of all this, the French are said to be in Nouzon, twenty kilometres away. I cannot believe it's really true, that the war is over. I can't concentrate on anything, I can't do anything. I only slept part of the night. I suppose this state of mind is understandable.

*

In the East Prussian town of Schneidemühl, Piete Kuhr and her family are taking in the hoped-for but nonetheless humiliating news of the war's end.

13th November

The Emperor has abdicated![1]

Grandma, who had managed to get a horsemeat sausage from Johr the butcher, already knew all about it. Nevertheless, she studied the announcement as closely as I had. Then she gave a deep sigh but said nothing. Again at supper we didn't say a word about the abdication of the Emperor. Gil and I exchanged glances. Gil was wearing his old, grey-striped jacket again. He had been playing the piano all afternoon. I was late getting back from the children's home. Half the people there are ill with flu.[2] They say that flu has flared up all over town; some people have died already.

14th November

People look at the ground when they pass each other in town, like they are ashamed. Soldiers go around without rank and unit markings or weapons; most of them stroll arm in arm, singing rousing songs. The war is over. Now all the bells should be rung. But all is quiet!

*

While millions of German soldiers rejoice at being able to return home alive, others, like young officer and future Nazi leader Rudolf Hess, cannot bring themselves to accept the defeat.

---

1 On 9th November 1918 Kaiser Wilhelm abdicates amidst a growing revolution.
2 Flu is the greatest killer that year. One in six German civilians falls ill and nearly a million die in 1918.

14th November

Dear parents,

I heard that the Armistice had been agreed. Though undefeated, we had to climb into our planes to withdraw, to flee. I can't tell you what was going through my mind. It was the hardest hour of my life. Now I read this note to America in which we grovel for moderation in the terms. Who would have thought that our compatriots could be so base, so mean, so shameless? I shan't waste my breath talking about the events in Germany, the collapse of the monarchy and the secession of Bavaria. The enemy's terms are so humiliating. I would not be coming back to Germany, were it not for you. Naturally they have taken neither my gun, epaulettes, nor insignia.

Shortly after his return home, Rudolf Hess will join German troops sent to suppress revolution in Bavaria, where a new government has been set up on 7th November 1918 aiming to establish a 'Free State of Bavaria' modelled on Bolshevik Russia.

*

On the same day Victor Guilhem-Ducleon records his first foray out of his underground hideout.

14th November

5 p.m. I couldn't write anything yesterday. What a day! In the morning we got our weapons out and in the afternoon I cleaned my gun. At three, I learn that all prisoners have been freed. We are free. Five French POWs came to spend the evening with me. The first ones I've seen in four years. Three of them slept with us in the hole. I couldn't sleep a wink. I'm getting ready to go to church. I haven't been able to attend mass since 15th August 1914. Thus, my first outing will be for God.

8.15 p.m. We are going to hoist the tricolour: to the flag, Vive la France!

The following day Victor begins his long journey home.

15th November

10 p.m. Noirefontaine. We meet a fellow from Lorraine who has left the German army and decided to come back to France with us. We haven't seen any Fritz. We met three of them earlier on tonight, they were pulling small wheelbarrows and said to us: 'Have a nice trip, gentlemen, we are the last Germans you will meet.' Tomorrow: France.

I went to the station to see the mayor and the head of the railway station and we organised the first train to Sedan to repatriate prisoners.

Two days later Victor helps to instigate the first train taking French prisoners back across the Belgian border. They arrive in Sedan just a few hours after the first French and American troops entered the town. Yves Congar's family have, in all likelihood, been taking part in the celebrations. While Yves's diary remains buried, Victor, newly unearthed from his underground refuge, records the whirlwind events with amazement.

17th November

6 a.m. this morning I woke up [in Sedan] very cold. I see my first French people, visit the ammunitions store, go to see a monument and a cemetery at Bazeilles. There is an ovation in the square and Americans photograph and film me. I talk with a lot of officers and then write to my wife. What a joy – I didn't even know what to write about. I am given somewhere nice to stay where I have my own bed. Marvellous! I have forgotten what it was like to sleep in a bed. In Bazeilles I inherited two blankets from the Fritz that will serve as bedding.

The next day finds Victor on the road again, desperate to get home after four years of virtually no contact with his wife and parents.

19th November

8 o'clock: in Le Chesne, near Vouziers. This morning I am trying to get to Quatre Champs by car. Right now, I am waiting for the captain so that we can leave. He is very young, twenty-six years old. To think I could have been a captain by now . . . This morning my captivity hits me hard even though it is over. As time goes by it should get easier. All hardships fade away eventually.

Victor is among the first soldiers and officers to get home. For millions of others there is still much work left to do.

*

Robert Cude's battalion is to stay on in France to clear up and patrol. Even though the war is over, on his last military leave Robert can't lose the habit of fighting and finds himself in a quarrel.

November 1918

I spend the night at Warloy, and whilst visiting a café that I was on familiar terms with occupants of, I am ordered out by the Yanks that are in occupation of the village. As I am on my own, I am given five minutes to clear out, and in that five minutes I have to listen to abuse of the British that even Jerry would not use. In return, they have a little to listen to and I get some truths home, especially the fact that the whole of the prisons of New York must have been emptied to fill the ranks of this division, that is the pride of that town. Again, I run through the fact, that there is not one but that has more than a little of German blood in him, this fact is openly spoken of, and not a little German sentiment. There is an uproar after this, and I have to fly for my life, ultimately putting up in the Barber's that night.

*

The regiment of Captain Paul Tuffrau is meanwhile marching through the towns and villages of Lorraine, lost to France in the

Franco-Prussian War of 1870–71. They finally reclaim this region for France and begin to clear up the devastation this war has wrought.

18th November, Bechy

What a moving welcome! We arrived feeling like an army of conquest, but were greeted as saviours. On the 17th we were back at our old front line in Villers-les-Moivrons. I saw again with a pang of anguish the trenches, with their damp and muddy corridors, and was amazed to think I lived there for four years.

This morning, the 18th, we crossed the river Seille at Ajoncourt and immediately entered a forlorn and desolate area. The silence was so moving – the thorny hedges, the now empty trenches, the machine gun slits looking out across the deserted land. Gloomy, vacant, abandoned. Our teams have begun to mend the roads, fill in the trenches and the ruts left by the tanks, and build new wooden bridges. There are deserted villages everywhere, with German inscriptions all over. Huge, beautiful farmhouses and old churches, every single one of them shattered, hollowed out. And so much barbed wire! Rusty clumps of it litter the streets of Claincourt.

The most beautiful moment was in Moncheux, whose inhabitants – about fifty of them – just looked so happy. Some were laughing, some were pale and cried as they watched our arrival, and saluted us. An old man pushing his wheelbarrow alongside our column, his brow all knitted, kept repeating: 'Vive la France!' Here and there, haycarts drove past us, their horses wearing rosettes pinned to their ears, while their drivers wore them on their lapels. They replied happily to our greetings in good French, which surprised us. The children formed a guard of honour, all of them shouting 'Vive la France!' Everybody is crying with relief! They can breathe again, these people! Tonight I could hear them saying: 'Poincaré, *our* President.'

They are real French people here. I feel guilty that I considered the question of Alsace-Lorraine as a purely political one. This is a human problem: it is about life and suffering, these people are our flesh and blood.

23rd November, Sarrelouis

There are endless columns on every road: artillery, infantry, stretcher-bearers, bridge crews. Streams of prisoners from the Entente flow back in the opposite direction. First the French, in red trousers, red kepis and thick blue capes. Despite all they've been through, they look delighted and wave happily. Then come the gloomy herds of men with long faces, in tattered, colourless clothes and high fur hats. Their skin is yellow and greasy: where do they come from? Russia, Serbia, Romania?

The sunset is magnificent, the sky's pastel colours offset by the hilly landscape. We reach the hamlet of Karlingen. We must be the first French soldiers to pass through here: all the young girls of the village rush to our car. So many outstretched hands! So many questions, all at once! This is the last Lorraine village. From here on everything is German, and in these villages the peasants stare at us with disdain.

While for the French-speaking inhabitants Tuffrau and his men are liberators, the province's German population fears reprisals and regards the French as forces of occupation. Both the French and the German sectors of Alsace-Lorraine will become French again after forty-seven years of German rule.

American Lieutenant John Clark is meanwhile marching towards Germany itself.

22nd November 1918, Essingen, Luxembourg

Again it seems the 2nd Division is indispensable, and, instead of being relieved, we are marching to Germany as part of the army of occupation. Quite an honour and a most interesting experience – but I should like to have had a couple of free weeks in France.

We crossed the lines on the 17th and since then have been closely following the evacuating Germans. Belgium and its people were splendid! Their reception of us was gloriously enthusiastic, for we were their deliverers and liberators, the conquerors of the Hun for whom they have only the bitterest hatred. On the whole, I like the Belgians even more than the French. They seem to be a cleverer and more wholesome race – though I have the greatest admiration for the French. Yesterday, we passed into another country – The Duchy of Luxembourg. The resemblance of the inhabitants to the Germans rather than the French is marked. I must say that I do not welcome the change. Thus far we have at least met with no demonstrations of antipathy. I fear they will soon appear however. Then we shall have to lay on with a heavier hand. My German, which I have most successfully managed to forget, must now be resurrected.

*

In German East Prussia, Piete Kuhr is feeling bitter, though more at the war's cost in human lives than her own nation's humiliating defeat. She goes to visit the local prisoners' cemetery on the outskirts of Schneidemühl. Piete first visited it back in September 1914, when she called it 'the little burial place for our enemies'.

29th November

Grandma grumbled a bit when she heard that we intended to go and said we would get our feet wet in the snow. Gretel trudged alongside me. The walk to the prisoners' cemetery had never seemed so far. Gretel said that many of the pupils at her school are ill with flu and I must on no account catch it, because I've become so thin that I wouldn't be able to get rid of it. I laughed and told her I would still resist it with all my energy. Then I pointed ahead: there was the first barbed wire fence surrounding the graves. The low mounds were hardly recognisable under the mass of white. We were amazed. As soon as we reached the fence, we saw so many crosses! We hadn't been there for a long while; since when the prisoners' cemetery had grown so big – so enormous! So many dead! It was nearly dark, but I could still read the names, not just of Russians as at the beginning of the war, but also French names, and English.

John Clark writes down his first impressions of the German civilians when his division finally goes across the border.

14th December, Fahr, Germany

We have crossed the Rhine! The thrill which we naturally felt at the event was somewhat dampened by raindrops trickling down our necks and filling up our boots; and the magnificent hills flanking the valley on either side were almost entirely obscured by the low hanging mists.

We crossed the German frontier on Dec 1st and the small villages we passed through in those first days were not prepossessing. The people appeared to be of a low type – by the soldiers commonly called 'square heads'. But as we entered larger towns we found people of quite another sort – cultured, graceful and friendly. The attitude of the German people has furnished the surprise of our lives. Instead of greeting us with dark scowls as hostile foe, they are most cordial and pleasant. I can only account for it by the fact that they are so sick and tired of war and Kaiser that they look upon us more as deliverers and forerunners of a better day, than as conquerors. And though they all realise that had the Americans not entered the war, Germany would have been victorious, they profess to prefer us to the French and English. So, while we came expecting to use stern measures, we find it hard to cut off the hands of women who offer us tea, and little children who sing and play for us. In spite of ourselves, we are becoming quite friendly and finding that the German people are very human. By this I do not mean that we forget Germany's wanton acts during the war, for every day I see a few men – some of them returned officers and soldiers still wearing uniforms, who look as if they were fully capable of performing degenerate acts of cruelty, and these I feel like striking down on sight, but the mass of the people are not like that.

*

German officer Rudolf Hess and his family reveal their feelings about the defeat in their letters. Gret Georg, Hess's cousin, writes to him from Schweinfurt.

16th January 1919

Dear Rudi,

No need to try and explain how you felt on your return home, I quite understand. We should look back on this time not with bitterness, but with gratitude. We must find in it the strength to help raise our country out of its wretched state. This is difficult, but very worthwhile, Rudi. As far as I am concerned, whatever sacrifice I am asked to make, I will do my duty. We are the young generation, so if we give in to despair, where does it leave our elders? I have fought to the end and seen it through. Come, follow me, Rudi!

26th June 1919, Munich

Dear Parents,

It is best not to think about the peace settlement. The only thing that keeps me going is the hope that we will reap our revenge one day, even though that day may be a long way off.[1] But perhaps I will live to see it. Our people are morally debased. But the same happened in other countries, where there was a revolution. There is no reason why our nation should not recover, it has so many strengths.

   Your Rudi

Rudolf Hess will stay in Munich where, in a few months, he will first hear the inflamed speeches of another embittered war veteran – Adolf Hitler. A year later Hess will join the newly formed Nazi Party as member number 16.

*

In late February 1919 Robert Cude hears he is finally going home.

18th February 1919

I receive notice that I am off tomorrow. Four out of six of the remaining runners, we are being demobbed together. Dumping my kit in the stores, I make my way back from Caudry to Logny,

---

1 In June 1919 General Hindenburg returned home and began writing his memoirs, where he would create the legend of 'stab in the back', insisting that the German defeat was not a military failure but the result of upheaval and revolution at home. This myth will be widely exploited by German politicians, most significantly, Adolf Hitler.

to the 'mess'. We have a splendid bust-up. 11 of us, all told, consume 12 bottles of whiskey, 2 bottles of Vermouth (French), also 2 Italian Vermouth, 13 bottles of Stout and 2 bottles of Port. What a glorious night, and I plus one full bottle of whisky find my way back to Caudry. 5.30 a.m. entrain, eventually arriving at Cambrai 9 a.m. March through Dieppe and straight on boat. Eventually arrive Wimbledon Station 2 p.m. Am in charge of 200 men. March behind uphill to the Camp on the Common and find it a maze of sheds. After a wash and a feed, we parade and are marched through first one shed then another, giving up part of our equipment in one and part in another. Finally I emerge from the last one 6.30 p.m. a free man. Arrive home 7.30. Am a civi at last after four years and five months of army life.

*

While Robert Cude's military service ends on the common of a quiet London suburb, thousands of soldiers, among them French Captain Paul Tuffrau, stay enlisted. Tuffrau has been appointed Military Administrator of Sarrelouis in the province of Lorraine, now once more part of France. Finding time to reflect upon the new world order taking shape in the aftermath of the war, Paul finds himself attracted to new ideas.

9th February 1919, Schlangenbad

Endless problems and political crises. Russian Bolshevism intrigues me. I don't think we really know the truth about it. It must be much stronger, better organised and more idealistic than we were told to believe, but evidently there are orders to silence these ideas so as not to let them spread. Nonetheless, the old world is breaking up and I believe that we will see in this century the emergence of the socialist state – by peaceful means, I hope, though I doubt it.

The following month Paul Tuffrau finally arrives home. He adds one last entry to his diary that now spans the entire war.

28th March, Paris

This morning I went to Fontainebleau for demobilisation. The weather was very beautiful. I was overjoyed to see the familiar landscape once again, this small town, a little emptier perhaps. Life goes on, things remain the same, it is only us that have changed . . .

*

Over 65 million people donned a military uniform during the First World War. Although precise figures remain contested by historians, by the war's end over 9.3 million soldiers and officers had died, 21 million were wounded and over 7.8 million captured or missing, a toll unprecedented in human history.

Among the Allies, 5.7 million soldiers perished, including an estimated 2.3 million Russians, 1.9 million French, 743,000 British, 690,000 Italians, over 200,000 Africans, 126,000 Americans, 63,000 Australians, 56,500 Canadians, almost 48,000 Indians, 45,000 Serbs and in excess of 18,000 New Zealanders. Thousands more combatants from places as diverse as China, Japan and the Caribbean also gave their lives in the conflict.

The Central Powers' losses exceeded 3.6 million soldiers, including nearly 2 million Germans, over 1.2 million Austro-Hungarians (including Czechs, Ukrainians, Poles and Slovenians among them), 325,000 Turks and 87,500 Bulgarians. The millions who survived on both sides were left to live with the war's physical and mental scars.

To this horrific toll must be added the civilian deaths, which moderate estimates place at over 6.7 million. While many ordinary people perished as a direct result of the conflict, others were claimed by indirect causes such as the flu epidemic, which in Germany alone killed nearly a million men, women and children in the final stages of the war.

At the war's end, four powerful empires had fallen and four monarchies toppled. Russian Tsar Nicholas II, his wife, Alexandra, and their four children were secretly executed by the Bolsheviks in

July 1918 and buried in unmarked graves in the dense forests of the Urals. The Tsar's German cousin, Kaiser Wilhelm, topped the Allied list of over a hundred wanted 'war criminals' but was allowed to remain an exile in Holland until his death in 1941. The last Habsburg Emperor, Kaiser Karl, was also exiled, firstly in the ancient seat of his ancestors at Habichtsburg Castle in Switzerland; later, after several attempts to reclaim his throne, Kaiser Karl died on Portuguese Madeira in 1922, aged thirty-four.

The defeat of the Ottomans marked the beginning of the end for this ancient empire of the east. Gallipoli hero Mustafa Kemal became leader of the Turkish liberation movement, fighting a successful war of independence and abolishing the Ottoman sultanate in November 1922. Mehmed VI, the last Ottoman Sultan, fled and died in San Remo in March 1926. The Sovereign Republic of Turkey was declared in 1923 and Mustafa Kemal, now known as Mustafa Atatürk, or 'Father Turk', became its first president.

Large sections of Germany's population refused to believe their country had been defeated on the battlefield. Rumours had spread that sabotage by traitors, pacifists and revolutionaries had led to the German army's failure to secure victory. And what Germany termed 'the unheard of injustice of the peace conditions' resulted in the delay of their final acceptance of the Versailles Peace Treaty. The acceptance arrived barely ninety minutes before the Allied deadline, which threatened a resumption of hostilities. The treaty was signed in the grandiose Hall of Mirrors at Versailles on 28th June 1919, exactly five years to the day since the Sarajevo assassination.

American President Wilson, who had begun initial peace negotiations with Germany based on his Fourteen Points peace plan, was also in disagreement with many of the terms of the Versailles Treaty. He believed that in the frenzied post-war atmosphere the European Allies had punished excessively rather than seeking to rehabilitate Germany. The United States did not ratify the Versailles Treaty and went on to make a separate peace with Austria and Germany in 1921.

Under the Treaty of Versailles, the Central Powers lost large amounts of territory and were no longer allowed to maintain close relations with each other, keep large armies or rearm. Germany lost 13 per cent of her territories and one-tenth of her population. The long-fought-over region of Alsace-Lorraine and the mineral rich Saar Basin went to France. The new states of Poland and Czechoslovakia received smaller territories and Belgium also gained some ground. Defeat in Europe ended Germany's brief period of empire-building, with Britain and France becoming prime beneficiaries of the 'second partition of Africa'. Additionally, Germany's reparations bill for war damages was set at a staggering 6,000 million pounds.

From the ruins of the Habsburg Empire, several new independent states emerged: Czechoslovakia, Poland, Hungary and Yugoslavia, the latter made up of Slovenia, Croatia, Bosnia, Herzegovina and much of Dalmatia. Sarajevo, where the war had been triggered in June 1914, was now under Slav rule. Austria itself became a small German-speaking republic of 7 million people, cut off from the sea and severely disempowered.

Italy and Romania received their shares of the Habsburg territories, yet Italy was dissatisfied with its gains. This 'mutilated victory' was denounced by many Italians, including Isonzo veteran Benito Mussolini, who, along with millions of others, believed his country had been deprived of land its citizens had paid for in blood. On 23rd March 1919 Mussolini founded the ultra-nationalist political party, Fasci di Combattimento. By October 1922 Mussolini had become Italy's prime minister.

The Treaty of Versailles will have lasting repercussions. Dissatisfied European nations will be at the mercy of those seeking a military solution to avenge defeat or make up for insufficient gains. Within fourteen years, the Nazi Party and its leader, Adolf Hitler, will come to power in Germany. It will take another horrifying global war to lay some of these ghosts to rest, yet the legacy of the First World War will continue to cast a shadow over the rest of the 20th century.

Postscript

In 1918 **Vaso Čubrilović**, the youngest of Archduke Franz Ferdinand's assassins was serving a sixteen-year prison sentence for his part in the plot. In the long letter of explanation he wrote to his sisters, Vida and Staka, telling of his motives and subsequent events, he closed by detailing the seemingly cursed fates of his six accomplices:

> Milović died following a couple of operations on the wounds he had received as a result of severe beatings in prison. Nedjo Kerović died of a stomach illness, having choked on his own blood. Cvjetko [Popović] developed tuberculosis and is still in the infirmary. Čabrinović contracted tuberculosis and died in 1916. Grabez went to the infirmary with pains in his stomach and was found dead the morning after he returned to his cell. Lazar Djukić went mad and in his delusion believed he was being poisoned. He died in a lunatic asylum in May 1917. You already know what happened to Gavro.[1] I myself got off lightly compared to the rest, using the money you sent me to bribe cooks and other prisoners. Yet I, too, developed a weak heart.

---

1 Gavrilo Princip, the only successful assassin, was sentenced to twenty years imprisonment and died in April 1918 from tuberculosis.

However, Vaso did not share the fate of his co-conspirators. Although his political idealism had led him to join the group that inadvertently catalysed a war which brought death to millions, he was to live to the age of ninety-three. Released from prison immediately after the war, Vaso became a national hero in the newly created kingdom of Serbia, Croatia and Slovenia. After the Second World War he was appointed Minister of Forestry in Yugoslavia's first socialist government, led by Josip Broz Tito. Vaso remained a much respected figure, dying in 1990. His last wish to be buried alongside his fellow accomplices at the Field of Blackbirds in Kosovo could not be fulfilled, however, for after the collapse of Communism Kosovo once again became a battle-field.

Belgrade doctor Slavka Mihajlović was one of the very few female doctors of her time. In 1919 Slavka went to Paris where she qualified as a gynaecologist. On her return, she continued to work at the General State Hospital and helped to establish the first maternity ward in Serbia. Together with her husband, surgeon Jovan Klisić, she co-founded the first sanatorium in Belgrade. Their son Predrag was born in 1921. A member of the Serbian Red Cross, Slavka was awarded the Order of Saint Sava. She was a co-founder of the Women's Party and a renowned member of the Women's Rights Movement in Serbia. She died in 1972, aged eighty-four.

British Private Robert Cude returned to his factory in South East London where he continued to work for the rest of his life. On retirement, Robert decided to do something different, however, and became a film extra in *Doctor No*, the first James Bond movie released in 1962.

French Captain Paul Tuffrau returned to Paris at the end of the war where he was reunited with his wife, Andrée. They had one daughter, Françoise. Paul went on to hold the Chair of

History and Literature at the École Polytechnique, yet, even while teaching the First World War to his students, he apparently never talked of his own experiences. He went on to fight and keep another diary, during the Second World War. In addition to teaching, Paul also wrote books on literature, poetry and history. He died in 1973, aged eighty-six.

Russian conscript Vasily Mishnin was happily reunited with his wife Nyura and their two young sons, Vasily and Yevgeny. Their third son was born soon after the war. Vasily went back to his job as a sales assistant at a Penza furniture shop and eventually became its Director. He died, surrounded by his family, in 1955, aged sixty-eight.

German schoolgirl Piete Kuhr left Schneidemühl in 1920 and went to live with her mother in Berlin, where she took singing and dancing lessons while earning a living as a typist. After her grandmother's death in 1924, Piete changed her name to Jo Mihaly and became a professional performer. In 1927 she married Leonard Steckel, a prominent Jewish German actor. Their daughter, Anja, was born in 1933. The same year, Piete declined to work as a dancer for the Ministry of Propaganda and the family fled to Switzerland where they remained until the end of the Second World War. In 1939 Piete published her first novel, *My Brother's Keeper*, again under the pseudonym Jo Mihaly. After the war, due to Piete's recurring health problems, the family moved to Ancona on the shores of Lake Maggiore where she continued to write. Piete died there in 1989, aged eighty-seven.

French schoolboy Yves Congar studied at the Rheims and Paris Catholic Seminaries in 1919 and joined the Order of Dominican Friars in Amiens on graduation. After completing his military training, Yves Congar served as an officer in the Second World War but was captured early on. During his three

Vasily and Nyura Mishnin and their three children

years as a German POW he made three foiled attempts to escape. In 1994, at the end of a long career in the Catholic church, he was made a Cardinal. Yves died the following year in Paris aged ninety-one.

The fate of Polish civilian Helena Jabłońska remains unknown, except for her death in 1936 at the age of seventy-two. Her diary was anonymously donated to the National Museum of the Przemyśl Region in Poland.

Serbian officer Milorad Marković returned home to Popović village south of Belgrade, where he lived with his wife, Anka, a teacher, and their four children until 1941. Milorad went back to teaching and was a prominent member of his local community. He joined the Yugoslav Communist Party in 1938. During the Second World War Milorad was captured by the Nazis; one of his sons was shot and his daughter died under German occupation. After the Second World War Milorad's second son, Dragoslav Marković, became a close associate of Yugoslav Communist leader Josip Broz Tito and rose to become President of the Socialist Republic of Serbia, one of Yugoslavia's new federation of republics. On 14th March 1965, Milorad's granddaughter, Mirjana, married Slobodan Milošević. Milorad died of a heart attack in October 1967, aged eighty.

Australian Corporal George Mitchell finished the war as a Captain. Though his First World War diary remained unpublished, George went on to apply his literary talent, and wrote several books about the war, including a memoir of fighting on the Western Front, *Backs to the Wall, a Soldier's Book* and *The Awakening*. During the Second World War George fought with the Australian troops in the Pacific. He died in 1961, aged sixty-seven.

Turkish officer Mehmed Fasih was released from an Allied POW camp in Suez at the end of the war. He escaped from

Milorad Marković in his village of Popović as a teacher in 1937

Allied-occupied Istanbul, apparently disguised as an egg-merchant, to join the Turkish War of Liberation in Anatolia. The new Turkish Republic was proclaimed in 1923 and Mustafa Kemal, Mehmed's Gallipoli commander and later leader of the National Liberation Movement, became the first Turkish President, known as Mustafa Atatürk. Mehmed rose swiftly through military ranks to become Deputy Commander of the Presidential Guards. During the Second World War, Mehmed became Director of Operations at the General Staff in Ankara. In 1955 he was appointed Chief of Staff of Turkish Land Forces. Mehmed's daydreams of having a family, which he wrote about in his Gallipoli dugout, also came true: he married in 1924 and had two sons. Mehmed died in 1964, aged seventy.

German doctor Ludwig Deppe returned to Dresden with his wife Charlotte after the end of the war, both writing memoirs of their experience in German East Africa. His subsequent fate is unknown.

Mehmed Fasih's wedding photograph in 1924

British officer Richard Meinertzhagen finished the war a colonel and was sent to the Paris Peace Conference and on to Versailles as a member of the British delegation. He was involved in negotiating the fate of the Middle East and of Germany's colonies. In 1919 Richard became Chief Political Officer for Palestine and Syria in General Allenby's administration. Richard was an ardent advocate for the creation of a National Jewish State in Palestine, clashing on the issue with some of his superiors. On return to Britain, Richard spent three years working in Churchill's Colonial Office and later briefly resumed his army career. In 1920 he married Anne Jackson and the couple had three children. When his wife died in a tragic shooting accident, Richard brought up their children largely on his own. He finally retired from his army career and followed his other passion, ornithology. In the early 1930s, Richard, still politically involved, had two audiences with Adolf Hitler. During his second informal visit he raised the question of Jewish emigration from Germany and supposedly sent Hitler into a rage. During the Second World War, Richard's second son, Daniel, was killed in action, aged nineteen. Richard died in 1967, aged eighty-nine.

Guinean soldier Kande Kamara returned home to West Africa at the end of 1919 and was overjoyed to be greeted by his father on arrival. Yet his father's praise and high esteem seem to have aroused jealousy and mistrust amongst his other siblings, who plotted to murder Kande fearing he would be made the next tribal chief by their father. Kande fled from the village. He never saw his father, family or wife again. Banished from home, Kande worked as a petty trader in Haute Guinea, Liberia and Sierra Leone for the rest of his life.

British First Lieutenant Robert Goldrich became a naval commander and continued to serve in the Royal Navy until retirement. Unfortunately, it has not been possible to establish any further details about his life.

U-Boat Captain Johannes Spiess wrote a book about his experiences, *Six Years of U-Boat Adventures*, published in Germany in 1932. Unknown to Spiess, his account was translated by US Military Intelligence, and evidently treated as a useful source of information.

British officer Duggie (Douglas) Lyall Grant returned home from captivity in 1918 and worked as a merchant banker and later as a paint and then a whisky salesman. In the Second World War he was Officer-in-Command of a troopship during the Sicily landings. Duggie had five children from two marriages. A member of many clubs, he became President of the London Scottish Rugby Club and played the bagpipes at its social gatherings. Duggie died suddenly of a heart attack aged seventy-eight after a cricket club dinner in Wimbledon.

French Lieutenant Victor Guilhem-Ducleon returned home to Bordeaux in November 1918 and was reunited with his parents and wife, Annick. In October 1919 the couple had their first son, Jean. Six other children followed in quick succession. For the rest of his life Victor lived and worked in Bordeaux as an engineer and later became a judge at the city's Tribunal de Commerce. He was mobilised again as a reserve captain in 1939. Victor died peacefully in Bordeaux in January 1970, aged eighty.

German officer Rudolf Hess joined the National Socialist Party on 1st July 1920 and became a close friend and confidant to Adolf Hitler during their joint incarceration at Landsberg prison in 1923 after a failed coup. While in prison, Rudolf transcribed the text of *Mein Kampf* under Hitler's dictation. On release, he became Hitler's secretary and in 1933 was appointed Deputy Leader of the Nazi Party. Using the pilot training acquired in the last months of the First World War, Rudolf made an unauthorised flight to Britain to negotiate peace in 1941, crash-landing in Scotland. He received a life sentence for war crimes at the Nuremberg Trials in 1946 and spent the next forty-one years in Berlin-Spandau prison. Rudolf was the only prisoner left there for the last twenty years of his life, having outlived all other inmates. He was found hanging in his cell in August 1987, aged ninety-three.

Dmitry Oskin (seated second from the left) as member of Tula Military Tribunal

Russian soldier Dmitry Oskin, who had risen fast through the ranks and became a Soldier's Deputy after the February Revolution of 1917, joined the Bolsheviks after the October Revolution. After the war, Oskin was appointed Military Commissar in his home province of Tula in Central Russia where he took part in food requisitioning and the suppression of peasant revolts during the ensuing civil war. He continued his swift rise through the Soviet ranks but died suddenly in 1934, aged forty-two. It has been suggested that he became a victim of one of the early Stalinist purges.

American officer John D. Clark and a certain Major Price had both fallen in love with Emma Marie Zangler, the American nurse who served with them on the Western Front and in John's words became 'the belle of the ball' in the French provincial town of Chaumont. When John left the US base hospital in Chaumont to pursue a military career at the front, Major Price arrived to serve on General Pershing's staff in the town and also became enamoured of the nurse. Emma Marie went home to the USA before them and both men sent radiograms asking her to meet them off the boat on their return. John Clark and Major Price travelled separately, but their two ships docked in New York on the same day in August 1919. Emma Marie evidently chose to meet John off his ship in Hoboken, for they married in 1920 and had, according to John, a 'wonderful life together' until her death in 1962.

A Note on the Sources

While every effort was made to include correct information, there is still much discrepancy in the First World War facts, figures and their interpretation. All unintentional mistakes and omissions are, of course, our own. Our main sources of historical reference were Hew Strachan's *The First World War Volume 1 To Arms* (Oxford 2001), the *Oxford Illustrated History of the First World War* (ed. Hew Strachan, Oxford 1998) and Holger H. Herwig's study of the Central Powers, *The First World War: Germany and Austria-Hungary 1914–18* (London 1997). We relied on Ian D. Hogg's *Historical Dictionary of World War I* (London 1998), *The European Powers in the First World War, An Encyclopaedia* (ed. Spencer C. Tucker, New York 1996) and *The Macmillan Dictionary of The First World War* by Stephen Pope and Elizabeth Anne Wheal (London 1995) for cross-reference and fact checking.

The original *Daily Telegraph Atlas of the First World War* published in 1918, *First World War Atlas* by Martin Gilbert (London 1994) and his *First World War* (London 1994) were most useful in tracing the movements of the diarists, while the essays in *Facing Armageddon: the First World War Experienced* (London 1996) edited by Hugh Cecil and Peter H. Liddle were especially helpful for their wide range of information. Malcolm Brown's *The Imperial War Museum Book of the Western Front* (London 1993), *The Imperial War Museum Book of the First World War* (London 1991) and *The Imperial War Museum Book of the Somme* (London 1996), were invaluable guides for our research into British primary sources. We also used John Ellis's *Eye Deep in Hell: Trench Warfare in World War I* (New York 1976) and Ian Ousby's *The Road to Verdun* (London 2002) for background information on the Battles of the Somme and Verdun.

Stéphane Audoin-Rouzeau and Dominic Congar's preface to Yves Congar's *Journal de la Guerre 1914–1918* (Paris 1997), Robert J. Young (ed.) *Under Siege* (New York 2000) and Helen McPhail *The Long Silence* (London 2001) deal with life under occupation and have helped to set in context the diaries of schoolchildren Yves Congar and Piete Kuhr. For the history of the siege of Przemyśl, several books by Mark Cornwall, in particular *The Last Years of Austria-Hungary: a Multi-National Experiment in Early 20th-Century Europe* and the above-mentioned volume by Holger Herwig proved most informative. *The Eastern Front 1914–17* by Norman Stone (London 1974) remains one of the main studies of the Eastern Front.

We are particularly indebted to Bill Gammage's *The Broken Years: Australian Soldiers in the Great War* (Ringwood 1980) for the details of the Australian experience at Gallipoli and to Turgay Erol and H. Basri Danisman for information on the Turkish side at Gallipoli contained in *Lone Pine (Bloody Ridge) Diary of Lt Mehmed Fasih, 5th Imperial Ottoman army, Gallipoli 1915* (Istanbul 2001). *Gallipoli* by Robert Rhodes James (London 1974) and Nigel Steel and Peter Hart's *Defeat at Gallipoli* (London 1994) provided many details of the campaign, while *Gallipoli 1915* by Peter Reid (Sydney 2002) was a source of visual reference.

The recent book by John R. Schindler, *Isonzo, the Forgotten Sacrifice of the Great War* (Westport, Connecticut 2001), was our main source for the history of this campaign. On the campaign in East Africa and the African contribution to the war effort, *A Modern History of Tanganyika* by John Iliffe (Cambridge 1979) and *Africa and the First World War,* a collection of essays edited by Melvyn Page (London 1987), were the sources of most of the facts and statistics. An additional source was *Eine Kopfjagd: Deutsche in Ostafrika. Spuren Kolonialer Herrschaft* by Martin Baer and Olaf Schröter (Berlin 2001). John Lord's *Duty, Honour, Empire: The Life and Times of Colonel Meinertzhagen* (Hutchinson 1971) provided some of the biographical details about Richard Meinertzhagen.

For the details of the naval conflict, the following books were helpful: Johannes Spiess' *U-Boot Abenteuer, Sechs Jahre U-Boot fahrten* (Berlin 1932) is the U-9 watch officer's and later U-Boat captain's own account of the war, while V. E. Tarrant's *The U-Boat Offensive 1914–1945* (London 1989) and John Terraine's *Business in Great Waters: the U-Boat Wars 1916–1945* (London 1989), provided historical background on the development and deployment of the early submarines.

Alon Rachamimov *POW's and The Great War: Captivity on the Eastern Front* (London 2002) was a welcome source of new information on this topic. *Black Bread and Barbed Wire: Prisoners in the First World War* (ed. Michael Moynihan, London 1978) was an invaluable guide to the diaries and accounts of British POWs during the First World War. We referred to *A People's Tragedy: the Russian Revolution 1891–1924* by Orlando Figes (London 1996) for the chapter on the Russian revolution.

Grateful acknowledgement is made for permission to reproduce extracts from the following copyrighted works:

Journal de la Guerre 1914–1918 by Yves Congar (le Cerf, Paris 1997), by permission of le Cerf, publishers of the edited French edition and the author's estate. The original diaries are held by the Dominican Archive in France.

Čubrilović i kasnije (ed. Dr Zdravko Antonić, Belgrade 1999), by permission of the editor.

Lone Pine (Bloody Ridge) Diary of Lt Mehmed Fasih, 5th Imperial

Ottoman army, Gallipoli 1915 (Denizler Kitabevi, Istanbul 2001), by permission of the publisher.

Quatre ans derriére les lignes Allemandes pendant La Grande Guerre: souvenirs et Journal de Victor Guilhem-Ducleon, introduced by Jacques Clémens (Agen Bordeaux 1984), by permission of the publisher and Jacques Clémens.

Rudolf Hess Briefe 1908–1933 (ed. Wolf Rüdiger Hess, Langen Müller, Munich 1987) by permission of the publisher.

Dziennik z oblężonego Przemyśla 1914–1915 by Helena Seifertóv Jabłońska (ed. Hanna Imbs, Poludniowo-Wschodni Institut Naukowy, Przemyśl 1994), by permission of the publisher.

There We'll Meet Again: the First World War Diary of a Young German Girl by Piete Kuhr (Gloucester 1998). English language translation by Walter Wright by permission of the translator's family and the author's estate.

Ratni Dnevnici 1912–1918 by Milorad Marković (Vuk Karadzić, Belgrade 2000), by permission of the author's estate.

The Letters of a Young Canadian Soldier During WW1 by P. Winthrop McClare of Mount Uniacke NS, edited by Dale McClare (Dartmouth, N.S. Brook House 1999), by permission of Dale McClare.

Army Diary 1899–1926 by Richard Meinertzhagen (Oliver&Boyd, Edinburgh, London 1960), by permission of the author's estate.

Oblaci nad gradom by Slavka Mihajlović (Belgrade 1955), by permission of the author's estate.

1914–1918 Quatre Années sur Le Front: Carnets d'un Combattant by Paul Tuffrau (Imago, Paris 1998), by permission of the publisher and the author's family.

Diary of Alexei Zyikov, by permission of *Klio* Magazine, St Petersburg.

Kande Kamara, manuscript of an oral history interview, by permission of Joe Lunn, University of Michigan-Dearborn, USA.

We are grateful to the following archives for permission to reproduce extracts from unpublished diaries in their collections:

Bibliotek für Zeitgeschichte, Paul Knoch collection, for permission to publish the diary of Ernst Nopper.

Hauptstaatsarchiv Stuttgart for permission to publish the correspondence of Paul Hub.

Kobarid Museum, Slovenia for permission to publish the diary of Virgilio Bonamore.

Vienna Kriegsarchiv for permission to publish the diary of Josef Tomann.

The photographs are reproduced by kind permission of the following:

We are indebted to the following individuals and archives for permission to reproduce photographs from their collections: The Archive of Bosnia and Herzegovina (Vaso Čubrilović); The Austrian State Military Archive (Archduke Franz Ferdinand and Sophie); Dr Ljiljana Klisić-Djordjević (Slavka Mihajlović); Hauptstaatsarchiv, Stuttgart (Paul Hub and Maria Thumm); Bibliothek für Zeitgeschichte, Stuttgart (Ernst Nopper, Officers Mess on U-9); Alexandra Mishnin (Mishnin family); Madame Cambon (Paul Tuffrau); Anja Ott (Piete Kuhr); Dominique Congar (Yves Congar); The National Museum of the Przemyśl Region, Poland and Marek Horwat (Helena Jabłońska diary); Tomasz Idzikowski (Przemyśl siege and occupation); Dragoljub Marković (Milorad Marković); Australian War Memorial (George Mitchell); Murat Culçu and Turgay Erol (Mehmed Fasih); Open-Air Museum of Lagazuoi (Isonzo Front); Museo Storico Italiano della Guerra (Austro-Hungarian artillery observation point; Italian soldiers with a 65A gun); Meinertzhagen Estate (Richard Meinertzhagen); Robert Hunt Picture Library (German askari riflemen on march); Joe Lunn (Kande Kamara); Dale McClare (Winthrop McClare); Daphne Robinson (Duggie Lyall Grant); Tula District Museum (Dmitry Oskin); USA Military Historical Institute, Carlisle Barracks (USAMHI) (John D. Clark and Emma Marie Zangler); Imperial War Museum (Q9582 French women welcoming a soldier); Historial de la Grande Guerre, Péronne (Empty Battlefield, 359; Barbed Wire, 364).

Every attempt has been made to contact copyright holders. Our apologies to any copyright holder who may have been inadvertently omitted.